Christmas, Ideology and Popular Culture

'This is an absorbing collection of essays, and it makes an impressive job of introducing ideological issues in an accessible way. In covering such diverse topics as family and home, cards and carols, religious beliefs, shopping, Christmas chart hits, TV and films, each author presents the reader with thought-provoking insight into much that usually goes unquestioned.'

Professor Derek B. Scott, University of Leeds

'Do they know it's Christmas? Sheila Whiteley and the other contributors to *Christmas, Ideology and Popular Culture* certainly do. The book traces the construction of Christmas from pagan ritual to Christian celebration, where charity, compassion, and goodwill compete with unreal expectations, family tensions, and the suffering of those less fortunate. Taking the reader behind the facade of festive follies and family values to reveal the crass commercialism and corporate chicanery that have always been part of the mix, this book is a must read for anyone interested in exploring the meaning and contradictions of this global festival ... and a great holiday gift to boot.'

Reebee Garofalo, University of Massachusetts Boston

Christmas, Ideology and Popular Culture

Edited by Sheila Whiteley

Edinburgh University Press

© in this edition Edinburgh University Press, 2008
© in the individual contributions is retained by the authors

Edinburgh University Press Ltd
22 George Square, Edinburgh

Typeset in 11/13 Ehrhardt
by Servis Filmsetting Ltd, Manchester, and
printed and bound in Great Britain by
Antony Rowe Ltd, Chippenham, Wilts

A CIP record for this book is available from the British Library

ISBN 978 0 7486 2808 7 (hardback)
ISBN 978 0 7486 2809 4 (paperback)

The right of the contributors
to be identified as authors of this work
has been asserted in accordance with
the Copyright, Designs and Patents Act 1988.

Contents

PART III: PEACE ON EARTH, GOODWILL TO ALL MEN

PART IV: WE WISH YOU A MERRY CHRISTMAS!

List of Illustrations

Acknowledgements

Figs 2.2, 2.4, 2.5 and 2.8   Images courtesy of Manchester Metropolitan University Special Collections, The Laura Seddon Collection of Victorian and Edwardian Greetings Cards. Photography by Tony Richards.

Figs 2.1, 2.3, 2.6 and 2.7   Personal collection of S. M. Dodd.

Fig. 3.1   Thomas Nast, *Harper's Weekly*, 1863. © Ohio State University Cartoon Research Library. Used with permission. George McKay is grateful to Professor Lucy Shelton Caswell and to Jenny Robb for arranging this; www.cartoons.osu.edu.

Figs 3.2–3.5   © Bob Beckerer/White Rock Collectors Association (WRCA). Used with permission. George McKay is grateful to Bob Beckerer and John Boucher for making these images available and to Bob for illuminating aspects of the social context of Prohibition and White Rock. Further information about WRCA is available at www.whiterocking.org.

Introduction

Sheila Whiteley

How do we understand Christmas? The ways in which this question can be answered depend very much on the status given to it. For the many, it is an unavoidable expense, one which emphasises giving but at a cost, as child-centred advertising creates often unrealisable expectations; the letter to Santa is quickly superseded by a list which not only details the identified gift but also the comparative price offered by catalogues and relevant stores. Yet despite an underlying cynicism about ever-increasing commercialisation and the tensions generated by family gatherings, Christmas continues to be accepted as an inevitable part of the annual cycle, a festival that is characterised by traditional rituals (family-centred events, the exchange of gifts and cards, parties and so on) from which, it seems, there is no escape. But, as John Storey comments later in this book, 'It was commercial from the very start. Part of what was being celebrated was the achievements of industrial capitalism – conspicuous consumption in a market economy' (p. 20).

The cultural activities associated with the festive season also have an interesting relationship with the idealised construct of family and community mapped out in Charles Dickens's seminal text *A Christmas Carol* (1843). Sentiments of benevolence and goodwill are mobilised and fused with the Christmas message of 'peace on earth, goodwill to all men', the implication being that this is a period when personal and social conflicts can be magically resolved. Reflected in the dual emphasis on compassion and optimism – the potential for individual acts of kindness to have a cumulative effect – Christmas also offers an idealised vision of a world without war, famine or disease. 'Feed the world. Let them know it's Christmas Time!' In essence, the festive season is about wish-fulfilment, but while the utopianism of world harmony and the ideals associated with Christmas have a certain synergy, it is how such themes are constructed (in the media, through cards, gift-giving, music and films, for example) and what it means (its cultural value) that continue to situate Christmas as '*the* global festival' (Miller 1993: 5, emphasis original). At the same time issues are flagged up around the ways in which Christmas has been mobilised to support particular political positions, not least at times of war.

The emphasis on harmony, hearth and home versus the bleakness of the outside world is ideologically powerful. For those without families, Christmas is all too often a time of acute loneliness; conversely, family life itself is often compromised by underlying tension and disagreements exacerbated by over-indulgence. It is also evident that the demands of conspicuous consumption, fed by a diet of advertisements and a heavily depleted cash card, highlight the problems associated with low-income families – itself a problematic concept in contemporary society. Meanwhile, the 'construction' of Christmas in the media often implies that its readers/viewers recognise that commercial interests override any real commitment to universal goodwill, and that the 'giving' associated with Christmas is better serviced by waiting for the January sales.

In spite of these underlying conflicts, the tensions inherent in wish-fulfilment versus reality, and the ever-increasing emphasis on secularisation, the phrase 'a traditional Christmas' continues to evoke an immediately recognisable picture of the way in which we spend or imagine an 'ideal' Christmas. Thus, while Britain is now a multi-cultural, multi-faith society (where the religious framework of Christmas is largely irrelevant to its many Jews, Hindus and Muslims – or, indeed, its atheists and agnostics), the associated sentiments of harmony and goodwill continue to provide an ideological discourse that informs its popular interpretation: a concern for the family, children and family-centred activities, the rituals and expectations framing gift-giving and receiving, and an idealised nostalgia for the past, which prioritises themes of neighbourliness, charity and community. As such, Christmas brings with it a sense of 'recognition' that is largely dependent upon a sedimented evocation of its history (both religious and commercial), albeit tempered by the social structure and customs of the country (as evidenced here in chapters discussing the development of and cultural practices surrounding Christmas in the UK, the USA and Australia, for example). More recently, as George McKay observes, iconic advertising figures like the Coca-Cola Santa and Rudolph the Red-Nosed Reindeer have generated a global appeal which includes such Communist countries as China and Cuba, so providing a uniquely rich focal point for the study of popular culture and its relationship to ideology.

The initial idea for *Christmas, Ideology and Popular Culture* emerged from the Open University's undergraduate course on popular culture (1982–8), for which I was a course tutor, and I am indebted to John Golby,

Ruth Finnegan and Tony Bennett, whose perceptive insights have informed my own writing. Subsequently, I used the theme of Christmas to introduce my students to popular culture, ideology, hegemony and semiotic analysis with particular reference to popular music – Christmas Number Ones, carols, Christmas songs focusing on the family and on romance, as well as those highlighting racism (Basement5, 'Last White Christmas'), dystopias (Crass, 'Merry Crassmas'), war (Jonah Lewie, 'Stop the Cavalry (Wish I was at home for Christmas)') and a refusal to engage with ritual sentimentality (Chas and Gromeski, 'Let's Burn the Christmas Tree'). Its success, as an introduction to popular culture and ideology, lies in the inescapability of Christmas. Students, practically without exception, go home to be with their families, seeing it as a natural, albeit not always welcome intrusion into the freedom of university life. As such, it comes as somewhat of a surprise to learn that 'Christmas was invented first and foremost as a commercial event. Everything that was revived or invented . . . had one thing in common: they could be sold for profit' (Storey, p. 20).

The topics explored in *Christmas, Ideology and Popular Culture* relate to major issues concerning cultural activity (watching Christmas films, television, listening or engaging with popular music and carols), its relationship to a set of basic values (the idealised construct of the family), social relationships (community) and the way in which ideological discourses are used and mobilised, not least in times of conflict and war. These are explored through a case study approach, with invited contributions from leading researchers within the fields of popular culture, communications, sociology, politics and music. For students of popular culture, the linked case study approach provides insights into how the themes surrounding Christmas are constructed (in the media, films, cartoons and music) through an often idealised nostalgia for the past; for media studies, the case studies offer a compelling account of how Christmas is shaped by the media, how this relates to social change and how it influences the public perception of the festival. Music is given a specific focus in chapters highlighting carols and Christmas chart singles, relating songs to the themes of family, community and goodwill. For visual culture, case studies offer a conceptual approach to the iconography of Christmas – including cartoons, Coca-colonisation, Christmas cards and films. What is evident is that the utopian is counterbalanced by the dystopian – that the contributors have chosen their case studies with an awareness of their ideological implications. As Thom Swiss explains in his personal recollection of Christmas in Illinois, the ideologies and customs of Christmas both mask and make painfully evident deep disagreements and family problems, not least during the lead-up to and following Christmas Day itself. Conversely, Tara Brabazon sees Christmas as the pivot of change in the twenty-first century's fight over fundamentalisms (p. 151). For the researcher, the analyst and, indeed, everyone experiencing Christmas, meaning is produced at many levels, and how one 'tells' the story is crucial to its interpretation, not least in times of conflict. 'Christmas . . . is what it has been *made* to *mean*, living in a particular culture at a particular moment in its historical development' (Bennett 1981: 49, emphasis original), and this is why meaning is always at issue.

An Overview of the Book

Our concern is to explore the ways in which the production of meaning is mediated by the social and cultural practices surrounding Christmas. As the reader will observe, certain texts and debates emerge across the range of chapters presented in the book. This is not surprising. Current writing on popular culture, popular music and ideology draw on earlier theoretical models which provide a starting point for diverse kinds of textual analysis. This is particularly evident in the discussion of ideology and its relationship to popular culture, including film, television and popular music. At the same time, contributors have been chosen for their investigative approach, and the conceptual frameworks discussed provide different insights into textual analysis which researchers and students can apply to their own investigations into popular culture.

Part I: 'Tis the Season to be Jolly

John Storey opens the discussion by taking the reader back to the 1840s, presenting a critical exploration of 'The Invention of the English Christmas' by the Victorian urban middle classes. As a utopian moment in their struggle for hegemony, Christmas was intended as both a celebration of the prosperity made possible by the achievements of the Industrial Revolution, and a recognition of the need to share that prosperity (if only temporarily and with clear limits) with those for whom industrialisation and urbanisation had not been an unqualified success. 'If what was invented was commercial out of instinct, it was charitable out of a sense of fear and guilt' (p. 22). The text at the heart of this aspect of the invention of the 'traditional' English Christmas is Charles Dickens's 'utopian' novel *A Christmas Carol* (1843). The story of Scrooge is a clear warning to the class he represents: share prosperity or face destruction. Even so, Dickens's emphasis is on charity rather than fundamental social change; charity relieves suffering, but what it does not do is change the causes of suffering. Rather it is a temporary redistribution of wealth, which works to safeguard the hierarchies of wealth (p. 26).

While philanthropy and charitable giving have remained central to its ideology, the iconography associated with the middle-class Victorian vision of Christmas focused on excessive consumption and pagan imagery, 'though there are warnings against over-indulgence and reminders of traditional Christian virtues', if not symbols, in both high art (Royal Academy paintings) and popular culture (*Punch* cartoons and Christmas cards) (p. 32). As Sara M. Dodd explains, in her chapter 'Conspicuous Consumption and Festive Follies: Victorian Images of Christmas', the creation of a Christmas 'tradition', with its associated symbols and rituals, originates in Victorian images of a nostalgic past – in a 'great house', for example – where the antics and activities of wassailers provide credibility and sustenance for the Victorian present. In general, the following of Christmas rituals in, for example, the sharing of festivities (decorations, trees, presents, enormous amounts of food and drink, and so on) or the simple exchange of cards, was seen as wholesome and improving. Thus, an article in *The Times* extols the 'cementing [of] broken friendships and strengthening of family and neighbourly ties in all conditions of life', betokened by the giving of cards, for example (p. 33). The portrayal of such rituals on cards themselves or in a variety of visual representations provides evidence of universal enjoyment. Winter games, such as sledging, skating or snowballing, for example, with Father Christmas or personified robins joining in at times (robins snowballing or the unfortunate Father Christmas rolled into a snowball himself), provide evidence of the emphasis on youth and fun in cards and cartoons up to the 1870s. Flirtation under the mistletoe is a popular motif in mid-century *Punch*, for example. Later cartoons, however, have an awareness of those less fortunate, particularly children, with the lack of Christmas warmth and spirit made explicit in contrasting images. Father Christmas is 'awakened' by a 'call to alms' (towards charitable acts) at the end of the century, and Ireland is personified by a woman receiving a Christmas stocking from a sheepish Father Christmas (with specific political implications at the time) (p. 37).

While the first two chapters focus on the Victorian English Christmas, George McKay turns his attention to the US, where the historical antecedents of Christmas advertising show that, as long ago as the mid-nineteenth century, a Father Christmas-style character had been employed for seasonal marketing. 'Consumption, Coca-colonisation, cultural resistance – and Santa Claus' takes the reader back to Philadelphia where, 'in 1841, a performer dressed as a character named "Criscringle" publicised a local store's merchandise to passers-by. A standardised visual amalgamation – white,

white beard, portly, jolly, wearing an identifiable fur or fur-trimmed uniform – developed through the century. It was this image that was most famously exploited by the Coca-Cola Company from the early 1930s on, in the corporate company colours of red and white, as part of its campaign to increase winter sales of its soft drink' (p. 57). The most successful of the Coca-Cola Santas was introduced in 1931 by commercial illustrator Haddon Sundblom, and in 1939 the dominance of Christmas within the American seasonal marketplace was confirmed by the introduction of Rudolph the Red-Nosed Reindeer as a marketing tool by the Chicago-based department store chain Montgomery Ward. The subsequent song, 'Rudolph the Red-Nosed Reindeer', further popularised this new character on the home front (p. 54).

By tracing ways in which iconic advertising figures like the Coca-Cola Santa and Rudolph generated appeal around the globe, McKay introduces key issues surrounding the Americanisation of Christmas, and reveals how 'external forms of American popular consumption (or the consumption of America) have inscribed within them variously power, pleasure and fear' (p. 63). Terms describing the process of the consumption of export pop cultures mix critical positioning, political accusation and emotive response: 'McDonaldisation', 'Disneyisation' and, of course, 'Coca-colonisation' (p. 63). Questions are raised as to whether Santa and Rudolph, and their loads of presents, can be considered as conscious global emblems of American consumption, and whether the fact that everyone likes receiving presents adequately explains their appeal. Finally, McKay's chapter explores forms of political campaigning around the contestation of Christmas consumption and their development in recent years in the so-called 'brand wars', from Adbusters to the annual Buy Nothing Day, extended recently to the Buy Nothing Christmas Day campaign.

While McKay's chapter is focused primarily on the valence of Christmas as an American socio-economic and cultural (export) practice, his consideration of the tensions between the secular commercial Christmas and the apparently increasingly religious society of the United States anticipates the problems explored in Part II, not least those concerning confrontation between the pagan roots of Christmas and the aggrieved majoritarianism of American Catholics and Evangelicals.

Part II: The Holly and the Ivy

Many of the mainstream traditions associated with Christmas had their origins in pagan practices, including Saturnalia, the greatest festival of the Roman year. Celebrating the passing of the old year and the birth of the new by marking the winter solstice, the feast honoured Saturn, the God of agriculture. Often overseen by a Master of Ceremonies, the festival included feasting, gift-giving, role reversal and dance. Homes were decorated, work was suspended, and ritual fires were lit to ensure the return of the waning sun. The significance of the winter solstice was also celebrated in Scandinavia and Northern Europe in the midwinter festival of Yule. A special log – most commonly birch, oak or holly – was chosen on Yule eve and lit by a small piece of the previous year's log, to symbolise hope and the return of the sun. Mistletoe, as a healing plant and as an invitation to kissing, is also related to Yule, this time celebrating the transition from the shortest day of the year and the return of the sun – a metaphor of death and rebirth. It commemorates Balder, the son of Frigga, the Norse Goddess of love, marriage and fertility, who was killed by Loki with an arrow made from mistletoe. When he was restored to life, Frigga blessed the mistletoe and established the tradition of kissing anyone passing under it. Ritual firs, holly, ivy and other evergreens were also important in ceremonies designed to placate the gods and goddesses and ensure the return of the sun. Their incorporation into the Christian festival of Christmas, together with the rituals associated with Saturnalia and Mithras, the God of light (whose birthday, the Day of the Birth of the Unconquered Sun, falls on 25 December), is a reminder of the acuity of the early church which, when confronted with pagan ceremonies, gave them Christian significance, assimilating them into the festivities surrounding the birth of Christ. The midwinter rituals of decorating the home with evergreens and lights, feasting and drinking were thus given a specific focus, transforming the feast of the solstice into the feast of the Nativity, the symbolic fire heralding the return of the sun and its life-giving force grafted on to Christian belief in the birth of Christ as the light of the world. Paganism was thus defused . . . or so the story goes. However, as Jennifer Rycenga reveals in her chapter, 'Religious Controversies over Christmas', the tussle between paganism and Christianity is still very much alive.

Basing her chapter on an incident from Christmas 2005, her analytical case study opens out the religious discourses surrounding Christmas and its relationship to contemporary America in a lively discussion of the controversy between the consumer hegemon, Wal-Mart, and Bill Donohue of the Catholic League. As Rycenga explains, 'this was a battle of structural cousins. Wal-Mart's world-view shows structural parallels to religious proselytising, for good reason: "it was the evangelical Christian publicists in the Bible and tract societies who first dreamed the dream of a genuinely mass medium . . . to deliver the same printed message to *everyone* in America" (Nord 1984: 2, emphasis original). Like an evangelising religion, Wal-Mart wants absolutely everyone worshipping at its temples, especially during the end-of-year blitz' (pp. 72–3). The 'inappropriate and inflammatory' blunder (Catholic League 2005c) committed by a seasonal employee defending Wal-Mart's decision to replace 'Merry Christmas' with 'Happy Holidays' thus provides a relevant context for a salutary Christmas tale. Exploring the ways in which 'playful neo-paganism nips at the heels of Christianity', Rycenga reveals how the 'majoritarian outrage at having their common sense challenged leads to a reinvigoration of a Christian compulsion to dominate' (p. 86). Yet, as Barry Cooper argues in his chapter 'Christmas Carols', a Christmas without Christ is, surely, 'a celebration without meaning' (p. 88).

Many people today encounter the true message of Christmas – which can be summed up in the single word 'Emmanuel' ('among-us-God') – only when they hear Christmas carols, which have become an almost inescapable part of the Christmas festivities. The 'carol as a genre has a long history, which has gradually become intertwined with Christmas hymns and songs of all types'. These have an even longer history, 'for Christmas hymns have probably been sung for as long as Christmas has been celebrated' (p. 88). The 'Christmas carols' of today are of extremely varied origin, both geographically and chronologically, and their theological content ranges from the profound ('Born to give them second birth') to the non-existent ('We will rock you, rock you, rock you') (p. 95). Most make at least some allusion to the biblical narratives of Christ's birth, but beyond that there is little that all have in common. The origins of the tunes now used are almost equally disparate. 'Some were composed specifically for the texts with which they are associated, while others were married to their texts only years or even centuries after the two were created' (p. 93). Nearly all offer a mainly syllabic setting of the text, in simple strophic form (p. 94). Although this music is today heard in a number of contexts, including as background music to such activities as shopping and dining, it is usually heard at its best in the context of the formal carol service.

While carols are the purest form of Christmas music, their mediation into mainstream music owes as much to the intervention of 1950s popular music as it did to the evangelistic zeal of Victorian England. As Sheila Whiteley explains, in her chapter 'Christmas Songs – Sentiments and Subjectivities', Elvis Presley's cover of the Rev. Phillips Brooks' carol 'O Little Town of Bethlehem' in his 1957 *Christmas Album*, took the Christian message into a secular context. The alignment of a carol describing Christ's birthplace with 'White Christmas' – a song situating Christmas within a nostalgic winter landscape – works to effect a shared romantic discourse which was heightened by Presley's crooning baritone (p. 101) and his well-publicised sex appeal. The inclusion of such romantic ballads as 'Santa Bring My Baby Back To Me' and 'Merry Christmas Baby' (the latter discussed in Freya Jarman-Ivens's chapter, pp. 124–5) provides a sexual undertow and, as such, it is not too surprising that the album was attacked by Bible belt America as amoral, profaning both Christmas and Christianity. Carols, however, are just part of the music associated with Christmas, and songs such as 'Feed the World', 'Driving Home for Christmas' and 'A Fairytale of New York' offer an abbreviated ideal model of the festive season, a condensed checklist of ideological themes (Bennett 1981: 54) that reminds us of what we should be doing (celebrating with the family and loved ones, giving to those less fortunate than ourselves) and what we should be feeling. In effect, there is an ideological discourse that governs the construction of the lyrics and arrangement of the music, which draws on the sentiments engendered by the religious basis of Christmas and such familiar texts as *A Christmas Carol*.

While the utopian of Christmas music prioritises romantic nostalgia and idealistic action, the competition for the Number One chart spot in the week encompassing Christmas Day has grown to be an annual ritual that is a significant part of the preparation for Christmas, the day which always promises more than it can deliver. As Freya Jarman-Ivens observes, in her chapter 'The Musical Underbelly of Christmas', rival songs and bands enact a battle for the coveted title of This Year's Christmas Number One – champion of Christmas Present – and in doing so also presumably hope to be included on the commercially available soundtracks to Christmases Future. A canon of Christmas tunes is thus repeated in varying combinations on collections of 'ultimate' Christmas music, perhaps assembled with a particular Christmas mood in mind: *Lifetime of Romance Christmas* (2004), *Ultimate Christmas Party* (2002), *A Family Christmas* (2004). Collections are also thematised according to musical genre: *A Motown Christmas* (1992), *R&B Christmas Party* (1999), *Christmas Crooners* (2003). While such albums exemplify the musical construction of those versions of Christmas deemed acceptable, Jarman-Ivens also delves into what she calls the 'musical underbelly' of Christmas, exploring 'the relations between musical signifiers and some of the "alternative" versions of Christmas that occupy positions on the outskirts of the festivities' (p. 116). These include 'Merry Christmas, Baby' (Elvis Presley, 1957), 'Mad World' (as recorded by Michael Andrews and Gary Jules for the soundtrack to *Donnie Darko* (dir. Richard Kelly) in 2001) and 'December Will Be Magic Again' (Kate Bush, 1979), 'where the slightly icy quality of Bush's voice places jagged melodies over unsettled harmonies, and the picture is more one of a sinister Jack Frost than of a cuddly Frosty the Snowman. It unsettles and discomforts, and this is far from what is usually demanded of our Christmas popular songs' (p. 128). However, as Jarman-Ivens concludes, while perennial favourites sing of friendship, love, peace and happiness, hidden amongst these banal vehicles of propaganda are occasional gems that confront, both lyrically and musically, the dominant Christmas values. 'These songs often do not find their way to the Christmas surface, but lurk beneath as a musical underbelly' (p. 131).

Whether utopian or dystopian, the centrality of music in the Christmas ritual is arguably attributable to its potential to define (and later recapture) a mood. Lyrical content is part of this, as evidenced by such songs as 'Mistletoe and Wine' (Cliff Richard, 1988) or the perennial best-seller 'White Christmas'. Performed by Bing Crosby, its timely release in 1942 provides a particular insight into the role of music during periods of conflict. As John Mundy writes, '[w]hile the 1944 musical *Meet Me In St Louis* contained a complex rendition by Judy Garland of "Have Yourself A Merry Little Christmas", which perfectly expressed the extent to which sentiment, nostalgia and wish-fulfilment were already part of Christmas, it was *Holiday Inn* (1942) which did most to establish the Christmas film. Though *Holiday Inn* was a celebration of all fourteen American public holidays including Easter, Independence Day and Thanksgiving, Christmas was given additional prominence through Bing Crosby's double rendition of Irving Berlin's "White Christmas". Written for the film on the condition that Crosby sang it, the song became what Berlin himself described as "a publishing business in itself" ' (Rosen 2002: 5), remain[ing] 'the all-time top-selling single until 1997. Recorded by hundreds of artists from Sinatra to U2 by way of Elvis Presley, Berlin's song retains its status as the Christmas anthem par excellence' (p. 167) evoking the transformative power of romantic nostalgia at times of both peace and war.

Part III: Peace on Earth, Goodwill to All Men

The construction of a shared imaginary utopia through, for example, an emphasis on family, hearth and home is central to the ideology sur-rounding Christmas, providing a touchstone, an idealised source which has the potential to influence social change. Compassion and friendliness are shown to be life-changing, exemplified, for example, in the game of football and exchange of gifts between British and German soldiers during the First World War, which provided a temporary resolution to the horrors of the battlefield in the so-called Christmas Truce of 1914. However, as Christine Agius explains, Christmas is also a device used to reinforce ideas about fighting the 'right' war, even if there are these momentary points in history where finer instincts and sentiments come to the fore.

'Christmas and War' explores the ways in which the gradual merging of ideology and patriotism with symbolic elements of Christmas is used to produce 'order' in society and correct responses to celebration at times of war. As such, while the Christmas Truce of World War I is widely held to represent the more positive, utopian associations of the Christmas spirit, there is also the dystopian. Exemplified in the Nazi appropriation of Christmas, which was taken over by the propaganda machine of the party, Christmas was 'absorbed into the ideological arm of National Socialism' and 'transformed into public expressions of the new *Weltanschauung*' (p. 141). It is also suggested that 'the "peoples" Christmas, or *Volksweihnachten*, was not simply the Nazi appropriation of a festival. Rather it melded "the twinned forms of the Führer and the Son of God, who promised national resurrection rooted in the primeval Germanic forest and the 'blood and soil' of the authentic *Volk*"' (Perry 2005: 572) (p. 143).

As Agius observes, the merging of Christmas rituals with the political or ideological 'offer[s] meaning in ambiguous, uncertain situations, and [is] crucial to the dynamics of identity construction and maintenance, particularly in periods of change' (Ross 2000: 54). The repercussions of September 11 on the American Christmas, for example, were reflected in the enhanced sales of GI Joes, police and firefighter toys, and decorations which commemorated the lives of those lost in the bombings. 'The powerful imagery of the collapsed towers of the World Trade Center was still imprinted on the nation's mindset and the direction of sentiment was one of support – support for troops, support for rescue services and support for ideas of liberty and freedom. To do otherwise would be "un-American"' (p. 147). The symbolism of the attacks was also important in this regard – the Pentagon represented America's strength as a nation in terms of defence; the Twin Towers of the World Trade Center, American prosperity and capitalism (p. 144). The billions spent on holiday decorations and ornamentation in 2001 thus gave some sense of normalcy to consumers that was critically needed after the terrible shock of September 11, 'the pulling together of the nation after the events of 9/11 being as important as confronting the terrorist threat' (p. 144).

As Tara Brabazon reflects in her chapter, 'Christmas and the Media', 'the banal acceptance of words and phrases like detention centres, asylum seekers and weapons of mass destruction alongside the exhausted sympathy in response to waves of tragedy from tsunamis to earthquakes and cyclones has created many moments to scream, rage, argue, fight or say no. Instead cookery programmes suggest that viewers pour another glass of wine, become immersed in the fascinations of frittata and feta cheese, and titter endlessly about celebrities rather than debating about how – precisely – a war can be won against fundamentalisms by constructing another set of fundamentalisms' (p. 161). 'You don't just give up. You make a stand. You say no' (*Dr Who*, 'Parting of the Ways' 2006). Her three case studies – *The Office*, *The Catherine Tate Show* and *Dr Who* – assemble a definition of Christmas through its mediations, showing that 'popular culture generally, and the popular media specifically, configure a secular Christmas that circulates meaning and interpretations of goodwill, love and generosity disconnected from religion' (p. 151). From news programming to soap opera, current affairs to drama, the goal is to show how notions of family, friendship, the home and consumerism are integrated into an ideological package of Christmas. One particular topic is the focus of this chapter. In the remaking of Christmas for the twenty-first century, the War on Terror – captured through September 11 and the second Iraq War – is an indicator of transformation. 'In the fight over fundamentalisms, Christmas is the pivot of change' (p. 151).

Films associated with Christmas – whether seen at the cinema or at home on the television – have also played a major part in effecting a popular consensus of what Christmas is all about, and the construction of the modern Christmas owes much to the moving image. As John Mundy writes, in his chapter 'Christmas and the Movies: Frames of Mind', though representations of Christmas in the cinema date back to the silent era, the commercial viability and dominant aesthetic sensibility of Christmas movies were established in Hollywood in the 1940s with films such as *Holiday Inn* (1942), *It's A Wonderful Life* (1946) and *Miracle on 34th Street* (1947). Though never short on romantic sentimentality, these and other films were able to reflect some of the tensions and conflicts inherent in our experience of Christmas. By the 1980s and 1990s, such films as *Gremlins* (1984) and *The Nightmare Before Christmas* (1993) placed greater emphasis on dystopian elements generated by profound shifts in social structure and the increasing commercialisation of Christmas. However, as an examination of two family entertainment-orientated films, *All I Want For Christmas* (1991) and *Jingle All The Way* (1996) reveals, Hollywood remains supremely efficient at both acknowledging and resolving ideological contradictions that characterise our experience of the modern Christmas.

'If, as Kris Kringle announces in *Miracle On 34th Street*, "Christmas isn't just a day, it's a frame of mind," such films reveal much about our contemporary frame of mind, conjuring visions in which divorce, structural changes in employment patterns and gender power, competitive pressures to acquire and consume, and the problems of being a parent compete with more positive, utopian images of Christmas. This contrast, the powerfully felt contradiction between the sentimental construct of Christmas as a time of peace, goodwill and family love, and the contemporary realities of divorce, the sense of guilt associated with commodity values and the mad rush to get the shopping done, accounts for much of the special poignancy of Christmas movies' (pp. 166–7). Such ideological contradictions, not least the problems associated with the family Christmas, are also the focus of the last two chapters, which explore personal responses to the festive season.

Part IV: We Wish You a Merry Christmas!
One of the central concerns of *Christmas, Ideology and Popular Culture* is to explore meaning, and while certain themes emerge across its twelve chapters, what they actually mean is subject to interpretation. As such, our final contributors explore the contradictions inherent in Christmas ideology and the pressures to take part in and enjoy the celebrations. Thom Swiss reflects on a family Christmas and brings together many of the themes and critiques discussed by writers in other chapters of this book. His discussion, 'Popular Culture and Christmas: A Nomad at Home', uses a variety of empirical materials – case study, personal experience, introspection, life story, artefacts, cultural texts, and interactional and visual texts. In deploying a wide range of interconnected interpretive practices, he provides a particular insight and understanding of the subject matter at hand: family Christmases in a middle-class suburban home near Chicago, Illinois, during the years 1958–68. The chapter's theme involves a consideration of how the ideologies and customs of Christmas both mask and make painfully evident deep disagreements and family problems, not least during the lead-up to and following Christmas Day itself.

But what if you do not need to conform or if your family faith is not (however loosely defined) Christian? Gerry Bloustien's evocative 'Reflections of a Jewish Childhood during Christmas' shows how the pressures to conform create their own specific pressures; you are always the outsider, the cultural tourist, looking in. On reflection, she wonders whether she has laid too heavy a responsibility on the celebration of Christmas, whether she has lost her own pleasure and enjoyment of Christmas completely.

Of course not! I find that I still enjoy sending Christmas cards to my non-Jewish friends and exchanging gifts. I still love the smells, sounds and excitement of Christmas time, especially when I am travelling in European and British cities where the snow somehow adds another layer of 'authenticity' to the magical mix. The difference is that I am able to remind myself and others that the rituals of Christmas, however splendid and exciting, are cultural creations and constructions alongside many others and as such are open to deconstruction and rejection. They are no less valuable or significant for that insight but neither are they superior or inevitable. (p. 195)

It is apparent, then, that Christmas is what we have made it mean, living in a particular culture in a particular historical moment, and that, surely, is one of the reasons why it continues to be such a rich and exciting area for research.

Part I
'TIS THE SEASON TO BE JOLLY

CHAPTER 1

The Invention of the English Christmas

John Storey

Introduction

The 'traditional' English Christmas was invented between the 1830s and 1880s. Its invention was directly connected to the processes of industrialisation and urbanisation and only indirectly connected to religion. To claim that the English Christmas was invented in the nineteenth century is to raise the objection that the Nativity was then almost two thousand years old. Although the Nativity may well have been two thousand years old, it and Christmas are not really the same thing.

Constantine the Great, who was Roman Emperor between AD 285 and 337, established Christianity as the state religion of the Roman Empire in AD 325. In AD 336 the new Christian Church of Rome established 25 December as the date of the Nativity, the central event in the developing Christian calendar. There is absolutely no scriptural evidence for this date. Moreover, 'historical' evidence suggested other dates, including 1 January, 6 January, 21, 28 and 29 March, 9, 19 and 20 April, 20 May, 29 September and 18 November (Harrison 1951: 15; Restad 1995: 4). So why 25 December? The answer is a rival religion called Mithraism. At the centre of this religion is Mithras, the god of light, whose birthday, the Day of the Birth of the Unconquered Sun (*Dies Solis Invicti Nati*), is 25 December. Mithraism, like Christianity, spread throughout the Roman Empire in the first three centuries AD and competed with Christianity as a potential state religion. As Payam Nabarz explains:

The Roman Mithraic practice was one of the greatest rivals to early Christianity for many reasons. As well as being a popular pagan religion practised by the Roman Army, it had many similarities to Christianity. These similarities frightened the Christian forefathers, as it meant that years before the arrival of Christ, all the Christian mysteries were already known. To combat

this, certain Christian writers said that the Devil, knowing of the coming of
Christ in advance, had imitated them before they existed in order to denigrate
them. As Christianity gained in strength and became the formal religion of
the Roman Empire, the cult of Mithras was one of the first pagan cults to
come under attack. (2005: 12–13)

The attack on Mithraism launched by the Christian Church consisted
of three strategies. First, Christians should separate themselves from the
rival religion. When this strategy did not work, they adopted a second. As
Manfred Clauss observes, 'When such evasions seemed impossible, they
effected a take-over, as in the case of the observance of Sunday and the festival of the god's birth on 25 December' (2000: 169). An account from the
fourth century makes clear the reason for the fixing of the Nativity as 25
December: 'But when the teachers of the Church realised that Christians
were allowing themselves to take part [in the celebrations of the Day of the
Birth of the Unconquered Sun], they decided to observe the Feast of the
true Birth on the same day' (quoted in Clauss 2000: 66). Therefore, it
seems quite clear that the intention of the Christian Church was to overlay
Mithraic rituals and ceremonies with Christian significance. This became
a common strategy. In the sixth century Augustine was sent as a mission-
ary to Britain. During the course of his work he received a letter from Pope
Gregory advising him to 'accommodate the ceremonies of the Christian
worship as much as possible to those of the heathen, that the people might
not be much startled at the change' (quoted in Harrison 1951: 28). The
third strategy was bloody persecution: what Clauss calls 'the Christians'
fanatical intolerance' (2000: 170). As Nabarz points out, 'In the fifth
century of the Common Era, temples of Mithras – like most other pagan
temples – were destroyed, and in some places churches were built on top
of them' (2005: 13). A letter written around the year 400 provides an
example: 'Did not your kinsman Gracchus . . . destroy a cave of Mithras a
few years ago when he was prefect of Rome? Did he not break up and burn
all the monstrous images there? . . . Did he not send them before him as
hostages, and gain for himself a baptism in Christ?' (quoted in Clauss 2000:
170).
    Although it is clear that 25 December is not the actual date of the
Nativity, it is possible to acknowledge this and to claim that it does not
matter, as the date was chosen to celebrate the Nativity without any corre-
sponding claim that this is the factual date of Christ's birth. In other words,
we do not know when he was born but we have chosen a date to celebrate
his birth. Whatever the argument, the fact remains that the fixing of the
Nativity by the Roman state was as much a political act as a theological one.

The circumstances of its origins have made it a problematic festival for some Christians. The Puritans, for example, the ideological engine behind the defeat of the army of Charles I, were literal readers of the Bible. Finding no evidence there for Christmas Day, they argued for its removal from the Christian calendar. Following the conclusion of the English Civil War, which established the Commonwealth or English Republic, Christmas was banned by Act of Parliament on 3 July 1647. On 24 December 1652 Parliament proclaimed, perhaps in the face of some ongoing resistance, that 'no observance shall be had of the five and twentieth of December, commonly called Christmas day; nor any solemnity used or exercised in churches upon that day in respect thereof' (quoted in Hearn 2004: 15). The ban remained in place until 1660. Parliament sat on Christmas Day, churches remained closed and soldiers were instructed to ensure that shops were open. Christmas was decriminalised as a religious holiday with the Restoration of the monarchy in 1660 but it did not return as popular festival. As Michael Harrison observes:

> Christmas came back . . . but he came back wearing something of the sober manner of the men who had temporarily driven him out. Old Christmas, in the twenty years [sic] that he had been officially outlawed, had lost much of his former jauntiness. It was a quieter Christmas who came back. (1951: 146)

By the first decades of the nineteenth century, what is now our major annual festival had almost disappeared. As J. M. Golby and A. W. Purdue point out:

> Christmas, in the first decades of the nineteenth century, was neither a major event in the Christian calendar nor a popular festival. Few magazines or newspapers referred to the festal day in any detail and many ignored it completely. In 1790 the leader writer in *The Times* had asserted that, 'within the half century this annual time of festivity has lost much of its original mirth and hospitality' and that newspaper's attention to the festival over the next half century bears witness to its general decline; in twenty of the years between 1790 and 1835 *The Times* did not mention Christmas at all, and for the remaining years its reports were extremely brief and uninformative. (2000: 40)

On 26 December 1826 *The Times* carried the following report: 'The due observance of Christmas-day was strictly enforced in the City yesterday, the Lord Mayor having given positive orders to the city officers, not to permit any shops to be open for the transaction of business . . . The order was strictly complied with in general.' The fact that the Lord Mayor of London felt obliged to enforce due observance clearly suggests that

Christmas was not really being observed. Further evidence of its decline is provided by responses to the Factory Act of 1833, which granted workers 8.5 days' holiday a year, plus Good Friday and Christmas Day. More enlightened factory owners allowed their workers to vote on which days they might have as holidays. Here is an example of the outcome of one such vote in 1833:

> [T]hey put it to the vote who were for Good Friday and who were for Easter Monday . . . the same with regard to Christmas-Day; in our part of the country Christmas-Day is not esteemed a workman's holiday, but New Year's day is, and the same process has been gone through of informing them that they were entitled to a holiday on Christmas-Day, and they have uniformly expressed a desire to take New Year's day in lieu of it. (Quoted in Cunningham 1980: 61–2)

The *Bolton Chronicle* reports a very similar attitude almost twenty years later in 1851:

> Not long ago the natal day of the Redeemer was pretty generally disregarded in this town, and a holiday was generally observed on New Year's Day. Now, though a holiday takes place on Christmas Day, the beginning of the New Year is looked upon as the Christmas season, and the inhabitants betake themselves to their festivities accordingly. (Quoted in Hudson 1997: 115)

In some rural areas it took even longer for the new invention to take hold. As late as 1867, a book on Lancashire folklore observed: 'In some rural parts of Lancashire it [Christmas Day] is now little regarded, and many of its customs are observed a week later – on the eve and day of the New Year' (quoted in Golby and Purdue 1981: 16).

Inventing Christmas

Commerce

Christmas was invented first and foremost as a commercial event. Everything that was revived or invented – decorations, cards, crackers, collections of carols, going to a pantomime, visiting Santa Claus and buying presents – all had one thing in common: they could be sold for profit. Therefore, it does not make historical sense to bemoan the fact that Christmas is too commercial; it was invented as a commercial festival. It was commercial from the very start. Part of what was being celebrated was the achievements of industrial capitalism – conspicuous consumption in a market economy.

Carol singing, for example, has a long history but it is only in the 1830s and 1840s that collections began to be made of old songs and new songs written with a specific focus on Christmas. Significant collections include William Sandys's *Christmas Carols, Ancient and Modern* (1833) and H. R. Bramley and John Stainer's *Christmas Carols Old and New* (1871). In these and other collections, recently composed carols easily outnumber the ancient or the old. Although the Christmas tree had been introduced into England by German migrants in the late eighteenth century, it is generally accepted that it was the *London Illustrated News*'s depiction of Queen Victoria's tree in December 1848 which popularised the practice. The first Christmas card was produced in 1843 (see Figure 1.2, p. 24). Within forty years, helped by the introduction of the ½d postage stamp, Christmas cards were in mass circulation. As *The Times* made clear in 1883 and applicable to the invention as a whole:

> This wholesome custom has been . . . frequently the happy means of ending strifes, cementing broken friendships and strengthening family and neighbourhood ties in all conditions of life. In this respect the Christmas card undoubtedly fulfils a high end, for cheap postage has constituted it almost exclusively the modern method of conveying Christmas wishes, and the increasing popularity of the custom is for this reason, if no other, a matter for congratulations. (Quoted in Golby and Purdue 2000: 70)

By the 1890s the Post Office was already finding it difficult to deal with the annual increase in mail. Significantly, like the first Christmas card, most cards ignored the Nativity and depicted instead evergreens, snowscapes, children playing, Father Christmas and robin redbreasts, providing further evidence of the decentred position of Christianity in the new Christmas celebrations.

Christmas crackers were invented by Tom Smith in 1846. Around the same period the pantomime first became associated with Christmas, its content becoming based on nursery tales. By the 1870s music hall stars were beginning to play the leading roles, anticipating the practice of contemporary pantomimes featuring pop and soap stars. Again, it is in the 1840s that Christmas presents first begin to be given at Christmas rather than at New Year. It is also at around this time that giving Christmas presents begins to lose its links to patronage: that is, giving as a confirmation of social status, giving without expectation of reciprocation. What is gradually established instead is an economy of giving amongst equals.

Father Christmas/Santa Claus is a latecomer to the new festivities. Significantly, he does not feature in the key ideological text of the new invention, Charles Dickens's *A Christmas Carol* (1843). He gradually emerges, mostly from the USA, between the 1860s and 1930s, most significantly in the drawings of Thomas Nast and the illustrations of Haddon H. Sundblom. The evolution of his image finally stops with Sundblom's Coca-Cola advertisements, which first appeared in 1931. Before then he might appear dressed in green, purple, blue or white. Moreover, he may appear human or as an elf. Although Coca-Cola did not invent Father Christmas/Santa Claus, it can claim to have finally fixed his identity. By the 1880s his presence is an important addition to the new department stores, where it is now possible to buy Christmas decorations.

By this time Christmas shopping, undoubtedly the central event in the new invention, is taking place a month or six weeks before Christmas Day. Two accounts from 1885 make this very clear:

> The presentation of 'boxes' and souvenirs is the same in America as in England . . . everybody expects to give and receive. A month before the event the fancy stores are crowded all day long with old and young in search of suitable presents, and every object is purchased . . . If the weather is fine, the principal streets are thronged. (Quoted in Miall 1978: 11)

> The note of preparation for the great festival . . . was sounded early in November when the windows of the stationers, the bookshops, and the railway stalls became suddenly gay with the coloured plates of Christmas numbers innumerable, has increased in volume as time went on. Now, on the eve of the great day, there is not a street in the capital containing a shop, from its broadest thoroughfare to its narrowest by-way, that has not decked its windows for the Christmas market. (11–12)

What the new urban middle class invented was a Christmas with a firm emphasis on commercialism. Its central organising figure was Santa Claus/Father Christmas and not Jesus Christ. If a nativity was being celebrated, it was the birth of a market economy underpinned by the new power of industrialisation. The profoundly commercial-secular nature of the invention has made possible its incredible international success. Even an officially atheist society like the People's Republic of China has no difficulty in embracing the festival (see Figure 1.1, p. 23).

'God Bless Us, Every One': The Politics of Charity
Charity is central to the Christmas invented by the new urban middle class. If what was invented was commercial out of instinct, it was charitable out of a sense of fear and guilt. The 1840s in England were known as the 'hungry forties', a period of economic slump, political unrest and

Figure 1.1 Christmas in Wuhan, China, 2006.

intense suffering and misery among the working class (Cole and Postgate 1976).

The first Christmas card (see Figure 1.2), commissioned by Sir Henry Cole and designed by J. C. Horsley, has at its centre not the Nativity but a representation of a typical middle-class family sitting down to Christmas dinner. On one side of the card we see the poor being given food, while on the other side they are being given clothes. The implication is quite clear; the celebration of the middle-class Christmas must include a consideration of the less fortunate. This argument is even more explicit in the text which is at the very heart of the invention of Christmas as an event organised around charity, Charles Dickens's *A Christmas Carol*, first published on 19 December 1843. The enormous popularity of the story of Scrooge's social redemption, not just as a novel (in its tenth edition by December 1844) but

Figure 1.2 The first Christmas card.

in theatre productions and public readings, made this the central text in the invention of Christmas. But to be clear, *A Christmas Carol* did not invent Christmas, as has been claimed by the *Sunday Telegraph* (18 December 1988), when it described Dickens as 'the man who invented Christmas'. His most recent biographer has made the same claim in slightly more guarded phrasing: 'Dickens can be said to have almost singlehandedly created the modern idea of Christmas' (Ackroyd 1990: 34). But what Dickens did do was to popularise what was being invented; in particular, he made material its organising ideology of charity. As Golby and Purdue say of Dickens's novel: 'in it Christmas becomes a bridge between the world as it is and the world as it should be' (2000: 45). The novel points 'to the social problems of the present and anxieties about the future' (45). When Dickens gave a reading of the novel in Boston on Christmas Eve 1867, it produced among his American audience what we might call the novel's ideal reader:

Among the multitude that surged out of the building came a Mr and Mrs Fairbanks (the former was the head of a large-scale factory), who had journeyed from Johnsburg, Vermont, for the occasion. Returning to their apartments in Boston, Mrs Fairbanks observed that her husband was particularly silent and absorbed in thought, while his face bore an expression of unusual seriousness. She ventured some remark which he did not appear to notice. Later, as he continued to gaze into the fire, she inquired the cause of his reverie, to which he replied: 'I feel that after listening to Mr Dickens's reading of *A Christmas Carol* tonight I should break the custom we have hitherto observed of opening the works on Christmas Day'. Upon the morrow they were closed. The following year a further custom was established, when not only were the works closed on Christmas Day, but each and every factory hand received the gift of a turkey. (Quoted in Golby and Purdue 2000: 48)

The story of Scrooge is a warning to the new urban middle class. Scrooge is continually presented as a representative of his class. When he is asked to give money for the poor at Christmas, he asks 'Are there no prisons [or] Union workhouses? . . . I help support the establishments I have mentioned: they cost enough: and those who are badly off must go there' (Dickens 1985: 51). A letter to the *Manchester Guardian*, written in the same year as the novel's publication, reveals how typical was Scrooge's response:

Mr Editor, – For some time past our main streets are haunted by swarms of beggars, who try to awaken the pity of the passers-by in a most shameless and annoying manner, by exposing their tattered clothing, sickly aspect, and disgusting wounds and deformities. I should think that when one pays the poor-rate, but also contributes largely to the charitable institutions, one had done enough to earn a right to be spared such disagreeable and impertinent molestations. And why else do we pay such high rates for the maintenance of the municipal police, if they do not even protect us so far as to make it possible to go to or out of town in peace? I hope the publication of these lines in your widely-circulated paper may induce the authorities to remove this nuisance; and I remain, – Your obedient servant, A Lady. (Quoted in Engels 1979: 303)

Above all, Scrooge is a typical middle-class businessman. His fault is not his meanness but his obsessive and typical focus on business. He appears honestly to believe what he says to the charity workers: 'It's not my business . . . It's enough for a man to understand his own business, and not to interfere with other people's. Mine occupies me constantly. Good afternoon, gentlemen!' (Dickens 1985: 51). His attitude is so similar to that of the bourgeois gentlemen Frederick Engels encountered in Manchester in 1844:

Ultimately it is self-interest, and especially money gain, which alone determines them. I once went into Manchester with a . . . bourgeois [gentleman], and spoke to him of the bad, unwholesome method of building, the frightful condition of the working people's quarters, and asserted that I had never seen so ill built a city. The man listened quietly to the end, and said at the corner where we parted: 'And yet there is a great deal of money made here: good morning, sir.' (Engels 1979: 304)

Scrooge has to learn what his former partner Marley had learned too late: 'The common welfare was my business; charity, mercy, forbearance, and benevolence, were, all, my business. The dealings of my trade were but a drop of water in the comprehensive ocean of my business!' (Dickens 1985: 62). Scrooge is, to use a phrase from Matthew Arnold, 'drugged with business' (quoted in Storey 1985: 224). As if speaking directly to Scrooge, Arnold argued: 'Money-making is not enough by itself. Industry is not enough by itself . . . The need in man for intellect and knowledge, his desire for beauty, his instinct for society, and for pleasurable and graceful forms of society, require to have their stimulus felt also, felt and satisfied' (ibid.). Like Dickens, Arnold was seeking to convert 'a middle class, narrow, ungenial, and unattractive' into 'a cultured, liberalised, ennobled, transformed middle class', one to which the working class 'may with joy direct its aspirations' (219).

The central idea of the novel is therefore the need for charity. Just like the middle-class family in the first Christmas card, Scrooge must share his prosperity. If he does not, he will be destroyed, the implication being that Scrooge's class must share its prosperity or it too will be destroyed. This is made absolutely clear in perhaps the most dramatic part of the story, Scrooge's encounter with Ignorance and Want (see Figure 1.3, p. 27):

'Spirit! are they yours?' Scrooge could say no more. 'They are Man's,' said the Spirit, Looking down upon them. '. . . This boy is Ignorance. This girl is Want. Beware them both, and all their degree, but most of all beware this boy, for on his brow I see that written which is Doom, unless the writing be erased. Deny it!' cried the Spirit, stretching out its hand towards the city. (Dickens 1985: 108)

Ignorance and Want instead of Exploitation and Oppression. This is an act of political displacement on Dickens's part. Education and charity rather than fundamental social change. Charity allows us to congratulate ourselves on the fact that we give. And charity certainly relieves suffering but what it does not do is change the causes of suffering. Charity is a temporary redistribution of wealth which does not disturb the hierarchies of wealth; in fact, it safeguards the hierarchies of wealth. The economic system which produced the suffering shown to Scrooge remains unchallenged. His 'conversion' to charity presents absolutely no challenge to the economic system which produces the need for charity. By embracing it

Figure 1.3 'Ignorance and Want'.

Scrooge will protect himself and his class from more fundamental social change. This is the conversion that he experiences: self-interest taking a more sustainable form. By learning to share a little, a great deal more will remain secure.

It is not that Dickens (and others like him) did not desire a better society, one with less squalor, less poverty, less ignorance and so on; rather that a better society could never be envisaged as other than a better middle-class society. Scrooge's nephew Fred unwittingly acknowledges the limits of what Dickens called the 'Carol philosophy' (quoted in Hearn 2004: 33) when he describes Christmas as 'a kind, forgiving, charitable, pleasant time: the only time I know of, in the long calendar of the year, when men and women seem by one consent to open their shut-up hearts freely, and to think of people below them as if they really were fellow-passengers to the grave, and not another race of creatures bound on other journeys' (Dickens 1985: 49). According to Ruth Glancy (1998), 'the story's strong social message' is an 'appeal to the people of England to lead less selfish lives, and the rich especially to take seriously their duty of care to those less fortunate' (x). This perfectly encapsulates the ideology of charity, the belief that all that is required is for the rich to share a little with the poor, as if these were natural orders of humanity, little related to exploitation, injustice and oppression.

Writing five years after the publication of the novel, Karl Marx and Frederick Engels in the *Manifesto of the Communist Party* (1848) reached a very different conclusion about Scrooge and his class:

> [T]he bourgeoisie is unfit any longer to be the ruling class in society, and to impose its conditions of existence upon society as an over-riding law. It is unfit to rule because it is incompetent to assure an existence to its slave within his slavery . . . What the bourgeoisie therefore produces . . . are its own grave-diggers. (Marx and Engels 1998: 23–4)

In the *Manifesto* version the boy and girl are reconfigured, not as Ignorance and Want, but as the capitalist system's 'grave-diggers'.

As George Orwell observed, 'It seems that in every attack Dickens makes upon society he is always pointing to a change in spirit rather than a change in structure' (quoted in Hearn 2000: 64). But Dickens was very clear about the consequences of doing nothing. As he expressed it in a letter written less than three months before the publication of *A Christmas Carol*, 'in that prodigious misery and ignorance of the swarming masses of mankind in England, the seeds of its certain ruin are sown' (quoted in Hearn 2000: 124). Whether the metaphor is grave-digging or an unwanted harvest, the message is the same: if social relations between classes do not change, society itself will undergo dramatic and revolutionary change. Marx and Engels wanted this; Dickens wanted to prevent it. Both despair at the current situation. But whereas Marx and Engels see revolution as the only means to justice, Dickens places his hope in reform. Here we see the playing out of a conflict between 'the Ghost of an Idea' (Dickens 1985: 41) and the 'spectre [which] is haunting Europe' (Marx and Engels 1998: 3).

Utopian Nostalgia

The invention of Christmas was driven by a utopian nostalgia: an attempt to recreate an imaginary past. Central to the urban middle class's invention of Christmas is the claim that they are simply reviving a 'tradition'. In their discussions of Christmas they look back longingly to 'Merrie England', a supposed lost golden age in which rich and poor lived in a glorious harmony of deference and subordination. The promise of Christmas was a temporary return to this golden age:

> The working man looked forward to Christmas as the portion of the year which repaid his former toils. (William Sandys, *Christmas Carols Ancient and Modern*, 1833; quoted in Connelly 1999: 24)

> The sports and festivities of the season were everywhere taken under the protection of the lord of the soil; and all classes of his dependants had a customary claim upon the hospitalities which he prepared for the occasion . . . The mirth of the humble and uneducated man received no check, from the assumption of an unseasonable gravity, or ungenerous reserve, on the part of those with whom fortune had dealt more kindly, and to whom knowledge had opened her stores. The moral effect of all of this was of the most valuable kind. Nothing so promotes a reciprocal kindliness of feeling as a community of enjoyment: and the bond of goodwill was thus drawn tighter between the remotest classes, whose differences of privilege, of education, and of pursuit, are perpetually operating to loosen it, and threatening to dissolve it altogether. (Thomas K. Hervey, *The Book of Christmas*, 1836; quoted in Hervey 2000: 50)

> Time was . . . when all were full of gladness and both serf and squire, baron and retainer, did their very best to keep their companions happy. All classes gave themselves up to frolic and revelry, with a thoroughness of spirit. (*Christmas in the Olden Times*, 1859; quoted in Golby and Purdue 2000: 53)

> It is hard to picture a more pleasant scene than that of Old English Christmas . . . Rich and poor discarded for a time all class distinctions and joined equally in merry-making. (*West Briton and Cornwall Advertiser*, 1900; quoted in Connelly 1999: 24)

These claims, and others like them, offered an imaginary past intended as a remedy for a dangerous present and an even more dangerous future. The utopian promise of Christmas is captured by Thomas K. Hervey, writing in 1836:

> [It] proclaimed peace on earth and goodwill towards all men, making no exclusions, and dividing them into no classes, rises [sic] up a dormant sense

of universal brotherhood in the heart . . . At no other period of the year are
the feeling of universal benevolence and sense of common Adam so widely
awakened; at no season is the predominant spirit of selfishness so effectually
rebuked; never are the circles of love so largely widened. (Hervey 2000: 88)

We should not take these writings as serious historical accounts of the
past but as nostalgic fantasies intended to promote in the present what had
never before existed. Middle-class nostalgia for Christmas past was a nostalgia for the feudal power relations of the past. What Christmas promised
was a return to feudal social relations in the new context of industrialisation and urbanisation. It was a utopia in which the working class would
once again embrace what Matthew Arnold, writing in 1867, had feared that
they had lost: 'the strong feudal habits of subordination and deference'
(quoted in Storey 2003: 23). Steve Roud summarises perfectly this aspect
of the invention:

In particular, Victorians had an uncanny knack of clothing their inventions
and remodelled traditions in an aura which implied that they were traditional
and ancient. They conjured up a curiously timeless Merrie England in which
the people were poor, but content, and were looked after by a benevolent local
baron or lord of the manor and equally benevolent clergy. Everyone knew
their place, and social hierarchies were not questioned. Such a time never
existed, but in rewriting the history of our major festivals and traditions, it
was this mythical Golden Age, which formed the backbone of the Victorian
world-view, to which they aspired, and to which they returned again and
again for ideas, ideals and legitimisation. (2000: 12)

Not only did the new urban middle class invent the English Christmas in
the nineteenth century, they also invented the 'tradition' which they
claimed only to be reviving.

Conclusion

The Christmas the new urban middle class invented was both a celebration
of the achievements of industrial capitalism and a temporary negation of
industrial capitalism, in which goodwill replaces competition, harmony
replaces conflict, abundance replaces scarcity, and desire replaces denial.
What was invented was a utopian version of industrial capitalism: a temporal and social space in which economic competition and exploitation are
softened by the temporary articulation of feudal relations of power. The
promise of Christmas is a middle-class utopia in which exploitation and
oppression can exist in harmony with deference and 'goodwill to all men'.

Instead of social equality and the redistribution of wealth, it articulates the mutual obligations of rich and poor permanently bound together in the best of all possible worlds – a sentiment embodied in the final words of *A Christmas Carol:* 'God bless Us, Every One!' (Dickens 1985: 134).

CHAPTER 2

Conspicuous Consumption and Festive Follies: Victorian Images of Christmas

Sara M. Dodd

This chapter explores the themes that came to be associated with the middle-class Victorian vision of Christmas and the iconography of its illustrations. Their emphasis is not so much on religious imagery as on pagan survivals and the associated consumption to excess, though there are warnings against over-indulgence and reminders of traditional Christian virtues like charity in both high art (Royal Academy paintings) and popular culture (cartoons in the magazine *Punch* and Christmas cards). The creation of a Christmas tradition, with its associated symbols and rituals, can often be seen in constructed images of a nostalgic past – in a 'great house', for example – where the happy antics and activities of wassailers in an ordered feudal world provide credibility and sustenance for the Victorian present as well as evidence of the link Thorstein Veblen makes between 'conspicuous consumption' and the honourable opulence of the wealthy (1899).

The festival began to be seen as highly moral, despite its pagan origins, in its celebration of conviviality and family life. A writer trying to identify the 'Spirit of Christmas' in 1930, A. Edward Newton, cites the American author Washington Irving's description of this attitude as early as 1819: 'shorn as it is of its ancient and festive honours, Christmas is still a period of delightful excitement in England' (Newton 1930: 7). Washington Irving's comments were to be republished as *The Old English Christmas* in 1876 by Macmillan with illustrations by Randolph Caldecott, a contributor to Christmas card designs. Newton goes on to examine the 'first' Christmas card (to be discussed later), which portrays 'a family group of three generations indulging in the Christmas spirit' (1930: 8). Articles in the middle-class press repeatedly promote the 'spirit of good fellowship which the Christmas festivities engender among every class', as a leader in *The Times*, 25 December 1883, puts it – though how true this optimistic picture was of the underclass is difficult to assess. The writer sees 'the universal practice of wishing one another the compliments of the season' as a 'wholesome custom [which] has been the happy means of ending strifes, cementing broken friendships and strengthening family and neighbourly ties in all conditions of life'. The *Art Journal* has increasingly lengthy articles on Christmas cards and the habit of exchanging them from the 1870s to the 1890s, with a repeated emphasis on the societal benefits of such a habit. An article (1873b, 12:379) applauds the giving of gifts, too: 'in anticipation of "the season" when pleasure becomes a duty and so many English homes are made happy by family gatherings [gifts] now fill the windows of the leading shops in the main thoroughfares throughout our cities and towns.' In what was to become a middle-class tradition after 1843, the reading of Charles Dickens's *A Christmas Carol*, the moral was reinforced throughout the Victorian period and beyond. Dickens is supposed to have confessed to being greatly influenced by Irving's nostalgic picture of an English Christmas: 'I don't go upstairs two nights out of seven without taking Washington Irving under my arm' (cited in Buday 1954: 64). The message was that self-indulgence was acceptable in the context of the family circle and friends; it was blessed not only to give, but also to receive.

Indulgence towards excess is pictured in numerous cartoons and Christmas cards from this time onwards. It is apparent in what has been identified as the first proper Christmas card, now dated 1843, designed by John Calcott Horsley, later to become a Royal Academician, at the behest of Henry Cole (later to be instrumental in the design of the Great Exhibition of 1851 and the founding of the South Kensington Museum), known as the Cole Horsley card. It proved instantly popular with those who could afford it; a thousand copies were lithographed, hand-coloured and sold for a shilling each, a price not readily affordable by the poorer classes. The central panel portrays a happy family feast, with the foreground figures toasting the viewer with goblets of what is presumably wine, and a small child being given some in the middle of the picture. It did attract some adverse comment for its encouragement of drunkenness. This was to set the scene for many card illustrations to come, though the side panels tell another story, portraying 'Clothing the Naked' and 'Feeding the Hungry'. John Leech's well-known illustrations to Dickens's *A Christmas Carol* take up a similar theme, of course. Leech faithfully follows the description of 'The Spirit of Christmas Present':

> Heaped up upon the floor, to form a kind of throne, were turkeys, geese, game, poultry, brawn, great joints of meat, sucking-pigs, long wreaths of sausages, mince-pies, plum-puddings, barrels of oysters, red-hot chestnuts, cherry cheeked apples, juicy oranges, luscious pears, immense twelfth-cakes,

A MERRY CHRISTMAS AND A HAPPY NEW YEAR!

Figure 2.1 'A Merry Christmas and a Happy New Year' (1858). Cartoon
by John Leech.

and seething bowls of punch, that made the chamber dim with their delicious
steam. (Stave III, 'The Second of the Three Spirits')

This leads on to the description of the Cratchits' meal ('There never was
such a goose,' 'Oh, a wonderful pudding!' and so on). On the last page,
Leech illustrates the reformed Scrooge serving Bob Cratchit from a
'Christmas bowl of smoking bishop' (Stave V, 'The End of It').

At the same time and later, John Leech was picturing slightly exaggerated, more humorous family gatherings for the middle-class magazine
Punch. In a cartoon of 1862, Leech depicts 'A family group – Baby Stirring
the Pudding', the group around the large table consisting of well-dressed
ladies, a soldier, children and Mr Punch himself, as was characteristic of
the magazine, holding the baby. In 'A Merry Christmas and a Happy New
Year' of 1858 (see Figure 2.1) Leech fills the page with what appears to be
a turkey (but also resembles a pudding) being led by children on a sledge
across the ice, accompanied by Mr Punch, as usual, and by fairies, clowns,
harlequins, dog, piglet and, in the background, dancing bottles and pies.

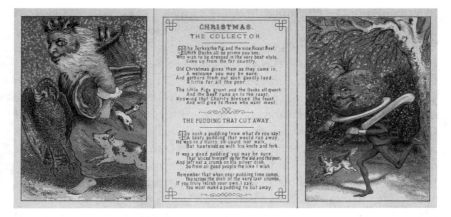

Figure 2.2 'The Pudding that Cut Away' (c.1870–5). Card
by Alfred Crowquill.

Interestingly, there is a decorated fir tree in the background and holly adornments (Leech 1887: 11).

George Buday in his comprehensive *History of the Christmas Card* points out that the sumptuousness of the Christmas dinner was a common theme in Christmas card design, citing, for example, 'a swineherd and a buyer looking at a fat pig and fatter piglets', with the caption 'The Compliments of the Season and All Good Things in Reason' and 'They're doomed for Christmas brawn and chine, for pigs must die that men may dine' (1954: 120). Many cards humorously humanise the food about to be devoured – joints of meat and bottles with arms and legs (as in the *Punch* cartoon mentioned above), and plum puddings running away, as in a series of cards produced by Charles Goodall and Son in the early 1870s (see Figure 2.2), where a pudding brandishing a knife and fork, running away with a plate around its neck, and a Father Christmas figure in blue carrying game and bottles are accompanied by some verses (entitled 'The Pudding that Cut Away'), which include:

> It was a good pudding you may be sure,
> That sliced himself up for the old and the poor;
> And left not a crumb on his silver dish,
> So from all good people the like I wish.
>
> (Seddon 1992: 24.9 [Alfred Crowquill])

Portrayal of family celebration with traditional repast was not limited to what were considered the less exalted forms of art. In 1868 the upmarket *Art Journal* illustrated and wrote about a painting by Thomas Webster,

R.A., entitled 'The Christmas Pudding', which had recently been exhibited. The accompanying article suggests that three generations of Webster's own family are being portrayed partaking in the 'old-fashioned custom of health drinking' (as in the Cole Horsley Christmas card), and attempts to link such customs to traditional Christian meanings: 'a plain unadorned representation of the simple way in which families of the middle classes were accustomed, half a century ago, to keep the great Christian festival commemorative of the Saviour's birth'. The article goes on: 'The origin of the "plum pudding" as an essential dish on the table is doubtful, but it may be presumed to have grown out of "plum porridge" which used to be served up on this occasion' (referring to a diary entry of 1801). This passage raises two issues: a desire to make Christmas festivities respectable through tradition and an awareness that there was a need to justify such excess.

A certain strand of guilt can be identified in the more popular press as early as Leech's cartoons for *Punch*: for example, in 'A Caution to Little Boys at a Festive Season' of 1853, where a decidedly sick-looking boy gazes aghast at the pudding being uncovered at the family table. The caption reads:

> *Mamma.* 'Why, my dearest Albert, what are you crying for? – so good, too, as you have been all day!'
> *Spoiled Little Boy.* 'Boo hoo! I've eaten so-much be-ef and t-turkey, that I can't eat any p–plum p-p-pudding!' *[Oh, what a very greedy little fellow!]*
> (Leech 1886: 119)

Later cartoons designed for *Punch* by John Tenniel depict a grimmer scene: the lack of Christmas spirit, food or warmth for many. For example, Tenniel's 'Ireland's Christmas Stocking (A Wish and a Suggestion)', 1881 (see Figure 2.3), shows a female personification of Ireland in rags, looking hopefully at a Christmas stocking (a relatively new custom) that has just been left at her door by a Father Christmas dressed in the old fashion of skins or fur. Out of the stocking pokes a scroll titled 'Mansion House Fund', and we are told in a later explanatory caption for this volume that 'A Defence of Property Fund had been started in defence of the Irish landlords Considering the distress still prevalent in the poorer districts, Mr. Punch, in this Christmas cartoon, suggests the propriety of starting a "Mansion House Fund" in the interest of the tenants – December, 1881' (Tenniel 1895: 146).

Similarly, Tenniel's 'The Awakening of Father Christmas; or, A Call to Alms' (with a deliberate double meaning in the subtitle) has an angel with a sash entitled 'Charity', holding by the hand two starving ragged children and trying to arouse with mistletoe over his head a dozing Father Christmas,

IRELAND'S CHRISTMAS STOCKING.

(A WISH AND A SUGGESTION.)

Figure 2.3 'Ireland's Christmas Stocking (A Wish and a Suggestion)' (1881). Cartoon by John Tenniel.

beside him a turkey and a box labelled 'toys'. The explanatory caption reads 'Poverty and distress were prevalent in the country at this time, the unemployed were numerous and clamorous, and Mr. Punch in this seasonable cartoon suggested that Christmas and charity should heartily co-operate for the relief of the children of the poor. – December, 1891' (Tenniel 1895: 146).

The theme of charity is very much to the fore in an oil painting exhibited in 1873 by Augustus Edwin Mulready. Called 'Remembering Joys that have passed away' (Guildhall Art Gallery, London, illustrated in Johnson 1986, Fig. 166), it shows two of the waifs and strays of Victorian London, a typical subject for him, a match seller and a crossing sweeper, gazing at a poster advertising the last night of 'A Grand Christmas Pantomime' while the snow deepens around them. The implication is that we should remember those who have no access to the joys associated with middle-class celebrations. Pantomimes, clowns and harlequins, as depicted on this poster, were common subjects for Christmas cards of the 1880s, for example, and were to be seen on another famous early card by William Maw Egley (1848). The Egley card has a similar theme to the Cole Horsley card of 1843, that of family feasting and celebration, and both have side panels showing charity to the poor. Charity was to be seen in cards such as another series produced by Goodall between 1870 and 1875. 'The Old English Gentleman' shows four scenes illustrating these verses:

The while he feasted well the great,
He ne'er forgot the small.
Nor was the houseless wanderer
Then driven from his hall.

(Seddon 1992: 24.6b)

Young waifs and strays – crossing sweepers, chimney sweepers, match sellers – though rather prettified, were consistently depicted on Christmas cards: for example, on a card both in the Seddon collection and selected by Buday, where a pretty but humbly clad girl holds an umbrella up against the snow (Seddon 1992: 6.8 – Sulman, 1870s). Chimney sweepers gaze cheerily at us through a basement grill, with the caption 'CLEAR YOUR DOOR-WAY, SIR' and 'A New Year full of merriment' (Seddon 1992: 68.20, c. 1890). A small boy grins at us as he sweeps a crossing, with the caption 'SPARE A COPPER SIR' and 'Wishing you a Happy Christmas' (Seddon 1992: 107.3, early 1880s). A small, ragged but pretty flower girl sitting by a railing holds up a nosegay of violets to an unseen passer-by, the caption being 'A PENNY A BUNCH' and 'With my best wishes for the coming year' (ibid.) (see Figure 2.4). All the children are portrayed as clean, well nourished and happy, but it must have been a constant reminder

Figure 2.4 'A Penny A Bunch' (card of early 1880s).

of those who could not enjoy Christmas while at the same time assuaging some guilt by the choice of image, perhaps.

Certainly, the *Art Journal* of 1872, in a long article praising the quality of the productions of Marcus Ward, a well-known Belfast Christmas card maker, goes on to extol the virtues of introducing such a trade into Ireland so as to provide employment. It is 'evidence of what Ireland may be when "agitation" ceases, and permits prosperity to be "at large" in that country'. If giving Christmas cards was actually helping the Irish poor, then it was a duty as well as a pleasure.

As has already been suggested by Tenniel's later cartoons of Father Christmas being enjoined to intervene in situations of dire need and poverty, the figure was identified by the end of the century with charity to all rather than simply giving gifts to the privileged classes. The transition from Criscringle to Santa Claus in America is traced by George McKay in his chapter, and the American Alfred Newton in his attempt to identify the 'Christmas Spirit' mentions the figure who became popular in Germany, Holland and England, who 'early took to Christmas: Santa Claus and Kriss Kringle, St. Nicholas and other forms of Father Christmas' (Newton 1930: 4). Buday traces his origins as 'Good King Wenceslaus, St. Nicholas, or Santa Claus, the latter being the American version derived from the early Dutch settlers' Sante Klass', Wenceslaus being King of Bohemia and St Nicholas Bishop of Myra, later patron saint of Russia and then New York (Buday 1954: 125). Laura Seddon, in her introduction to Volume 12 of her Christmas card collection, suggests that the images of Father Christmas in these cards of the early 1870s are linked to portrayals of the Lord of Misrule, particularly when portrayed in white with a holly wreath (Seddon 1992: 12.12). Indeed, he is seen in various colours – green, brown and blue – as well as in what was to become the traditional red robe. The role of the mythical Bacchus is sometimes invoked in, for example, cards that depict him proffering barrels, flagons or goblets of wine (Seddon 1992: 12.1 or 54.4).

In one example, the 'Christmas Aged King' portrayed is dressed in white, with the caption 'Ring forth the bells in triumph ring, To welcome Christmas aged king'. The usual goblet of wine and Christmas pudding accompany him (Seddon 1992: 12.32). Some links can be made with the 'Spirit of Christmas Present' in Dickens's *A Christmas Carol*, perhaps, with the author's description and its faithful illustration by Leech:

> It was clothed in one simple deep green robe, or mantle, bordered with white fur . . . on its head it wore no other covering than a holly wreath set here and there with shining icicles. Its dark brown curls were long and free: free as its genial face, its sparkling eye, its open hand, its cheery voice, its unconstrained

demeanour, and its joyful air. Girded round its middle was an ancient scabbard; but no sword was in it, and the ancient sheath was eaten up with rust. (Dickens 1843b: 78)

This genial and benevolent image was one which survived to the end of the century, and may well have inspired various illustrated versions of Father Christmas. Raphael Tuck's Christmas card productions of the 1880s and 1890s include cut-out cards for children, one of which has a benevolent red-robed and fur-trimmed Father Christmas laden with gifts and a Christmas tree (see Figure 2.5), while a boy and a girl holding each arm clutch in theirs a sailboat and a doll – suitably gender-specific, of course (Seddon 1992: 91.20). There is a more unusual rendition of 'Santa Claus' in the first edition of the *Strand Magazine* in 1891; Santa is portrayed as a delicate, angelic child, with a halo, barefoot, carrying a Christmas tree through some snow-laden woods above a picturesque snow-covered village (see Figure 2.6). The traditional St Nicholas is obviously being reincarnated here and, like the child, the tree is aglow, but with candles and baubles (frontispiece [unattributed] of the *Strand Magazine*, 1891). In the final illustration in the *Strand* of 1892, there is a Christmas puzzle picture, wherein the reader is supposed to 'Find Old Father Xmas', who is pictured on the right, carrying a fir tree (*Strand Magazine* 1892: 68).

The Christmas tree has a well-known provenance, of course. Newton traces the habit back to Egypt via Germany (Newton 1930: 4). Queen Charlotte, the German wife of George III, had apparently decorated a tree for her family in the 1790s, and Prince Albert is supposed to have introduced the German habit of bringing a decorated fir tree indoors at Windsor Castle in 1841, though the custom was not to become popular with the middle classes for the next twenty years. The children's magazine *St. Nicholas* contains several references to the Christmas tree, which was evidently by now well established in the middle-class home at Christmas (1895: 23:2, opposite p. 91). In the frontispiece, 'Ho for the Christmas Tree!', the focus is on five children, a maid and a dog, all gazing out of the glass half of a front door, either eagerly awaiting the delivery of a tree or admiring it outside. Wreaths and mistletoe hang over the door. A few pages further on, the story 'A Christmas White Elephant' by W. A. Wilson is introduced:

'Papa', asked Cecie, whose blond curls scarcely reached the lowest branches of the tree, 'it never moves, does it?'
'No, dear.'
'And it is alive just like us?'
'Yes. That is – well, yes; not exactly, you know, but it is quite alive.'
'What does it feed on all the time, then?'

Figure 2.5 'Father Christmas' (cut-out card of late 1880s/early 1890s, produced by Raphael Tuck).

Figure 2.6 'Santa Claus' (frontispiece, *Strand Magazine*, 1891).

'The juices of the earth', said Fred, with the air of an experienced gardener. That is why we must give it water.'

(Wilson 1895: 113)

The giving of water is illustrated in 'The tree was ceremoniously watered, to the complete satisfaction of its patroness' (ibid.: 117). Cecie has been full of admiration for the baubles, chains and candles that are pictured, but had worried that it would hurt the tree:

She was wondering if it would care to be lighted up with candles within an inch of its life like that, and covered with glittering ornaments till it could scarcely breathe; whether it liked to have molten wax run all over its fresh green branches; and whether it were being treated with proper respect in being made to hold up such a load of things. (ibid.: 115)

All this is indicative of an established custom by that time.

A later edition of *St. Nicholas* of 1896 contains a serialised story, 'Betty Leicester's English Christmas' by Sarah Orne Jewett, which had been started in the December number. It is a construction of 'Ye Olde English Christmas' at an aristocratic country house, some time in that or the previous century – or so the illustration would suggest. 'The great hall was gay with holly and Christmas greens [. . .] as if Christmas had never been so warm and friendly and generous in a great house before [. . .] such splendour and warm-heartedness of the old English fashion' (Jewett 1896: 315). The illustration is of 'Old Bond, the butler, bearing the plum-pudding aloft', with musicians and singers 'in quaint costumes' in the background, singing a beautiful old English song' (ibid. and 317). It must have become clear that the story is that of a nostalgic, sentimentalised, feudal – and quintessentially English – Christmas. The assumption of English traditions long established was common in Christmas cards. The *Art Journal* of 1871, singling out the cards produced by Marcus Ward for high praise, lists topics such as 'quaint borrowings from medieval games and costumes' as very successful. Buday also singles out Marcus Ward's output, mentioning T. Walter Wilson's designs for 'Christmas Cabinets', which were folding triptychs in a series called Christmas in the Olden Times (Buday 1954: 67). He cites the productions of the printer Vizetelly, too: for example, his *Christmas with the Poets*, with illustrations by the Royal Academician Myles Birket Foster, as contributing to the 'popular revival of the "old Christmas" atmosphere, customs and traditions' of mid-Victorian England (ibid.: 63). The book was apparently compiled from old poems and carols, with depictions of Anglo-Norman carol-singers, a boar's head being brought into a great hall, 'Old English hospitality to the Poor', the wassail bowl, the yule log, tenants bringing presents to the landlord and 'Christmas sports'. Reviewing the Christmas card productions of de la Rue and Co., an article in *The Times* (1880) mentions that amongst the variety of subjects 'a knight of the 14th century is bending over the hand of a lady who may well inspire him with a sentiment stronger than mere friendship'. There are many examples of supposedly traditional Christmas practices in the Seddon Collection: for example, amongst the Charles Goodall volumes of the early 1870s, some medieval indoor scenes, set in a baronial hall with a yule log (Seddon 1992: 24.33, 28), or a card dated 1878 produced by the American publisher Louis Prang of children dressed in what looks like sixteenth-century costume, playing a dancing game (Seddon 1992: 62.25). The accompanying verse begins 'Merrily, merrily, to and fro, / Under the holly and mistletoe', and ends 'Dear, dear CHRISTMAS! come ever so'.

The enduring and reassuring trimmings associated with Christmas were all part of the child's eye vision reproduced in Victorian Christmas cards. Holly and ivy had been associated with the old winter solstice and mistletoe was linked with the Druids and Norse mythology, when former enemies sealed their reconciliation with a kiss beneath it. Holly and mistletoe had first appeared in the 1840s – for example, on the Egley card – and continued to be popular decorative motifs on letters, magazine titles and simple cards. The Egley card also portrays the apparently traditional 'Sir Roger de Coverley' dance, which is pictured by Leech in his illustration of 'Mr. Fezziwig's Ball' for *A Christmas Carol* (Dickens 1843, frontispiece, Stave II): 'the great effect of the evening came after the Roast and Boiled, when the fiddler . . . struck up "Sir Roger de Coverley".' Sir Roger de Coverley himself, the rakish philanthropist, had become a renowned measure of Christmas benevolence and charity after the articles by Joseph Addison in *The Spectator* of 1711 and 1712, his grandfather supposedly inventing the dance, 'Roger of Coverly [*sic*]'. It was fiction but the dance itself was real enough, and was obviously considered traditional by Addison's time. Mr Fezziwig's room is garlanded and wreathed, and there is flirting under the mistletoe. The effects of mistletoe were much ridiculed in Leech's later illustrations for *Punch* magazine. In his cartoons of social mores, young people are mercilessly lampooned; 'Caution During the Mistletoe Season' (1855), for example, shows a disconcerted young man who has obviously just tried to kiss a young woman under the mistletoe, with the caption: '*Pretty Cousin.* "What a tiresome great awkward boy you are! – just see how you have scratched my chin!" [*Young gentleman apologises amply*]' (Leech 1887: 1).

In 'None but the Brave Deserve the Fair' (1858), a small boy is trying to hold a bunch of mistletoe up to a young woman, without much success, crying 'Now, I've got you!' (ibid.), while in 'Miss and Mistletoe' (1858) a smug-looking elderly spinster, as she would have been termed, sits expectantly under some mistletoe, looking at a young man, the caption being:

> *Miss Gushington.* 'Oh, don't you like Christmas time, Mr. Brown, and all its dear old customs?'
> *Brown.* 'Don't seem to see it.'

(ibid.: 4)

A delighted Mr Punch is trapped by a group of young women under a bunch of mistletoe (1864) (ibid.: 5), and in 'Volunteer Movement' (1861), 'That distinguished rifle shot, Mr. Punch, having done his duty like a man, throws himself under the mistletoe, and receives his just reward' (presumably from the young women surrounding him) (ibid.: 10). That Mr Punch's hairstyle and features resemble those of Benjamin Disraeli may be simply a coincidence. Slightly more sinister to modern eyes is the depiction of Mr Punch leaping up and trapping a young woman under the mistletoe as he forces a kiss on her, saying 'Rooti-Tooit – I've Got Cher!' (1859) – but she doesn't seem to mind (ibid.: 8) (see Figure 2.7). In the same series is a depiction of 'A Christmas Party. – Grandpapa dances "Sir Roger" – and may he dance it for many, many years to come' (1856), which seems to have a more serious sentiment attached, despite the fact that 'Grandpapa' seems to resemble Mr Punch again. Mid-Victorian family celebration is the ostensible subject matter, at least.

Children's games, particularly those associated with winter, abound on illustrations. On Christmas cards, in particular, skating, sledging and snowballing reinforce the Christmas spirit of fun and frolics. Examples are plentiful. For example, from the Seddon Collection a boy and girl skate, ignoring the 'Dangerous' sign (Seddon 1992: 6.10, early 1870s, J. Mansell); a girl in blue is skating on a card probably by W. Tasker Nugent for Marcus Ward between 1875 and 1880 (Seddon 1992: 33.41); one of the American producer Prang's cards shows a boy sledging downhill (Seddon 1992: 63.22). Robins sometimes take on the roles of naughty children. In a card of the early 1870s, good robins sing while a naughty one aims a snowball at the 'grown-up' (Seddon 1992: 26.14). Robins snowball a Father Christmas in some designs. According to Buday, robins were popular motifs from the 1850s onwards (Buday 1954: 99), with their traditional associations (some cited the legend of Christ's blood dropping on to a robin's breast). The Spode factory,

ROOTI-TOOIT—I'VE GOT CHER!

Figure 2.7 'Rooti-Tooit – I've Got Cher' (1859). Cartoon by John Leech.

one of the first ceramic manufacturers to produce Christmas designs on their ware, in about 1861 issued one of a robin standing on a snow-covered branch, after a painting by Harrison Weir which had been illustrated in the *Illustrated London News* on 5 December 1858.

Religious associations were not so popular as secular and even pagan survivals, though. Religious cards could be commissioned by societies such as the Society for the Promotion of Christian Knowledge, the Religious Tract Society and the Sunday School Union, or by producers such as Raphael Tuck for the Artist Series (reproducing Renaissance images by Titian, Correggio and others). An example of an angel image that became extremely popular is by Rebecca Coleman, a prize design of 1880 (Seddon 1992: 67.7) (see Figure 2.8). Gleeson White, a contemporary critic, said

Figure 2.8 'Angel Head' (1880), one of a series of cards by Rebecca Coleman, produced by Raphael Tuck in 1881.

that her angel series 'almost broke the record for popular success' (Seddon 1992: 76). She may well have been inspired by the unusually popular portrayal of an angel head in an oil painting by Joanna Boyce, exhibited in 1861. The gap between 'high art' and 'popular design' was closing. Royal Academicians were sometimes brought in by publishers to raise the status of Christmas cards – even though their designers were consistently praised in the *Art Journal*. 'They are very beautiful – examples of a high order in Art', says the *Art Journal* in 1869. 'Excellent examples of art' is the verdict in 1871. 'Pictures of great merit by artists who have rare skill in designing [. . .] we are considering these Christmas cards as pictures,' states the *Art Journal* in 1872 (11:313). 'Examples of Art works of a high order' was the following year's judgement (1873a, 12:30).

Nevertheless a certain snobbery, based partly on the perceived gap between art and design (or craft), and partly on the popularity of the market, pertained – most noticeably towards the end of the century. 'Christmas cards and crackers' in *The Times* of 19 December 1895, for example, begins: 'During the past few years the fashion of dispatching indiscriminately large numbers of Christmas cards – a fashion which had become little more than a mere form and was regarded by most people as an infliction – has, fortunately, been dying out.' It continues, 'Christmas is, by common consent, the most appropriate season for the exchange of kindly wishes with far-off friends, for recalling and renewing old ties of union, but those who have such commendable objects in view can generally be counted on for a warmer token of good will than a mere slip of painted pasteboard.'

A middle-class and upmarket publication, *The Graphic* magazine of 2 January 1886, reported 'the abundance of berries on both holly and mistletoe made the internal decoration of most houses unusually bright and cheerful and it was to be observed that the regular Christmas plants were generally used, to the exclusion of laurel and other aids to decoration in ordinary seasons' (p. 11). By the later 1890s, the taste associated with many of the decorative images and the decorations themselves was being questioned within a certain 'aesthetic' section of the middle class – 'cheap and nasty tinsel' was cautioned against in an article on the appropriate decoration of a church in a journal associated with the 'Aesthetic Movement' (*The Studio* 1898, 2:105). Equally heinous were 'paper banners, shields, scrolls, etc.' and the custom of 'smothering the lectern, pulpit, font, still more the altar, in 'jack-in-the-green fashion'. Tasteful textile hangings were seen as 'more seasonable'. A highly stylised Christmas card design, reductive to the point of absurdity, is included in Volume XV. For this artistic circle, affirming the seductive glitter of the commodity would disqualify the status of readers of *The Studio* as a distinct aesthetic group, whereas for the middle-class majority the 'traditional' decorations and images were welcomed uncritically.

CHAPTER 3

Consumption, Coca-colonisation, Cultural Resistance – and Santa Claus

George McKay

At least four of the seven deadly sins against which Christianity once railed are now seen by some to be venerated in Christmas celebrations: avarice, gluttony, lust, and envy. The conflict is by no means uniquely American . . . but America has contributed the uniquely American Santa Claus and has become an arbiter of Christmas celebrations around the world, primarily because of its part import of European emigrant traditions and its present export of popular culture. (Belk 1993: 75)

In what ways has the iconography and practice of Christmas been shaped, understood and consumed as an American experience? This chapter explores, explains and questions the ideological valence of Christmas in part as an American socio-economic and cultural (export) practice. I do acknowledge the fact that Daniel Miller has identified a number of the inter-national strands of influence operating transatlantically on Christmas from the mid-nineteenth century on whereby '[t]his syncretic modern form extracts the Christmas tree from the German tradition, the filling of stockings from the Dutch tradition, the development of Santa Claus mainly from the United States, the British Christmas card' (Miller 1993: 4). It is telling that the two American artists responsible for the most influential visual representations of Santa Claus had strong European backgrounds: in the nineteenth century, cartoonist Thomas Nast (born in Germany in 1840), and in the twentieth, advertising illustrator Haddon Sundblom (Sweden). I recognise too the shifting relationship America has had with Christmas, it being historically sometimes hugely antagonistic; in early modern America Christmas was actually banned by the Puritans (Miller 1993: 3), though by the late eighteenth century some Americans were celebrating St Nicholas in part as an anti-British sentiment (Carrier 1993: 66). In recent years the replacement of the seasonal greeting of 'Happy Christmas' by the faith-neutral 'Happy Holidays' is a further small sign of the shifting relationship. Yet overall there are a cluster of issues around (American) consumption in

Figure 3.1 Thomas Nast's influential Christmas 1862 depiction of Santa Claus in *Harper's Weekly*.

relation to seasonal advertising, the global or hemispheric spread of secular and commercial Christmas, and some gestures of resistance towards this spread, which are important if debatably residual national aspects of Christmas, even as it has become 'today *the* global festival' (Miller 1993: 5; emphasis original). Following close on in the American calendar of 'festivals of consumption' from Hallowe'en (sweets, beer) and Thanksgiving (turkey) is 'the festival of festivals, the only festival to achieve transcendental status – Christmas' (Twitchell 1996: 172). Rather than 'his evil twin Scrooge' (Twitchell 1996: 176), the key visual figure here is Santa Claus, born (kind of) in the United States in the nineteenth century.

Christmas Shopping, Department Stores and Santa Claus: The Festival of Consumption

Modern Christmas brought together a cluster of practices and innovations in social and commercial life alike, and indeed these became intertwined through developments in Western capitalism in both domestic and public urban spheres. These include the fact that the production/consumption economy was facilitated by the increasingly common practice of gift-giving (and vice versa: gift-giving – moving into gift exchange (Fowles 1996: 247) – pushed on the economy); the development and then rapid expansion of the department store made a new shopping leisure experience and consumerist lifestyle possible; advertising became a dominant mass media form of public communication and persuasion, predicated in large part on shifting the new products available from the 'cathedrals of consumption' (Crossick and Jaumain 1999).

Christmas, the season of both gift-giving and 'intensive shopping' (Miller 1993: 21), was relatively rapidly recognised by store owners for its potential impact on increasing sales. This was capitalised on in various ways until the now familiar seasonal spike in sales and turnover was established. On Christmas Eve 1867, for example, R. H. Macy first extended the opening hours of his New York department store until midnight, and in doing so 'set a one-day sales record of more than $6,000' (Twitchell 1996: 173). An 1874 promotion in Macy's of $10,000 worth of imported dolls led to 'Christmas window displays of manufactured goods [becoming] a part of the promotion of Christmas buying and gift-giving' (Belk 1993: 90). The offering of Christmas bonuses to department store employees at the end of the nineteenth century – even if it was for no more munificent reason than to avert industrial action at Woolworth's in the first instance – would effectively introduce a further mechanism to swell the seasonal marketplace (Twitchell 1996: 173).

Figure 3.2 Santa Claus, advertising and consumption: White Rock mineral water advertisement, Christmas 1916, *New York Herald*.

Besides its emphasis on materialism, consumption and display, the rise of the department store in nineteenth- and early twentieth-century America and Europe could have wider social resonance. Meg Jacobs has noted that 'department stores legitimized public loitering. . . . Their free entry policy along with their grand physical construction and accessible lay-out of merchandise encouraged shopping as a leisurely activity. Even if one could not afford to purchase, looking was free . . . *[D]epartment stores democratised desire*' (2001: 228; emphasis added). There was too a compelling gendered perspective around issues of consumption and the act of shopping and its adjacent new social opportunities available inside department stores. '[T]he many non-shopping activities that stores offered [ranged] from afternoon tea and classical music to public libraries to public debates over women's suffrage. Breaking from an older ideology of separate spheres that had confined them to private arenas, women now moved in many commercial public spaces' (Jacobs 2001: 228). A note of caution is introduced by Hosgood with regard to Christmas shopping, in which 'women's role as Christmas shoppers promoted a healthy new image of the woman shopper' in the popular imaginary: 'while shopping did enable women to escape the domestic sphere, it did not automatically empower them . . . Indeed, it left them open to the taunt from men that they were simply parading and massaging their petty vanities' (1999: 103, 99).

In 1939, the dominance of Christmas within the American seasonal marketplace would be confirmed by the introduction of the character 'Rudolph the Red-Nosed Reindeer' as a marketing tool by the Chicago-based department store chain Montgomery Ward. Over two million copies of the story of 'Rudolph' were sent out with Montgomery Ward catalogues that first year alone (Twitchell 1996: 175), apparently in spite of concerns from executives that a Bardolphian red nose was not the symbol with which a family business should align itself (Mikkelson and Mikkelson 2004). A decade later, the eponymous song sung by Gene Autry, based on the Montgomery Ward character, became a major hit. It remains one of the most popular of Christmas songs, a key part of the sonic landscape of the season, even if with a provenance that is, in Twitchell's term, signalling the imbrication between advertising and popular culture generally, 'pure Adcult' (1996: 175). In fact such a provenance confirms its centrality in the Christmas festival landscape.

This is the case even more with the figure at the heart not only of Christmas but of the profound transformation of this festival season: the overweight and elderly superhero, the 'deity' of materialism' (Miller 1993: 20), known as Santa Claus, with his amazing sackful of magic powers – flight, shape-shifting, time travel, omniscience . . . For, as Twitchell has observed, 'You can keep Christ out of Christmas but not Santa' (1996: 174). His preferred location – in representation, in a snowy landscape of Norway or the North Pole; in 'reality', ensconced in the grotto of the department store – illustrates for us the centrality of myth and marketing, which I will look at further in due course. In his 1952 essay entitled 'Father Christmas executed', Claude Lévi-Strauss points out that '[t]he variety of names given to the person who distributes the children's toys – Father Christmas, Saint Nicholas, Santa Claus – shows that it is a result of a process of convergence and not an ancient prototype preserved everywhere intact' ([1952] 1993: 42). While to an extent the syncretic hero matches the syncretic season of Christmas itself, there are also more specifically national contributions to be considered. For example, Russell Belk has contrasted what he calls the modern 'American Santa Claus' with other traditional (mostly European) Christmas figures, identifying the following key differences:

1. Santa Claus lacks the religious associations of such gift-bearing figures as Santa Lucia, Saint Nicholas, Christkindlein . . .
2. Santa Claus lacks the riotous rebelliousness of figures such as Saturn and Knecht Ruprecht.
3. Santa Claus lacks the punitive nature of Sinterklaas (with his companion Zwarte Piet) . . .

Figure 3.3 White Rock advertisement showing Santa Claus,
Christmas 1923, *Life* magazine, relaxing with
a whisky and water.

4. [W]ith his many appearances on street corners, in stores and shopping malls, and in homes, Santa Claus is a more tangible character than his predecessors and counterparts.
5. Santa Claus is a bringer of numerous and substantial gifts, not merely the fruits, nuts, and simple homemade toys of [tradition]. (Belk 1993: 78)

A normative whiteness – the Caucasian appearance, white hair and beard, white fur trim – and reassuring masculinity – unthreatening, paternal (Father Christmas) or avuncular – can be understood as being embodied by representations of Santa Claus. This is so from the early popularisation of a visual image in January 1863 (marking the Christmas 1862 season – perhaps we can say that Santa Claus was also born at Christmas) by political cartoonist Thomas Nast, at a period of social crisis in the USA (see Figure 1.2, p. 24). In Nast's drawings in the magazine *Harper's Weekly*, collected and published in book form within a few years as *Santa Claus and His Works* (1869), Santa is introduced as a stabilising figure. After all, as Carrier reminds us, 'it was during the [American] Civil War that the modern image of Santa appeared' (1993: 68). Even from these early familiar times, then, Santa was already ideologically located; constituting part of the Union imaginary during the Civil War, the implication was that Southern children would be made to wonder why Santa was not visiting them (Whyte 2005). Santa commented on some of the ideological terrain in which he has found himself implicated in a 2005 interview:

When, for example, the Ku Klux Klan used my image, it was their way of recognizing the fact that I stand for benevolence and decent human behaviour, even though that's hypocritical on their part. When the Viet Cong threw down propaganda brochures to be found by American troops in Vietnam to weaken their morale, it was acknowledgment of just how big a role I play in the fabric of American families. So, while I certainly am not happy to see myself used by the Nazis, nonetheless it's kind of a backhanded compliment. (Quoted in Whyte 2005)

The strange man mysteriously breaking into the house in the middle of the night, often visiting children in their bedrooms, unseen by all, came to evoke not nightmare but dream and desire. Portly rather than obese, jolly and rosy-cheeked rather than inebriated (even after several whiskies, as in Figure 3.3), Santa is predominantly a domesticated rather than saturnalian festival figure. Interestingly, in spite of his distinctive appearance and dress and the consistency of the claims of his American origins, Santa is not in fact easily visibly identifiable as an American figure – most obviously, clothing is red and white rather than (starred) red, white and blue, for example.

The one pivotal exception to this is that first Santa of Nast's, from 1863; the cover illustration of *Harper's Weekly* shows Santa at a troop camp, standing beneath the Stars and Stripes flag with stars on his jacket and striped trousers (see Figure 3.1). Overall, though, is it rather in the products (gifts and merchandise) and his locations (stores and advertisements) that we must recognise and seek to understand his Americanicity?

The historical antecedents of Christmas advertising in the USA show that, as long ago as the mid-nineteenth century, a Father Christmas-style character had been employed for seasonal marketing; in Philadelphia in 1841 a performer dressed as a character named 'Criscringle' publicised a local store's merchandise to passers-by. A standardised visual amalgamation – white, white beard, portly, jolly, wearing an identifiable fur or fur-trimmed uniform – developed through the century. It was this image that was most famously exploited by the Coca-Cola Company from the early 1930s on, in the corporate company colours of red and white, as part of its campaign to increase winter sales of its soft drink. It is widely recognised that it is from this long-running campaign that Santa's place and most familiar representation have been concretised in the contemporary Christmas imaginary. Twitchell, for example, argues that '[t]he jolly old St. Nick that we know from countless images did not come from Macy's department store, neither did he originate in the imagination . . . of [Thomas] Nast . . . *He came from the yearly advertisements of the Coca-Cola Company*' (1996: 175; emphasis added). Indeed, the Coca-Cola Company was itself so confident of this that it reintroduced Santa in an international advertising campaign during Christmas 2006 to mark the seventy-fifth anniversary of the Coke Claus. This was accompanied by a range of official Coca-Cola merchandising, including not only glasses and trays, but also Christmas tree baubles, showing favourite Sundblom Santa images. Such a revival speaks to the sense of historicity of the advertisements and of the figure himself. It is clear that these advertisements, appearing most years over three decades and featuring over forty different Santa images painted by Sundblom, were very influential in the dissemination and popularisation of the visual figure of Santa Claus – and of the connection between Christmas, Americana, advertising and commerce – but intriguingly there was at least one major precedent here. I want first to look at that before moving on to discuss the Coke Claus.

White Rock mineral water, produced by the beverage company established in Wisconsin in 1871, first used Santa Claus in its seasonal advertising in 1915. Monochrome newspaper advertisements depicted Santa delivering children's presents in a wintry landscape, while also taking the opportunity to deliver crates of White Rock (see Figure 3.2). This campaign

Figure 3.4 White Rock advertisement, Christmas 1924, *Life* magazine,
showing Santa savouring a gift of alcoholic liquor
and water.

developed so that each December from 1923 to 1925 colour advertisements appeared in *Life* magazine, with Santa in now familiar garb and setting: fur-trimmed red and white clothing, white beard, portly and jolly, in comfortable and warm domestic Christmas settings (usually contrasting with a winter scene outside, visible through a window). The further familiarity, of course, is that the images are advertisements, that Santa exists in the meta-context for material commercial transaction, that he is pimping his product. Together the three advertisements tell in order the important stages of Santa's annual narrative of activity, so there is a neat and presumably considered continuity to the series. In the first from 1923 (see Figure 3.3) he is at home reading through wish-letters sent to him by children, a third of the way through an open bottle of whisky, with White Rock mixer; in 1924 (see Figure 3.4) he is shown in the act of delivering presents to a house – while also gratefully consuming the present the household has left for him, a bottle of White Rock (and accompanying uncorked bottle of spirits); in 1925 (see Figure 3.5) he is back at home after a hard night's work delivering presents, sitting by his fridge enjoying one of several bottles of White Rock (with no hint of alcohol this time). In the social context of 1920s USA these advertisements are fascinating, as Bob Beckerer of the White Rock Collectors Association explains:

> This was the middle of Prohibition [1920–1933] – no booze and no ads for booze. Yet, here is a group of ads showing a liquor bottle. White Rock became so popular that its name became synonymous with soda water. Much like today, where some people ask for a 'Coke' when they mean any 'cola'. Being primarily a mixer, during Prohibition a request for 'White Rock' took on a secondary meaning as a coded request for a mixed [alcoholic] drink. (Personal correspondence, 20 March 2007)

A bucolic Santa in the White Rock advertisements, aimed firmly at parents, the struggling present-buyers and givers of the season, recognised and confirmed the adult encoding only too well.

It is, though, the soft (drink) Santa, the Coca-Cola Claus, depicted in a long-lasting series of colour advertisements illustrated by Haddon Sundblom from 1931 on, that has maintained a central place in the public Christmas imaginary (and, judging by collectors' enthusiasms and websites, possibly too in the public's affection). The seasonality of sales is a key issue for chilled products – sales peak in hot weather and drop in cold. The Christmas Coke adverts were intended to boost sales at the annual flagging time of the year. Some products have an articulated seasonal marketing strategy – the gift-giving period of Christmas being most important for sales of wristwatches, cosmetics and children's toys, for instance, as well as

Figure 3.5 White Rock advertisement, Christmas 1925, *Life* magazine,
showing Santa refreshing himself with a chilled drink
by the fridge, predating Coca-Cola Santa.

for the business of advertising itself. Coca-Cola wanted both to raise sales figures at a notoriously quiet time and to tap into the spending spike becoming associated with the consumerist celebration of the festive season. Twitchell describes the process:

> 'Thirst knows no season' was their initial winter campaign. At first [Coca-Cola's advertisers] decided to show how a winter personage like Santa could enjoy a soft drink in December . . . They started showing Santa relaxing from his travails by drinking a Coke, then showed how the kids might leave a Coke (not milk) for Santa, and then implied that the gifts coming in from Santa were in exchange for the Coke. Pay dirt. Santa's presents might not be in exchange for a Coke, but they were 'worth' a Coke. Coke's Santa was elbowing out other Santas. *Coke's Santa was starting to own Christmas.* (1996: 175; emphasis added)

To what extent, over the succeeding decades, did Sundblom's Coca-Cola Santa figure in the construction and cementation of the (American) experience of Christmas itself? As with the White Rock advertisements, the innovation in the widespread use of colour in the print images of popular media (which included not only magazines but also seasonal greetings cards, though this was more of a European practice) was significant, and the red-clothed (rather than white or green) Santa became the definitive one. This was a gesture of powerful but simple branding, since such colour coding became and remains part of the enduring transnational, extra-linguistic and possibly even subconscious recognition of Coke brand identity: '[t]he eye decodes what stymies the mind, hence . . . the red of Coca-Cola' (Twitchell 1996: 22).

'Coca-colonisation' and Santa

In the 1943 Sundblom Coca-Cola Christmas advertisement, Santa is shown trudging happily through the virgin snow with a heavy sack of presents over one shoulder and a bottle of Coke in the other hand. His boots are covered in snow, so it is a long journey. The slogan 'Wherever I go' (itself in quotation marks – his speech) refers both to his current journey through the snow to unseen houses and to the ambitious global reach of the company's business plan. For behind his image, in the direction he is walking, floats a globe on which America, Africa and Europe can be easily identified. Further, the globe is marked as a seasonal gift, wrapped with ribbon and a label. The label, covering the USA on the globe, has the 'Coca-Cola' logo. The previous decade the Coca-Cola Export Corporation had begun to market the drink outside the USA, employing a franchise system in which the home company in Atlanta, Georgia, 'supervis[ed] quality and advertising' while each local producer made drink and profits. Within a few years in Europe business was considerably enhanced by the presence of so many GIs drinking bottles of Coke, 'mostly at government expense' as part of the war effort (Kuisel 1993: 53). One publicity slogan from 1945 went: 'Whenever you hear "Have a Coke", you hear the voice of America' (Digger History 2007).

After the war, Coca-Cola plants were established in many Western European countries, to the extent that a 1950 *Time* magazine cover depicted the globe drinking a bottle of Coke – effectively little more than a finesse of the company's own 1943 advertisement. While 'almost everywhere in postwar Europe Coca-Cola's arrival provoked opposition' (Kuisel 1993: 54), it was in France in particular that what became known as the 'Coca-Cola affair' illustrated and dramatised the tensions within the easy embrace of American popular culture, and where the phrase 'Coca-colonisation' occurred in both left-wing and mainstream print media. From 1949 until 1953 a battle raged in Communist circles, within the French and later American governments, and in the French agriculture and viniculture industries, about national culture and identity – against a backdrop of the Cold War and the Marshall Plan. *Le Monde* expressed it sardonically in 1950: 'We have accepted chewing gum and Cecil B. Demille, *Reader's Digest*, and be-bop. [But i]t's over soft drinks that the conflict has erupted. Coca-Cola seems to be the Danzig of European culture. After Coca-Cola, *holà*' (quoted in Kuisel 1993: 65).

Over the decades many of the Sundblom Santas were depicted in domestic environments – by the roaring fireplace or the decorated Christmas tree, or, most favoured, by the refrigerator (which contained chilled bottles of Coke). Such adverts seem designed to confirm Miller's view that, while 'Christmas may be everywhere . . . the only true Christmas is within one's own home' (1993: 30). They also, though, imply the valorisation and acceptance of models of domestic consumption; that the fridge was an essential item of American everyday life (even in midwinter) was normalised. This could have curious repercussions. In France, for example, Communist-led anti-Americanism actually attacked the fridge as a symptom of Americans' excessive and redundant consumption. According to Kuisel, 'The Frigidaire, militants were informed, was a useless gadget most of the year, except for making ice cubes for whiskey cocktails. It was usually cool enough in France so that a traditional *garde-manger* "placed on the window keeps the leftovers of Sunday's lamb until Wednesday"' (1993: 40).

In what ways can iconic advertising figures like the Coca-Cola Santa help us to address questions of the Americanisation of Christmas? Can we consider Santa, and his load of presents, as a global emblem of American-modelled or led consumption? In Belk's view there can be a connection: '[t]his diaspora of the American Santa Claus is not unlike the diaspora of Coca-Cola as an emblem of American modernity' (1993: 82). In general, external forms of American popular consumption (or the consumption of America) have inscribed within them variously power, pleasure and fear. Exported American popular culture is criticised for its homogenising effects. Through this process of Americanisation, cultural dopes and dupes are produced, who value novelty over tradition, nostalgia over history. There is little room in this dismal analysis for originality or individualism; mass media and commodification deny us agency in our own cultural choices; nor is there recognition of the subversive potential of the appropriation or localised reinscription of cultural meaning. Admitting to the pleasures of Americana is merely proof positive of one's dopey-ness (signifying infantile, ignorant, narcotised). As Twitchell casually articulates it, '[p]roducts that symbolise America cross borders with ease. Coke, Hershey bars, Levi's jeans, Marlboro cigarettes, Nike shoes, and Wrigley's gum are bought worldwide simply for being American. The packaging is the ad' (1996: 246). The critical, sometimes pejorative, terminology employed here is, as we have seen, 'Coca-colonisation', of course, but also 'McDonaldisation' (Ritzer 1996), 'Disneyisation' (Bryman 2004) – and even, in the context of consumption, 'Wal-Martisation' (explained and challenged in Wrigley 2000: 232–6). The twentieth century, for instance, was punctuated by regular moral panics around the latest pop cultural craze emanating from America, which would generally also involve youth pleasure and autonomy and a generational disruption. European elders railed against the symptoms of what they perceived as a febrile, vacuous, immature export culture, whether in the form of hot jazz, gangster films and gun culture, streamlining, soft drinks, comic books, juvenile delinquency, rock 'n' roll, pop art, LSD, fast food, video nasties, gangsta rap and gun culture, both jogging and obesity . . . all happily nibbling away at Old World social consensus and cultural hierarchy through the century (Hebdige 1988; Kuisel 1993; Campbell et al. 2004; McKay 2005). Though each alone may appear a relatively minor novelty, and some are demonstrably more dangerous in perception or practice than others, reactions to them contributed to a current of distrust of the USA and its pop cultural pleasures from significant sectors of European society and, importantly, across the political spectrum. A 1957 Sundblom Coca-Cola Christmas advertisement shows Santa by a space rocket: a fairly direct statement of the alliance of Coke, Christmas and the Cold War, merging the space race with a politics of pleasure and plenty. In Kuisel's view:

> [I]n retrospect the war over Coca-Cola was a symbolic controversy between France and America. Its emotional energy derived from French fear of growing American domination, in a political, economic, and cultural sense, during a bleak phase of French trade and a tense moment of the Cold War. (1993: 68)

This is not simply a historic phenomenon, for in some European countries a class-centred aesthetic and practical seasonal struggle continues to take place precisely in this frame of the national popular:

> A recurrent theme in middle-class narratives has to do with the constant threat of the invasion of an 'Americanised' Christmas, the ultimate vulgarity with blinking red, green and yellow lights, plastic trees, canned Santa Polyester Snow, taped muzak carols, and 'Christmas Home Memories Fragrance Spray'. (Löfgren 1993: 230)

Further, in the twin contexts of Coke and Christmas, a minor but telling international controversy over the Sundblom Santa paintings occurred when they were exhibited in Canada in 1991, precisely because of their links with Coca-Cola. (The company lent the paintings for the exhibition and had numerous promotions tied in for those attending.) One local critic thundered: 'It is sad that an august institution like the Royal Ontario Museum would put its imprimatur on junk food . . . This further links the birth of Christ with Santa Claus, with consumption' (quoted in Belk 1993: 76).

Conclusion: Fulfilling Each Other's Needs or Greeds

I want to return to the starting point for much of this chapter: the issue of Christmas as the season of consumption and, in particular, the charge that such consumption not only is excessive but also undercuts the traditional religious tenet of the festival. There are contrasting views on this. Mary Searle-Chatterjee, for example, suggests that the commercialism of contemporary Christmas is a major problem identified by many of its practitioners. Indeed, this is so much the case that, in her view, '[b]elievers *and non-believers alike* lament the commercialism of the Christmas season . . . The festival is "sacred" in so far as it can be profaned by commerce.' She contrasts Christmas with '[t]he summer holiday season [a]s a time of equally extravagant and commercialised expenditure yet no one deplores this fact for nobody expects the summer holiday to be sacred' (Searle-Chatterjee 1993: 182–3; emphasis added). On the other hand, considered historically and compared with earlier versions of the festival, for Jib Fowles:

[T]he charge of 'commercialism', with the implication that Christmas used to be less so and now is more, is not profound. The holiday was not much celebrated in the English-speaking world for the two centuries before the arrival of the production/consumption economy in the 19th century. As the holiday re-emerged, it used as gifts the goods that were at hand – in this case, manufactured ones. (1996: 251, n. 7)

Michael Schudson has taken this kind of pro-'commercialism' argument further. In his view, in contemporary society '[t]he prevalence of gift giving suggests that people very often buy things not because they are materialistic but because they are social . . . We have not forsaken traditional family values for material consumption; we consume materials very often to preserve families' (1993: 139).

Such qualifications as these are helpful in delineating the grand and dismal narrative of 'Coca-colonisation' in the Christmas context, enabling us to move beyond that most obvious of deconstructions: Santa/Satan. How far should the Santa figure, even with a full sack, let alone the ideologically overloaded thing that is the soft drink of Coke, (continue to) bear the weight of too much meaning and power? Yet it is the case that a later Coca-Cola advertising campaign would demonstrate even further the company's ecumenicism – the counterculture lite pop and youth idealism of the early 1970s' 'I'd like to teach the world to sing in perfect harmony' (Falk 1997) can be viewed as a relatively early, not to say brazen, articulation of what Naomi Klein sees more critically as 'the equalising promise of the logo-linked globe' (2000: xvii). In a contemporary world of transnational mediation, according to Charles Acland:

[F]rom the IBM commercials of quaintly remote locations (a convent, a Middle Eastern desert, etc.) to Microsoft's 'Where do you want to go today?', from Benetton's racially obsessed images of diversity to Coke's vaguely neo-hippie multiculturalism and Pepsi's dance internationalism of 'Generation Next', a dominant representation is that of geographic and cultural borders being transcended by commodity forms that draw the interest of young people. Such images construct a form of fetishism – affixed to both commodities *and* young people – that carries a magical 'one worldness', in the end a pure ideological reverie of individual empowerment. 'One worldness' is seen as a determining characteristic of a unique generational phenomenon. (2000: 45)

By historicising Coca-Cola and Christmas consumption via its advertisements and the key figure of Santa Claus from the 1930s on, I have suggested that in some ways it confirms the argument that the 'association of materialism and Christmas is often viewed . . . as part and parcel of a global

"Americanisation" of popular culture, which has promoted materialism under the umbrella of other forms and values' (Miller 1993: 18).

Finally, those twins I mentioned at the top of the chapter, Scrooge and Santa, reappear in campaign groups and movements dedicated to the contestation of and opposition to Christmas consumption. It is in such activist spaces that the ideological struggles of Christmas can be clearly seen. Some have sought to campaign against what they view as the rampant materialism of Christmas – in one critique, Christmas gifts help us to 'fulfil each other's greeds' rather than needs (quoted in Belk 1993: 93) – though from different political positions. For instance, a campaign group called SCROOGE was founded in the USA in 1979 – the Society to Curtail Ridiculous, Outrageous, and Ostentatious Gift Exchanges. According to Belk, SCROOGE 'encourages "sensible spending" at Christmas and gives suggestions such as buying gift certificates for self-improvement classes, smoke alarms, and first aid kits' (1993: 96). More politically radical perhaps, working under the umbrella of the Canadian-based anti-advertising and creative anti-capitalist group and magazine Adbusters, the so-called 'brand wars' have targeted Christmas in part precisely because of the festival's connections with advertising and consumerism. For groups like Adbusters the fact that certain ideologies of Christmas have been promulgated via massively influential (therefore successful) advertising campaigns is justification as well as rationale for their campaigning counterblasts in the form of what have been called not advertisements but subvertisements. An annual global day of action – an alternative Thanksgiving – was launched by activists rejecting consumerist consumption. Known as Buy Nothing Day, from the 1990s on it has become one of the regular events in the activist's calendar. Since at least 2001 an offshoot has targeted the subsequent seasonal 'festival of consumption' specifically with the Buy Nothing Christmas campaign. As some of the 2006 BNXmas publicity put it:

> Dreading the holiday season? The frantic rush and stress? The to-do lists and sales hype? The spiritless hours trapped in malls? This year, why not gather together your loved ones and decide to do things differently? With the simplest of plans *you can create a new rhythm, purpose and meaning* for the holidays. Why not try a Buy Nothing Christmas? If that's too extreme for grandma and the kids, maybe try a Buy Less Christmas. Or a Buy Fairer Christmas. Or a Slow-Down Christmas. Whatever you decide, 'tis the season *to reclaim our celebration from the grip of commercial forces.* (Adbusters 2007; emphases added)

To state, or reinstate, the possibility of the carnivalesque irruption of festival was the aim, to be achieved by stepping out of the social frame of consumerist culture and practice. In malls and shopping streets, Zentas rather than Santas began to appear, the idea being for the anarchist – robed for the day in red and white rather than red and black – to project an ironic Zen-like calm rejection of frantic consumption, with the handy extra activist practicality that adopting the position of cross-legged meditation was also effectively a sit-down protest blockade. At Buy Nothing Christmas actions, Santa/Zenta Claus reaffirmed his place in ideological and social debates, just as he had in Nast's Civil War illustrations of 150 years before or, as I hope to have shown, in Sundblom's Coke-fuelled domestic American utopias of fifty years back.

Part II
THE HOLLY AND THE IVY

CHAPTER 4

Religious Controversies over Christmas

Jennifer Rycenga

The biblical canon remains active today . . . but primarily as a totem or talisman, an increasingly empty gesture. It has become an icon of religiosity, a sign in its own right, apart from the texts that it contains and controls. Its value as a catalog of scriptures is coming to an end. (George Aichele, in Black 2006: 200)

It Is a Wide Wide World

The stresses of the contemporary holiday season – gift-giving, travel to visit family, increased requests from charities, year-end financial worries – are not calculated to bring out the best in people, despite hymns that extol 'good cheer'. Contemporary identity politics, especially in the hands of a vocal and aggrieved majority, only makes matters worse. Holidays become major sites of ideological posturing, quite distant from the pious practices ideally imagined. Christmas in America has now become a stage for both commercial excess and majoritarian Christian identity.

Whether fortuitous or strategic, the placement of the Christmas season at the winter solstice and end of the calendar year ensures its role as economic saviour to American consumer capitalism. Retailers cherish this time of year as the opportunity to navigate their bottom lines to finish, not in festive red, but in classic black. While some decry the loss of religious solemnity, the 'traditional' Christmas in the United States has always been commercialised; nostalgic laments for an earlier family intimacy and religious authenticity have been a component of Christmas rhetoric from the early nineteenth century (Nissenbaum 1996: 318; Schmidt 1995: 124–6; Golby and Purdue 1986: 9ff; Rycenga 2000). The religious roots of Christmas did not slow its mercantile growth, creating instead 'a market for manufactured crèches, cards with religious messages, and recorded sacred music' (Moore 1994: 205).

The religious and secular protocols of the holiday can clash, however. This often takes standardised form, typified by campaigns to 'Put Christ Back into Christmas', to ensure that the holiday maintains some dignity instead of being given over to orgiastic indulgence. This antinomy between matter and spirit is as old as Christianity and the Christianised Christmas itself. Despite the prominence of Nativity accounts in the Gospels of Matthew and Luke, the early church focused on the resurrection. The birth of Jesus is not the self-evident cosmological linchpin that Easter is, and therefore giving Christmas prominence in the Christian calendar calls for explanation. Some Christian groups – most notably the Puritans and Jehovah's Witnesses – scorn Christmas as inherently and irredeemably pagan (Watch Tower 2006). Whether accepting or opposing Christmas, though, no Christian group has denied that there are pagan roots to holiday customs (Moore 1994: 205; Count 1948: 1).

The pagan versus Christian battle over the celebration of Christmas has reached a new stage, where seeming contradiction between the humble birth of Jesus and the frenzy of shopping no longer stokes the main controversy. A group of largely right-wing agitators have declared that there is a war against Christmas being waged by secular liberals. Their alarmism, with its frankly dualistic language of battle, issues from polemical media outlets. The loudest amplifiers (and feedback loops) are Bill O'Reilly and John Gibson of the politically and socially conservative Fox News network. They and their minions maintain that, largely through the courts, the very mention of Christmas in public settings is discouraged and even banned. Gibson wrote a full-length book on the subject in 2005, *The War on Christmas*. Concentrating on local governments and school boards, Gibson outlines cases in which he discerns an animus against Christmas resulting in censorship. His globalising conclusion is as follows: 'The war on Christmas . . . (is) really a war on Christianity,' fomented by secularists and 'minor religionists' whose antipathy to Christian proselytising pushes them to limit free religious speech (Gibson 2005: 132, 160, 162–3; Menendez 1993: 83–163).

In November 2005, the consumer hegemon, Wal-Mart, enraged the right's defenders of Christmas when one of its customer representatives outlined the pagan roots of the holiday. This was a battle of structural cousins. Wal-Mart's world-view shows structural parallels to religious proselytising, for good reason: 'it was the evangelical Christian publicists in the Bible and tract societies who first dreamed the dream of a genuinely mass medium . . . to deliver the same printed message to *everyone* in America' (Nord 1984: 2; emphasis original). Like an evangelising religion Wal-Mart wants absolutely everyone worshipping at its temples, especially during the end-of-year blitz. To accommodate increased demand, Wal-Mart hires seasonal employees (known by the euphemism of 'Associates'). Not all recent hires are fully integrated into Wal-Mart's ideologies and practices; it can be expected that some of the more sardonic among them will commit what Wal-Mart counts as mistakes or, more precisely, 'inappropriate and inflammatory' blunders (Catholic League 2005c).

A New Christmas Story for a New Century

Some time in early November 2005, a Wal-Mart customer wrote to complain that 'Happy Holidays' had supplanted 'Merry Christmas' as a greeting and advertising phrase at the giant chain. A 'Temporary Associate', known only as Kirby, answered her letter. Here is Kirby's reply, in full, as reproduced in numerous media outlets:

> Walmart is a world wide organization and must remain conscious of this. The majority of the world still has different practices other than 'christmas' which is an ancient tradition that has its roots in Siberian shamanism. The colors associated with 'christmas' red and white are actually a representation of the aminita mascera mushroom. Santa is also borrowed from the Caucuses, mistletoe from the Celts, yule log from the Goths, the time from the Visigoth and the tree from the worship of Baal. It is a wide wide world. (Catholic League 2005a; all sic)[1]

On Wednesday, 9 November, Bill Donohue, President of the Catholic League for Religious and Civil Rights, sprang into action. Donohue merits special attention from John Gibson as a hero in the culture wars (Gibson 2005: 156–9); he is best known to the public as the single-minded enemy of the American Civil Liberties Union. Donohue's para-church Catholic League cultivates controversy, and could not resist the sugar plum Kirby deposited into their stocking; Donohue published Kirby's email in a press release calling for a boycott of Wal-Mart. Donohue describes the situation:

> This statement was signed by someone called Kirby. When I read it, I thought he might be drunk. But I was wrong. We sent Kirby's response to Wal-Mart's headquarters only to find that Dan Fogleman, Senior Manager, Public Relations, agrees. (Catholic League 2005a)

Donohue has exaggerated the extent of Fogleman's agreement with Kirby; this Senior Manager would not have risen to such hierarchic prominence by carelessly answering questions directly.[2] No; Fogleman instead performs a corporate feint with the skill of a fencing champion as he replies to Donohue's initial outrage:

As a retailer, we recognize some of our customers may be shopping for Chanukah or Kwanza gifts during this time of year and we certainly want these customers in our stores and to feel welcome, just as we do those buying for Christmas. As an employer, we recognize the significance of the Christmas holiday among our family of associates . . . and close our stores in observance, the only day during the year that we are closed. (Catholic League 2005a)

Donohue disdains Fogleman's false inclusion, and so he deploys sarcasm and statistics to force Fogleman's capitulation:

It's nice to know that Wal-Mart is closed on a federal holiday. Now here is why I am asking the leaders of 126 religious organizations that span seven religious communities to boycott Wal-Mart. Go to its website and search for Hanukkah and up come 200 items. Click on Kwanzaa and up come 77. Click on Christmas, and here's what you get: 'We've brought you to our "Holiday" page based on your search.' In other words, Wal-Mart is practicing discrimination. (Catholic League 2005a)

The sarcastic opening is disingenuous; Fogleman has just said that Christmas is the only day on which the mighty Wal-Mart rests (a better ratio than the deity of Genesis!). Obviously, that means that Wal-Mart is ecstatically open to hordes of shoppers who fill its aisles on every other federal holiday (even, ironically, on Labor Day). But Donohue's rhetorical misstep here may be his own feint, as he turns not to Wal-Mart's hours, but to the politics of website representation. Armed with the outrage that Kwanzaa and Hanukkah are given more respect than Christmas by Wal-Mart, Donohue ends the press release with Fogleman's email address. The call to action is clear.

It is perhaps helpful here to consider Donohue and Fogleman as duelling functionaries of two universal constituencies: consumer and retailer, buyer and seller, customer and employer. But Donohue represents more than an outraged consumer; he has the tincture of religion to anoint his side. He needs this added boost, of course, for capitalism's market-driven imperatives have an inexorable trajectory toward profit, well capable of 'drown(ing) out the most heavenly ecstasies of religious fervor' (Marx 1848). Representing Christianity, the dominant religion in the USA (between 80 and 93 per cent, depending on the survey used), Donohue is unashamed to use the veil of religious illusion, but he does not do so to ameliorate the worst effects of capitalism. Instead, Donohue will use the cultural capital of religion to constrain the crass capitalists at Wal-Mart to enunciate the shibboleth of 'Christmas' instead of 'holiday'.

The three-day war continued on Thursday, 10 November. Joe Kovacs, editor of the conservative WorldNetDaily, kept the rhetoric spinning. He contacted another Wal-Mart corporate employee, Jolanda Stewart, who protested that Wal-Mart was not trying to ban Christmas, but merely 'serve a diverse customer base . . . and help them to celebrate their individual needs and wants' (Kovacs 2005a). To his credit, Kovacs double-checked the Wal-Mart website and his numbers did not precisely corroborate Donohue's. He agreed that 'Christmas' led to a 'Holiday' page, but that a secondary link gave access to almost 8,000 items matching the term 'Christmas'. Despite finding this flaw in Donohue's logic, Kovacs was still frustrated by the euphemistic 'holiday' splayed over most of Wal-Mart's website. There was one humorous note: he found the phrase 'War on Christmas' brought up Gibson's book, out just in time for seasonal jollity (Kovacs 2005a).

Apparently Donohue did not find Kovacs's fact-checking abrasive because he quotes from Kovacs's article in the Catholic League's 10 November press release. Donohue scoffs at Kirby's 'insane statement regarding the origins of Christmas', and repeats his demands that Wal-Mart reject Kirby and revise its website. Rather than attack a conservative cousin in Kovacs, he directs his scorn at Jolanda Stewart. Calling her comments 'flatulent', he provides evidence that Christmas is singled out for discrimination:

> If Wal-Mart had a 'Holiday' section on its website that directed customers to its Christmas, Hanukkah and Kwanzaa sites, that would not be objectionable. What is objectionable is its steadfast defense of the statement about the origins of Christmas as crafted by its Customer Relations department, and the way its customers are directed online to find Christmas items. Searches for Hanukkah and Kwanzaa direct customers to the Jewish and African-American holiday sections, but searches for Christmas are directed to the 'Holiday' section. Ergo, Wal-Mart discriminates in its treatment of Christmas. (Catholic League 2005b)

The argument appears to be that if it takes Jewish and Kwanzaa celebrants only one click to get to their impoverished amount of holiday merchandise, while it takes Christians two clicks to get to an overwhelming amount of merchandise (including their own polemical literature decrying attacks on Christmas), then that second click is discriminatory ('Jim' 2005). Donohue ends with a threat: 'Now that Wal-Mart is standing by its position, I hope you're ready for our next move. Don't forget, we have the next six weeks to pull out all the stops, and we will' (Catholic League 2005b).

'Wal-Mart Caves', trumpets the final serial press release from the Catholic League on 11 November. Overnight, Kirby had been dumped into the dustbin of history. Fogleman's apology actually has more passion than the usual corporate-speak, directed, of course, against the ex-worker: 'We sincerely apologize to any person or organization that was offended by the inappropriate and inflammatory comments made by this former associate.' Kirby was fired for a factually defensible, if slipshod and not incontrovertible, outline history of pagan Yuletide origins. In the press release the triumphant president of the Catholic League is uncharitable to his fallen foe – 'Alas, Kirby has been fired' – and basks in 'a sweet victory for the Catholic League, Christians in general, and people of all faiths' (Catholic League 2005c).

Despite the quick turn-around at Wal-Mart, Fogleman has not surrendered the field entirely. Employing the royal 'we', he clears his company of any complicity: 'We at Wal-Mart believe this e-mail between a temporary associate and one of our valued customers was entirely inappropriate. Its contents in no way represent the policies, practices or view of our company. The associate, who was hired less than three weeks ago, is no longer employed by our company' (Kovacs 2005b). But even while he condemned Kirby's 'inflammatory' readings of history, Fogleman embraced the diversity that ensures the largest customer base: 'Wal-Mart is proud to welcome customers of all faiths, and celebrants of all holidays' (Kovacs 2005b). Donohue's parting shot mocked Fogleman one more time, decrying that Wal-Mart was not changing the 'policy of encouraging employees to say "Happy Holidays" instead of "Merry Christmas". This is dumb, but it was never part of the Catholic League's complaint' (Catholic League 2005c).

Back at WorldNetDaily, Kovacs takes the next logical step, speculating that Kirby was part of a pagan renaissance: 'Today, followers of ancient paganism strive to remind the public about the heathen origins of traditions that many may never have questioned.' He cites Selena Fox's website in particular, including 'a list of suggestions on how 21st century citizens can take part in the ancient rituals, to "re-paganize" Christmastime' (Kovacs 2005b: Selena Fox).

So who was Kirby? This personage's real identity remains a mystery; no one can definitively say what gender Kirby was (though most commentators default to male) or what religion s/he practised, rejected, invented or despised. What can be said is that the range of references cited in the infamous customer service email reflects a passable survey of pagan roots, albeit one poorly transcribed (for which the blogosphere crucified Kirby).[3] Kirby's overall tone, especially the sarcastic finial 'It is a wide wide world', rings sophomoric and condescending. While it could be read as mean-spirited, the email is more playfully smarmy and certainly fully conscious; I imagine Kirby participating in an in-joke amongst the Temporary Associates burdened with inane consumer complaint letters.

Since Kirby's own religious background is unknown, why link the reply to neo-paganism? Because it is a resurgent, articulate, self-conscious and playful neo-paganism that makes such a reply possible, as Joe Kovacs intuited. It does this on the material level, by providing ready access to arcana on the pagan roots of Christmas. It also makes Kirby's response possible on the ideological level, because rather than seeing these pagan roots as something to be transcended, expunged and used as an embarrassment or as an excuse to condemn Christmas as irrevocably pagan (as Puritans did and Jehovah's Witnesses do), Kirby sees these pre- and non-Christian solstice traditions as mere diversity. As one anti-Kirby blogger picked up, the Siberian shaman is to be respected ('G as in Good'). Kirby swims in a world where pagan is descriptive, not polemical, where all religious traditions have the same (potential) legitimacy.

For instance, one possible source for Kirby came in a newspaper article connecting Santa Claus's flying reindeer to hallucinogenic mushrooms. While some scholars have cast doubt on a direct influence between Siberian shamanic practices and the modern, commercial Santa Claus, the evidence is intriguing (Bowler 2005: 190–1; Ott 1993). The *Amanita muscaria* mushroom (also known as fly agaric), and its hypothetical connection to Christmas via altered states of consciousness, was featured in Janice O'Leary's *Boston Globe* article from 6 November 2005 – a date intriguingly close to Kirby's controversial email. O'Leary's article followed veteran mycologist Lawrence Millman into the mysteries of Boston's urban mushrooms. The climax of the article comes when Millman makes 'the crowning discovery' of 'the lovely, hallucinogenic *Amanita muscaria* . . . atop which the caterpillar in "Alice in Wonderland" smokes his hookah'. Millman then entertains the mushroom-hunting hikers with this conjectural spin on

> the mushroom's possible connection with Santa Claus. In its Siberian and West Coast versions, the *Amanita muscaria* is red with white splotches, the colors of Christmas.
>
> He explains that Siberian shamans valued them for healing powers and delivered the mushroom to the yurts of the ill at night, entering and leaving through their chimneys. (O'Leary 2005)

Christmas Presents from the Past

Backing away from the overheated cleverness of the blogosphere, a brief survey of Christmases past will provide some context for seeing Kirby's actions, and the reactions it provoked, as more than a tempest in a teapot. This incident recapitulates significant fault lines of Christianity, of American religious history and of class differences in America.

All sources agree that the celebration of Christmas was not central to the earliest centuries of Christianity. In fact, it appears to have been controversial, because the midwinter time was connected with the Roman Saturnalia, a time of feasting, role reversals and general licentiousness. Yet the two sources most often quoted by historians of Christmas as evidence of the opposition of the early church to the holiday are ambivalent. The first oft-quoted source is Origen (185–c. 255), whose Homily number 8 on Leviticus contains a general condemnation of birthday celebrations. Significantly, though, this condemnation is directed against the celebration of birthdays for those born from sexual union; Origen is explicitly concerned to separate the virgin birth from other forms of birth (Origen 1990: 154–5). He writes:

> Scripture also declares that one himself who is born whether male or female is not 'clean from filth although his life is of one day.' . . . ([T]herefore) not one from all the saints is found to have celebrated a festive day or a great feast on the day of his birth . . . Only sinners rejoice over this kind of birthday. For indeed we find in the Old Testament Pharaoh, king of Egypt, celebrating the day of his birth with a festival (Gen 40:20), and in the New Testament, Herod (Mark 6:21). However, both of them stained the festival of his birth by shedding human blood. For the Pharaoh killed 'the chief baker' (Gen 40:22), Herod, the holy prophet John 'in prison' (Mark 6:27). But the saints not only do not celebrate a festival on their birth days, but, filled with the Holy Spirit, they curse that day. (Origen 1990: 156)

Origen seems more concerned with keeping human ego in check and denigrating the body, than with regulating celebrations of Christ's nativity. Similarly, the equally famed St Gregory Nazianzen (329–389) articulates the Nativity's importance to the Christian doctrine of Incarnation, citing many scriptural references. He focuses on modifying the festival so it will be sombre, decorous and focused on the spiritual. He exhorts his listeners to 'keep the Feast, not after the manner of a heathen festival, but after a godly sort; not after the way of the world, but in a fashion above the world' (Gregory). He then gives an impressive (perhaps tempting?) list of wild practices to be abandoned:

> Let us not decorate our porches, nor organise dances, nor adorn the streets; let us not feast the eye, nor enchant the ear with music, nor enervate the nostrils with perfume, nor prostitute the taste, nor indulge the touch, those roads that are so prone to evil and entrances for sin; let us not be effeminate in soft, flowing clothes, whose beauty consists in their uselessness, nor with the glittering of gems or the sheen of gold or the tricks of colour . . . not in rioting and drunkenness, with which are mingled, I know well, bed-games and wantonness . . . let us not strive to outdo each other in intemperance. (Gregory)

Gregory of Nazianzen merely sets up a dualistic paradigm of spirit versus flesh, arguing for the former against the debased latter. Christian opposition to Christmas has its roots and branches in anti-pagan polemics. This is true for Origen, who finds deplorable pagan birthday celebrations in the Bible, as well as for Gregory of Nazianzen, who would likely find contemporary American Christmas trees and carolling distasteful.

As with many other popular practices, Christmas gained legitimacy in the post-Constantinian church. The date was investigated and set by Pope Julian I (337–352) as 25 December, first officially observed in 350 in Rome (Krythe 1954: 2). Once Christmas was on the church calendar, the next step was exploiting the holiday's simultaneity with the winter solstice. In nature-based religions, past and present, the changing lengths of day and the extremes represented by the solstices generate sacred attention. When an expansive Christian proselytising reached the shores of Northern Europe, it found solstice celebrations just waiting to be baptised. St Gregory the Great (c. 540–602) instructed St Augustine of Canterbury (d. 604), in his conversion of Britain, to retain pagan temples, reconsecrating them for Christian use after destroying their statues. Concerning festivals, he suggests that the converts

> are no longer to sacrifice beasts to the Devil, but they may kill them for food to the praises of God, and give thanks to the Giver of all gifts for His bounty. If the people are allowed some worldly pleasures in this way, they will more readily come to desire the joys of the spirit. For it is certainly impossible to eradicate all errors from obstinate minds at one stroke, and whoever wishes to climb to a mountain top climbs gradually step by step, and not in one leap. (Bede 1965: 86–7)

Gregory's flexibility, enabling partial conciliation with pagan traditions, emerged from the proselytising imperative of the Christian Great Commission to spread the gospel to all lands (Matthew 28:16–20). Gregory's decision to utilise the resources of existing pagan cultures as stepping stones to Christian belief is reminiscent of Mahayana Buddhism and modern advertising: get your truth-claims to everyone possible, by any means possible.

With this conciliation in place, the flowering of medieval European Catholicism could occur, in which all sorts of blendings, especially around holidays, arose. But this overflowing creativity affects our story only as a backdrop to the anti-Catholic polemics of the Reformation. The Puritans could not endorse Christmas practices, which they interpreted as simultaneously popish and pagan. In both Massachusetts Bay Colony in the New World and the Puritan Revolution back in England, Christmas was forbidden. The logic behind this position is stated by Hezekiah Woodward (1591–1675), whose 1656 pamphlet lambasted Christmas as

> 'The old heathen's feasting day, in honour to Saturn their idol-god, the papist's massing day, the profane man's ranting day, the superstitious man's idol day.' He also complained of 'heathenish customs, popish superstitions, ranting fashions, fearful provocations, horrible abominations committed against the Lord and His Christ on that day and the days following'. (Menendez 1993: 45)

So the Puritans knew that Christmas had pagan roots. But they also were concerned about the 'misrule' common to Christmas celebrations, especially among the working class in England. In the early modern era, Christmas often involved 'rowdy public displays of excessive eating and drinking, the mockery of established authority, aggressive begging (often involving the threat of doing harm), and even the invasion of wealthy homes' (Nissenbaum 1996: 5). The Anglican bishop and martyr Hugh Latimer (d. 1555) once commented that 'Men dishonour Christ more in the twelve days of Christmas, than in all the twelve months besides' (Nissenbaum 1996: 8). While this dishonour may have been mere rowdiness, there was deliberate role reversal, in which social hierarchy was inverted along lines of class, gender and age (Nissenbaum 1996: 8). Order was further threatened by sexual licence; apparently little had changed since the 'bed-games and wantonness' proscribed by Gregory of Nazianzen. Massachusetts Bay's storied Cotton Mather harangued Christmas revellers: 'Let the Night of your Pleasure be turned into Fear!' This stern warning did not achieve its desired effect; demographic research shows a 'bulge' in colonial New England's birthrate in September and October (Nissenbaum 1996: 22).

Puritans in power forbade recognition of Christmas; 25 December was a day of work like any other, and any caught celebrating it could be subject to legal penalties. Working-class people, mainly fishermen, resisted this control. One most intriguing case involves William Hoar, who in 1662 was brought before a magistrate for allowing drinking amongst friends who were visiting his house on Christmas Day. Mr Hoar's refusal to capitulate to Puritan Scrooges, though, epitomises a larger family pattern, which eventually brought his wife to misery. Dorcas Hoar had let it be known that she was a fortune-teller, maybe even a witch, and so she eventually became one of the victims of the Salem witch-hunt, executed in 1692 (Nissenbaum 1996: 15–16). The Puritans and pagans re-engaged an old battle, in which joyous celebration of Christmas was perceived as innately, and dangerously, pagan.

What does this have to do with Wal-Mart, John Gibson, Bill Donohue and the redoubtable Kirby? Quite simply, early Christmas celebrations in

Christianity skated along the tension between the natural diversity of people and the command to make the faith universal. If you compromise with the existing culture, you have more converts but you lose the purity of Christian spirit against pagan flesh. If you adopt the masochistic mood of Origen and curse the fact that you were born, or celebrate Christmas with Gregory of Nazianzen by avoiding all revelry, you may achieve theological purity but you lose a significant percentage of the masses. Dan Fogleman and Wal-Mart are in a parallel position; they want a universal market and they are willing to compromise with the diversity of their culture to get it. But when a significant part of their customer base – conservative Christians (whether Catholic or evangelical) – voiced preferences for a shibboleth (Judges 12:4–6) of the word 'Christmas' and a denial of origin narratives not to their liking, Wal-Mart blinked. However, capitalism is a most exacting task-master, since the bottom line is calculated in the here, not the hereafter; hence, Wal-Mart refused to capitulate in the greeting of its customers with 'Happy Holidays' in lieu of 'Merry Christmas'. What differentiates the modern story is its regrettable nominalism; far from defending some alleged theological truth, the Christmas warriors defend the Americanised (and secularised) holiday, crushing the spirit of religious (and cultural) pluralism by an assertion of majoritarian might (Menendez 1993: 159).

Common Sense Christmas

Eugene, Oregon, home of the University of Oregon Ducks, occupies one of the more intriguing chapters in John Gibson's *War on Christmas*. Establishing a simplified dualism, Gibson contrasts the 'everyday common sense of the logging industry' against 'the airy ecothinking of the university' (2005: 77), as he charts the exile of Christmas trees from municipal offices. These Oregon loggers resonate culturally with the young Gibson, who sets his default vision of Christmas in his youthful hometown, 1950s Redding, a modest city in the logging areas of Northern California (xxiv–xxix). Gibson's nostalgia imagines a time when cultural norms and expectations about Christmas went unquestioned. Whether in contemporary Eugene or in the hoary reaches of a remembered Redding, Gibson and his fellow defenders of a 'traditional' Christmas are playing an old game in American philosophical and religious thought: the triumph of common sense, the notion that ethical (and cultural) norms are obvious to any (honest) working man. The ultimate roots of common sense unite the impulses of the Protestant Reformation and the American Revolution: first, a demand that the Bible itself should be readable and interpretable by all believers, and, second, that men should be able to govern themselves. A very specific school of eighteenth-century thought, Scottish Common Sense Realism (SCSR), became crucial to the development of a distinctly American outlook, through the American Revolution and notions of American self-reliance. Ironically, common sense realism had a paradoxical effect; by empowering citizens to think for themselves, it germinated anti-intellectualism.

Based in Enlightenment rationalism but posing a direct challenge to Calvinism, common sense ethics were developed by Francis Hutcheson (1694–1747) and Thomas Reid (1710–96). For these thinkers, ethics were 'grounded upon universal human instincts' (Noll 2005: 94), and they 'favored these intuitions over traditional, historic, or ecclesiastical authority as the ideal basis for morality' (Noll 2005: 95). Evangelicals, ranging in style from Jonathan Edwards to John Wesley, objected to this philosophical innovation that 'reduced the agency of God by exalting the self-sufficiency of humanity' (Noll 2005: 100). The original American Christmas detractors, the Puritans, were no fans of human intellectual autonomy, as can be heard in more haranguing from Cotton Mather, who tagged 'the new moral philosophy "a vile Peece of Paganism"' (Noll 2005: 102).

By the latter half of the eighteenth century, though, American leaders needed intellectual cover for the radical undertaking of the revolution. In order to be successful, they had to encourage a vigorous questioning of traditional forms of authority (monarchy, state, church, home country). The rationalism of the Enlightenment found shared ground with the very evangelical Christianity that would have condemned its arrogance a generation earlier. The place of unity – for sceptics and believers – was the patent common sense of everyday people. George Marsden finds this principle at the very root of Protestantism, which from its inception 'had to stress the sufficiency of Scripture as the only rule of faith and practice' (Marsden 2006: 111). The Protestant Reformation had a similar agenda to the American Revolution: to overturn an existing, long-standing authority. 'If, as the Protestants argued against the Catholics, neither the church nor tradition was essential to understanding the Biblical message, then it was necessary to claim that even simple Christians could understand the essential message of the Bible on their own' (Marsden 2006: 111). While Marsden sees that common sense realism was 'above all democratic or anti-elitist' (2006: 14), he also acknowledges its incipient anti-intellectualism:

> Everyone in his sense believes such truths as the existence of the real world, cause and effect, and the continuity of the self. The ability to know such

things was as natural as the ability to breathe air. If philosophers questioned such truths, so much the worse for philosophers. (2006: 15)

The cultural pattern that will yield Gibson's dismissal of 'the airy ecothinking of the university' starts here. The lumberjack-as-plain-thinking-hero can be heard in Jefferson's advice to his nephew Peter Carr: 'State a moral case to a ploughman and a professor. The former will decide it as well, & often better than the latter, because he has not been led astray by artificial rules' (Jefferson 1787).

The rise of consumer capitalism in the early nineteenth century created the modern 'traditional' Christmas. Marsden notes that America did not experience anti-clericalism in the nineteenth century, instead responding to secularism by blessing 'its manifestations – such as materialism, capitalism, and nationalism – with Christian symbolism' (Marsden 2006: 49). Ann Douglas suggests that the clergy surrendered their position of actual cultural power to facilitate the defeat of the anti-intuitive cosmology of Calvinism (Douglas 1977: 12). As she trenchantly points out – with obvious correlates to the story of Christmas – clergymen and middle-class women in the early nineteenth century knew they lacked real power, and so instead they claimed

> to exert 'influence,' which they eulogized as a religious force . . . 'influence' was to be discreetly omnipresent and omnipotent. This was the suasion of moral and psychic nurture, and it had a good deal less to do with the faith of the past and a good deal more to do with the advertising industry of the future than its proponents would have liked to believe. (Douglas 1977: 8)

When consumer capitalism creates (in order to satisfy) myriad needs in ever-increasing comfort, the need for application of difficult thought – whether on matters of sin, state or morality – is no longer apparent. In fact, rigorous intellection may obstruct creature comforts and so it is often abandoned. Influence overtakes realism, and common sense realism devolves into 'I know what I like, I know what I want, and I don't have to give any reasons.' This is the anti-intellectualism that Hofstadter made famous, when he espied a 'decline from . . . the vernacular to the vulgar' (1962: 112) in American religious thought. This waning leads to a point where the 'vernacular style' will 'merely confirm, or even exaggerate, the coarsest side of popular sensibility' (Hofstadter 1962: 113–14). The battle over Kirby's history lesson, engaged to defend a Christmas that is already a hodgepodge of secular and sacred practices (mostly to the benefit of business), shows that American Christianity has reached this point of exaggeration as surely as it did with Hofstadter's chief example, Billy Sunday (114–16). As

Christmas developed – from the elaboration of wisps of tradition like the Christmas tree and Santa Claus, to the invention of Christmas cards and holiday department store displays – it artfully combined the imperatives of capitalism with sentimentality (Nissenbaum 1996; Schmidt 1995). What we are now seeing, with the impassioned assertions of the Christmas warriors, is a debased common sense realism that has replaced intuitive ethical norms with a false naturalising of culturally bounded traditions, in the name (and only the name, as in a talisman) of a bland Christianity.

Christmas: Supernatural or Expected?

In the 1950s – icon of normality in twentieth-century American culture – many Christians were aware of the pagan tint surrounding Christmas. In 1950, Rev. Del A. Fehsenfeld of the Argentine Baptist Church in Kansas City, Kansas, noted that 'Some people are more interested in teaching their children there is a Santa Claus and an Easter Bunny than in teaching about the Virgin Birth and the Resurrection' (Barnett 1954: 39). The *Hartford Courant*, in the holiday season of 1949, quoted Rev. Martin F. Clough condemning Santa as 'the most popular hoax of the age . . . a modern representative of the heathen god Nimrod who is a defiant hater of God and Satan's earliest effort to produce Anti-Christ' (Barnett 1954: 39). Even more intriguingly, a storied battle over biblical translation perspectives erupted into the Christmas season. The much-awaited Revised Standard Version (RSV) of the Bible was released – with President Truman accepting a copy at the White House – in November of 1952 (in time for Christmas gifts). However, a key passage, Isaiah 7:14, had demoted the King James' version's 'virgin' Mary into a mere 'young woman'. This launched some dramatic attacks against the RSV as a liberal translation of the Bible, with primarily fundamentalist preachers denouncing this alteration of prophecy. Criticisms escalated, until the House Un-American Activities Committee investigated members of the translation team, and an Air Force Training Manual labelled the RSV a 'Communist Bible' (Thuesen 1999: 4, 13–14, 94–103). However overwrought it might seem, this battle over Christmas concerned a key concept: the notion of supernaturalism, a sticking point between fundamentalist and modern liberal Christianity (Marsden 2006: 25, 62, 121).

Protests against Santa Claus were ridiculed, perceived as outside the mainstream, vestigial remnants of a dying fundamentalism. The contrast, though, between the protest against the RSV and the protest against Kirby's revised version of Christmas origins reveals how much less intellectually and theologically substantive the latter controversy is. Neither the supernatural truth claims of Christianity nor the historic truth of the pagan roots of Christmas serve as motivating factors today. The outrage precipitated by Kirby's comments expressed itself in a defence of an intellectually flabby notion of an American cultural Christmas, tied to the majoritarian status of titular Christianity. This intellectual flabbiness emanates from the marriage of a sentimentality utilised by market forces (advertising in particular) to a common sense realism descending toward a least common denominator. Hofstadter noted how in the nineteenth century 'rational discussion of theological issues . . . came to be regarded as a distraction,' replaced by emotion (Douglas's 'influence'). All was subordinated to the goal of marketing/proselytising, wherein 'simple people were brought back to faith with . . . the simplest of alternatives: . . . heaven or hell' (Hofstadter 1962: 83–4).

Consider how the rhetorical warriors who defend Christmas double as anti-gay crusaders (Gibson 2005: 138, 141). The nuclear hetero-normative family was the earliest market for the sentimental Christmas. As Richard Wightman Fox suggests, it was the ability of nineteenth-century Protestants to embrace a sentimental view of childhood that made it possible for them also to abandon their Puritan scruples and embrace Christmas's highlighting of the man-God Jesus as an infant (Fox 2004: 261). When Kirby introduced the Siberian shaman, hallucinogenic trance and other visceral pagan possibilities, he revealed a more adult, embodied and frankly dangerous version of the midwinter festivities than the family-values parents wanted for their children. In fact, when one considers the plethora of role reversals along gender, age and status lines, let alone out-and-out fun, in many midwinter festivities (recall the condemned 'bed games' of Gregory of Nazianzen and Mather's 'Night of Pleasure' [to 'be turned into Fear']), the pagan Christmas is non-normative enough to be queer. This queerness, the defenders of Christmas have intuited in common sense style, is just plain wrong; in fact, it is, as Donohue said of Kirby, 'insane' (after rejecting intoxication as an explanation).

While Kirby v. Donohue is just another chapter in the epic of Pagan v. Christian, this time the class markers have been reversed. Where once the working class scorned the anti-revelry strictures of the educated elite (recall Dorcas Hoar's husband William), now the educated elite have embraced an eclectic mélange of religious traditions and encourage a ludic anarchy. Gibson's lumberjacks prefer a Luddite destruction of the pretensions of the university machine, to reinstate the 'traditional' Christmas, the one celebrated in self-validating stories and songs (and reminiscences of small-town normality in 1953).

Interestingly, the conservative defenders of Christmas know something of the history of Christmas, including the Puritan objections to it (Gibson

2005: 162), but they will not acknowledge that a culturally homogenous and visibly religious Christmas presumes a majoritarianism that willingly tramples minority sensibilities and rights. Kirby's ideas on the origins of Christmas were ridiculed and silenced, and cost the unfortunate Associate a job. This was not a necessary outcome, except that Kirby, and the Paganism bubbling under the surface of the subsequent controversy, appeal to such a small market share that Wal-Mart had no interest in defending them. (Note how Fogleman defended Kwanzaa and Hanukkah instead of Kirby's actual comments in his initial response.) Furthermore, from the viewpoint of the Christmas warriors, Kirby's latent paganism was an obstacle to the Great Commission, to the monopolisation of the religious environment, a unification parallel to the standardisation of the capitalist market that Wal-Mart projects. In a very telling passage near the end of his history of fundamentalism, George Marsden endorses the practice of evangelism, saying that 'Evangelicals of all sorts have believed that sharing' the Christian message 'is the kindest thing one can do for one's neighbor' (2006: 252), while he decries the 'stridency of radical feminists (and) gays' (2006: 256). Gibson hammers a similar point in his Christmas diatribe: 'The central tenet of 84 percent of the country's religion is evangelization, which requires free speech in public' (2005: 163). Both the scholar and the rabble-rouser seem either unaware of, or perfectly at ease with, the coercive aspects of proselytising. Evangelisation explicitly intimidates, even more than advertising, by claiming that failure to accept their perspective/product condemns one eternally. A robust pluralism, even when represented in the bungling form of Kirby's email, provides a viable counterweight in the form of a feasible set of alternative world-views that blunt the absolutism of evangelical claims.

Battles over Christmas in America have mined many themes, most of them legal, but the Kirby incident provides a particularly rich prism for the early twenty-first century. No court case is pending, to my knowledge, in Kirby v. Christianity. Instead, the ground has shifted to rhetorical sparring. Playful neo-paganism nips at the heels of Christianity, and majoritarian outrage at having their common sense challenged leads to a reinvigoration of a Christian compulsion to dominate. Gibson laments the existence of that 'great annoyance', the 'offended observer, the one minor religionist who complains' about Christmas (2005: 132). Apparently, even if written in jest, Kirby's email was perceived by Bill Donohue and his allies as the work of such an 'offended observer', whom they cast as a thorough irritation: the smarmy Grinch who rewrote Christmas. But rather than defending any substantive theological point about the nature of Christmas and the Incarnation, or arguing for a Christian asceticism (or even dignity) against pagan celebration of the body, Donohue, Gibson and their ilk defended the majoritarian understanding of the consumerist Christmastide, a desire on the part of their audience to enjoy Christmas in the way they did as children, without any interference from uncomfortable facts. The ultimate aim is homogenisation, whether in Wal-Mart consumerism or Christian triumphalism. The aggrieved majority prevails through rhetorical pouting, claiming to be injured by Kirby or by Wal-Mart's website when, in fact, Christmas went on, celebrated by millions of Americans expending millions of dollars. An aggressive proselytising majority religion claims that its marketing is kindness itself, while Kirby's mere enumeration of an alternative religious history is assailed as insane, perhaps because of its uncommon sense.

Notes

1. This text exists in only one version – the one published by Kirby's opponent, the Catholic League. All versions of the story that I accessed had the exact same text, right down to the misspellings, word repetitions and lack of punctuation.
2. Fogleman is well known to opponents of Wal-Mart across the political spectrum. He is especially despised by unions, and by feminist activists who are advocating the availability of over-the-counter birth control products.
3. Bloggers pointed out the repeated 'of of', the misspelling of the 'Caucuses', the rather tortured 'aminita mascera' instead of the correct '*Amanita muscaria*' mushroom, and the odd turn to the singular in naming 'the Visigoth'. As a professor at a state university, I find this rate of error to be ruefully unsurprising. One left-leaning blogger even pointed out that 'Walmart' is not in the preferred corporate format of Wal-Mart in Kirby's letter (Rodney Anonymous).

Acknowledgements

The author would like to thank Sheila Whiteley for her patience, liberality and deft editorial hand. Janice O'Leary was kind enough to correspond with me about her *Boston Globe* article. Dan Williamson, Louis Mazza, Eliza Rentschler, Todd Ormsbee, Scot Guenter, Donald Hines and Shantanu Phukan all contributed ideas, witticisms or needed slack en route to the completion of this paper. Thanks above all to Peggy Macres, my partner, for her boundless understanding and her intuitive agreement to spend every holiday season as far from the traditional Christmas as possible.

CHAPTER 5

Christmas Carols

Barry Cooper

Christmas without Christ is like *Hamlet* without the prince, and a celebration without meaning. Yet in the secular world of today, many people rarely encounter the true message of Christmas except when they hear it proclaimed in Christmas carols, which have become an almost inescapable part of the Christmas festivities in Britain, America and elsewhere. The carols recount and interpret the message and the original Christmas story in a great many ways, sometimes at great length, other times more succinctly. The essence of the Christmas message can in fact be summed up in a single word – Emmanuel (Hebrew for 'among-us-God'), for the central theme of Christmas is that God, the Son of God, the second person of God the Trinity, 'came down from Heaven and was incarnate' (as stated in the Athanasian Creed), living among human beings and taking the form of a newborn infant. This central point is present, or at least understood by implication, in almost all Christmas carols of all periods.

The Christmas carol as a genre has a long history, which has gradually become intertwined with Christmas hymns and songs of all types, so that almost any short vocal piece that has a religious text relating to Christmas can now be loosely regarded as a carol. If this wider definition is embraced, as will be done here, then the history of the Christmas carol becomes very much longer still, for Christmas hymns have probably been sung for almost as long as Christmas has been celebrated. Among the earliest are the fourth-century hymns 'Veni, Redemptor gencium' ('Come, thou Redeemer of the earth'), by St Ambrose, Bishop of Milan (c. 340–97), and 'Corde natus ex Parentis' ('Of the Father's heart begotten'), by Aurelius Clemens Prudentius (348–c. 410).[1] Neither of these hymns, however, is sung to its original tune today, for no musical notation is known to date from this period, and the original tunes must have been at least modified during transmission over several centuries before the invention of notation, if not replaced by another tune altogether. Today, 'Veni, Redemptor' is sung (usually in translation) to a variety of tunes, none of which was written down before about the tenth century at the earliest. Meanwhile 'Corde natus' is usually sung to a tune that has been taken from the Swedish publication *Piae cantiones* of 1582. Tune and words were brought together only much later, in 1854, by J. M. Neale and Thomas Helmore.[2] This practice of grafting a new tune on to existing words, or alternatively bringing together the words and an existing tune composed for some quite other text, is typical of the carol genre; relatively few of the older texts have been retained with their original melody, and there are several cases where, as with 'Corde natus', tune and words were brought together only after both had led separate existences for a century or more.

As Christianity spread throughout Europe during late Classical times, local traditions of celebrating Christmas inevitably arose, and with them, local Christmas carols (in the broadest sense). In medieval times, many more such carols were written, while increasing devotion to the Virgin Mary tended to reinforce this trend. An example is the popular carol 'Angelus ad virginem', which is mentioned by Chaucer and was perhaps written and composed by Philippe the Chancellor,[3] a thirteenth-century Parisian, though the sources of the carol, including one version in middle English, are all British. Most of the text concerns the Annunciation rather than the Nativity, while the final is addressed directly to Mary. Another medieval example still popular today is the fourteenth-century German carol 'In dulci jubilo', which was written in a mixture of Latin and German. Here, however, the Marian element has been significantly reduced since the Reformation.[4]

In England, meanwhile, a type of song known as the 'carol' was emerging. This type of carol was initially a religious but non-liturgical strophic song, distinguished by the presence of a refrain or 'burden' at the end of each stanza and not necessarily related to Christmas. The regular rhythms of these carols (in contrast to freer plainchant rhythm) imply an early association with dance music, as does the word 'carol', which is related to the French 'carole', a type of dance-song,[5] though any connection with dancing gradually disappeared in later times. One of the earliest such carols is the famous 'Deo gracias Anglia', which celebrates the English victory at the Battle of Agincourt (1415) and must have been composed shortly after the battle. The religious content is limited, with the text simply giving thanks to God for the victory. Most of the 'carols' (in the more limited sense of this period), however, relate to the Virgin Mary, Christmas or related subjects, so that the word 'carol' eventually became synonymous, for many, with 'Christmas carol'; thus they can be seen as true precursors of our modern carols. Nevertheless the carol, Christmas or not, of the late Middle Ages was essentially a part of popular culture rather than an ecclesiastical conceit, and the quality of both music and text was mostly far more simple and direct than the complex theological hymns of St Ambrose and Prudentius. This can be seen by a comparison of Prudentius's 'Corde natus', replete with scriptural allusions, with that of one of the more interesting fifteenth-century English carols.[6] Prudentius's first verse includes references to Christ being born 'before all worlds', which is a paraphrase of the Athanasian creed ('ex Patre natum ante omnia secula'), and being Alpha and Omega, the first and the last, the beginning and the end (Rev. 22:13):

Corde natus ex Parentis	Of the Father's heart begotten
Ante mundi exordium,	Ere the world from chaos rose,
Alpha et O cognominatus,	He is alpha and omega,
Ipse Fons et Clausula	He is the fount and he the close
Omnium que sunt, fuerunt,	Of whatever is or has been
Queque post futura sunt,	Or the future years disclose
Seculorum seculis.	Evermore and evermore.

By comparison, the carol 'Alleluia. A nywe werk', though perfectly sound theologically, is much less sophisticated:

Alleluia.
A nywe werk is come on honde
Thorw myght and grace of Godys sonde [messenger],
To save the lost of every londe,
Alleluya.

The first verse describes the coming of Christ as a 'new work' – in other words a new event – announced by God's messenger (the Angel Gabriel), to save lost mankind (cf. the parable of the lost sheep, Luke 15:4– 7). The refrain or burden is simply 'Alleluia', whereas Sedulius's refrain 'Seculorum seculis' relates to concepts of eternity already alluded to in the verse. Thus the level of theological content in Christmas poetry was already quite variable, and this diversity continued to increase in later centuries, as will be seen.

Christmas carols (in the broad sense) sometimes also appeared in medieval mystery plays, though few have survived with music. The best-known one is the so-called 'Coventry Carol' ('Lully lulla, thow little tyne child'),[7] which derives from the Pageant of the Shearman and Tailors and survives in a three-voice setting from the late sixteenth century. Of all carols commonly sung today, this is the oldest that can be heard, in both words and music, in something like its original form (though the older 'In dulci jubilo' has retained much of its original medieval state).

One feature of the Reformation was a great reduction in the attention given to the Virgin Mary, and therefore also to celebration of Christmas in music. In churches that developed along Calvinist principles, only strictly biblical texts could be sung – normally just metrical psalms. This principle applied also in the Church of England until at least the mid-eighteenth century. There were even attempts to abolish Christmas altogether during the Commonwealth period (1649–60). The range of popular attitudes to the festival at that time is neatly summed up in the title of a pamphlet by Hezekiah Woodward published in 1656 (London: Henry Cripps): *Christ-mas Day, the old heathens feasting day, in honour to Saturn their idol-god. The Papists massing day. The prophane mans ranting day. The superstitious mans idol day. The multitudes idle day. Whereon, because they cannot do nothing: they do worse then nothing. Satans, that adversaries working-day. The true Christian mans fasting-day. Taking to heart, the heathenish customes, Popish superstitions, ranting fashions, fearful provocations, horrible abhominations committed against the Lord, and His Christ, on that day, and days following.* Although Christmas Day itself was still clearly regarded as special by most people, there was clearly no general agreement that it should be celebrated in song, and some Christians were even prepared to fast, as Woodward appears to recommend in the pamphlet. With attitudes like this permeating popular culture, it is hardly surprising that Christmas carols, like hymns in general, failed to flourish in Britain at that time, for any religious songs that were not purely scriptural were regarded with suspicion.

In 1700, however, Nahum Tate published a paraphrase of part of the Christmas narrative as related in St Luke's gospel (Luke 2:8–14), to be sung either as a kind of congregational hymn in church or alternatively in more informal contexts. This paraphrase was allowable even for strict Puritans, since it was in essence purely scriptural. The text, 'While shepherds watched their flocks by night', quickly became extremely popular in the eighteenth century, as is evident partly from the large number of tunes with which it can be found – no fewer than seven are printed in *The New Oxford Book of Carols*.[8] The tune now sung almost universally today, Winchester Old, is actually much older than Tate's words, dating back to the late sixteenth century. It was some years after 'While shepherds watched' had been published before the text became associated at all with this tune, and it was not regarded as the standard tune until the nineteenth century. By that time hymns had become acceptable again, and several notable new Christmas hymns had been written, such as Byrom's 'Christians, awake' (c. 1749) and even the Latin 'Adeste, fideles' (c. 1740), later translated as 'O come, all ye faithful'.[9]

Northern Germany was also largely Protestant, but there the orthodox Lutheran church always allowed simple chorales (hymns), including Christmas chorales. Some of the chorales consisted of newly written verses, while others were based on older texts; 'Nun komm, der heiden Heiland', for example, is a translation of St Ambrose's 'Veni, Redemptor' mentioned above. More elaborate music was also allowed, both vocal and instrumental, and such music for Christmas eventually culminated in Bach's Christmas Oratorio of 1734, which consisted of a series of six cantatas to be performed on six different days from Christmas Day to the Feast of the Epiphany (6 January). These cantatas included several individual verses from chorales.

Meanwhile in Catholic countries during this period Christmas continued to be celebrated in church with often elaborate ritual and music, with Midnight Mass sometimes adorned by pastoral-style music. Corelli's 'Christmas' Concerto, Op. 6 No. 8, published in Rome in 1714 but composed some years earlier, concludes with a pastoral-style movement specifically 'fatto per la notte di natali' ('made for Christmas night'). In France, a similar tradition of elaborate ecclesiastical ritual was supplemented by a flourishing tradition of popular Christmas carols or *noëls*. These *noëls* were so popular, in fact, that they were occasionally even incorporated into elaborate art music for the Midnight Mass, as in Charpentier's *Messe de minuit pour Noël*, which dates from about the 1690s and incorporates some dozen *noëls*.[10] Numerous *noëls* were also published in the eighteenth century in various arrangements – particularly as sets of variations for the organ by such composers as Louis-Claude Daquin and Michel Corrette. Examples include such titles as 'Bon Joseph écoute moy' and 'Laissez paître vos bestes'.

In England, despite the absence of a comparable written tradition, folk carols from the eighteenth century were sometimes invented and transmitted orally, and luckily several were rescued from oblivion by later collectors, notably Davies Gilbert (*Some Ancient Christmas Carols*, London, 1822) and William Sandys (*Christmas Carols, Ancient and Modern*, London, 1833). Similarly in other countries popular Christmas songs might be collected orally and then published as part of a collection. For example, a volume of Austrian folk songs published in Pest in 1819 includes a section of seven *Weihnachtslieder*, complete with their melodies.[11] These were essentially folk carols collected from the neighbourhood of Vienna by the editors. It was within this tradition that the most famous carol of all, 'Stille Nacht' ('Silent Night'), was written and composed by Joseph Mohr and Franz Gruber, probably for their village's annual Midnight Mass at Christmas.[12]

By the twentieth century, although the term 'carol' had become closely associated with Christmas in English-speaking countries, there were still some who felt that such a restriction of the term was unjustifiable. Consequently, when the pathbreaking *Oxford Book of Carols* was published in 1928,[13] a different stance was adopted by the editors, as is evident from Percy Dearmer's preface. Taking a somewhat partisan approach to the subject, he views carols as 'songs with a religious impulse that are simple, hilarious, popular, and modern', and condemns the view that had allegedly emerged by 1848 that the term 'had come to mean printed matter suitable for Christmas', including hymns and poems without music.[14] Thus the book included carols for all seasons of the year, including Christmas, as well as many for no particular season; nearly all were arranged with four-part harmony suitable for choirs. The book also included some Christmas texts that were not true carols. The old biblical paraphrase 'While shepherds watched', described as a 'carol, which is better known as a hymn', was included merely so that a traditional eighteenth-century tune 'proper to the words' could be included, rather than Winchester Old; and 'O little town of Bethlehem', was described as a hymn that was 'so much a carol that we feel bound to include it in this book also'.[15] Meanwhile many fine Christmas hymns were excluded, such as Wesley's 'Hark! the herald angels sing'. A substantial section was devoted to foreign carols, with a considerable number of countries represented (though the words were always translated into English); but 'Silent night' was omitted, to the chagrin of many subsequent users of the book. Indeed carol singers in the following decades were often frustrated by the absence of well-known carols and the inclusion of large numbers of carols for other seasons. Thus they commonly supplemented their *Oxford Book of Carols* with hymn books and other smaller collections. Not until the appearance of *The New Oxford Book of Carols* in 1992 did a single book appear that included almost all the carols that were in common use in English-speaking countries.

The Christmas carols of today, therefore, are of extremely varied origin, both geographically and chronologically. The origins of the tunes now used are almost equally disparate. Some were composed specifically for the texts with which they are associated, while others were married to their texts only years or even centuries after the two were created. Each country has its own way of celebrating Christmas, and nowhere is this more apparent than in music, where the *noël* of France, the *Weihnachtslied* of Germany and the Christmas carol of Anglo-Saxon countries include very different repertories, as do the Christmas songs of other countries and languages. Although *The New Oxford Book of Carols* is strikingly eclectic in its selection, with an impressive variety of countries and languages represented, including Czech, Polish, Provençal, Basque, Spanish and a good number of old Lutheran chorales, a sizeable majority are settings of English texts. What nearly all have in common is that they are settings of multi-stanza texts with largely syllabic settings in simple strophic form – in other words, with the same or almost the same music to each stanza.

Within this uniformity of structure and diversity of language, there are features worth noting. Almost all carols make at least some allusion to the biblical narratives contained in the gospels of St Luke (1:26–38, which describes the Annunciation, and 2:1–20, relating the birth of Christ and the angel's appearance to the shepherds) and St Matthew (1:18–2:18, which describes the birth of Christ, the coming of the magi and the flight into Egypt). But apart from these features, there is little that most carols have in common. Certainly the level of theological content varies enormously. Different levels have already been noted in connection with medieval and pre-medieval hymns and carols, but more recent carols are even more diverse. In some there is virtually no theological element, as in 'We wish you a merry Christmas', with its obscene demand for 'figgy pudding'. Another example is 'The twelve days of Christmas', which derives from a traditional forfeits game,[16] although some have endeavoured to interpret the numbers from one to twelve as metaphors for Christian symbols (e.g. four colly-birds can represent the four gospels). Christmas songs such as 'Jingle, bells' have even been regarded as carols by some, despite their patently secular subjects.

At the other extreme, some carols are deeply theological, with allusions to many aspects of man's redemption as well as to the standard Christmas narratives of St Matthew and St Luke. A fine example is 'Hark! the herald angels sing', where almost every line is full of rich content. In what is now the second half of the third stanza (originally it was the sixth of ten four-line stanzas), Wesley develops the idea of Christ's birth by ingeniously relating it to other births and to death:

> Mild, he lays his glory by;
> Born that man no more may die,
> Born to raise the sons of earth,
> Born to give them second birth.

In the first line Wesley reflects on how Christ, who has dwelt in Heaven in eternity, has laid aside his glory to descend to earth (cf. John 1:14) as a mild infant. In the second, Wesley recalls Christ's assertion that his followers will never die but inherit eternal life (John 6:50), with the neat opposition of 'born' and 'die' at the beginning and end of the line. In the next line there is again neat opposition; whereas infants are normally born and raised, Christ is born not to be raised but to raise others. Then in the final line Christ's birth is linked with his later command that one must be 'born again' to enter into the Kingdom of God (John 3:3). It is all too easy to overlook most or all of these concepts and references when listening to these words being sung to Mendelssohn's rousing tune (which, incidentally, was originally composed for quite another purpose and only united with Wesley's text in 1856, after both composer and poet were dead). The difference in quality between this and the following, which appeared in *The Oxford Book of Carols* (no. 87) as a rather loose translation of the Czech carol 'Hajej, nynej, Ježišku', is all too evident:

Little Jesus, sweetly sleep, do not stir,
We will lend a coat of fur,
We will rock you, rock you, rock you,
We will rock you, rock you, rock you,
See the fur to keep you warm,
Snugly round your tiny form.

This banal text, charming though it may be, has no theological content and only the most indirect of biblical allusions, painting a wholly imaginary scene in which the singers are somehow present beside the newborn Christ, and in a position to rock him (interminably) and to offer a fur coat as a largely superfluous addition to the swaddling clothes that Mary had already provided to keep the baby warm. Yet popular culture scarcely distinguishes these two carols, and will happily include both within the same performing context.

What are these performing contexts? They are actually quite diverse, for carols can often be heard as recorded background music to such activities as shopping and dining, and recordings for domestic listening are plentiful. Live performances are less frequent, for the days when bands of carol singers would roam the streets during the Christmas season have long since passed – largely due to the increasingly easy availability of high-quality recordings, as well as the increase of traffic noise. The main context for live performance of carols in recent years, where the music can be heard at its best and purest, has been the carol service. Carols began to be incorporated into church services during Victorian times, and eventually services were being held that were constructed specifically around a series of carols. Dearmer even suggested that churches might hold a carol service every Sunday throughout the year, with about six hymns or carols interspersed with readings and prayers,[17] but this suggestion has not caught on.

Far more successful was the invention of the 'festival of nine lessons and carols', as it has become known. This became firmly established through the lead given by King's College, Cambridge, under A. H. Mann in the years after the First World War, and has been widely imitated in churches and chapels throughout the United Kingdom. The nine lessons are more or less fixed, and lead from a reading from Genesis, through the prophets, to the narratives of St Luke and St Matthew and ultimately the opening of St John's gospel, where the mystery of the Incarnation is unfolded. Interspersed with the readings are at least nine carols and sometimes many more. The attraction is that some of these carols (or hymns) are so well known that everyone can join in confidently, while other carols are less well known or more sophisticated, and are performed by a trained choir. Almost any suitable Christmas music can be included here, whether an excerpt from Bach's Christmas Oratorio or Berlioz's oratorio *L'enfance du Christ*, or a little known but attractive carol, or a new composition written for the occasion, or a slightly sophisticated arrangement of a popular carol, where the well-known tune is heard in versions that differ from verse to verse, with the arranger either varying which voice has the melody or changing the harmony or organ accompaniment. Although a few of these choir carols are through-composed and resemble an anthem or motet rather than a normal carol, many are no more complicated than the congregational ones, and most still have the familiar carol structure of a series of stanzas set to essentially the same melody. Even the excerpts from the Bach and Berlioz oratorios are of relatively simple sections that bear some relation to the strophic carol.

A boost to the use of this more complex type of carol music was given in 1961 with the appearance of a volume of *Carols for Choirs*, edited by Reginald Jacques and David Willcocks,[18] which included nearly all the favourite congregational carols and a fair selection of popular choir carols. The volume was so successful that three further volumes were published in the next few years. A fresh boost for carol singers came in 1992 with the above-mentioned *New Oxford Book of Carols*, which besides containing over 200 carols – some in several different settings – includes a very useful and detailed account of the history of the Christmas carol and several of the various traditions that have embodied it, as well as a history of each individual carol.

In recent decades carols and carol services have, like the rest of the Christmas festivities, increasingly infiltrated the period before Christmas, rather than the traditional twelve-day period of Christmas itself. This was partly due to the desire of schools and colleges to hold a carol service before the Christmas holidays, and partly by a general tendency to anticipate events rather than look back on them. Thus there are today relatively few carol services held during the actual twelve days of the Christmas season, but a great proliferation of them from early December onwards, including the occasional Advent carol service, a more austere form with different readings and a more limited selection of carols. King's College, Cambridge, however, still holds its main carol service in the afternoon of Christmas Eve, from where it can reach the whole country – and nowadays even the whole world – through broadcasts by the BBC. For many people, these broadcasts from King's are an essential and integral part of their Christmas celebration, and a timely reminder that there is a deeper significance to what might otherwise become an orgy of eating and drinking.

Notes

1. These are to be found in many modern hymnbooks, and at nos. 2 and 19 respectively in Hugh Keyte and Andrew Parrott (eds) (1992) *The New Oxford Book of Carols [NOBC]*, Oxford: Oxford University Press, from which all translations are taken unless otherwise indicated.
2. Ibid., p. 58.
3. Christopher Page (1983) 'Angelus ad virginem: a new work by Philippe the Chancellor?', *Early Music* xi:69–70.
4. See *NOBC*, p. 198.
5. See John Stevens, 'Carol: 1', *Grove Music Online*, ed. L. Macy. www.grovemusic.com. Accessed 21 June 2007.
6. *NOBC*, nos. 19 (translation altered) and 30.
7. *NOBC*, no. 40.
8. *NOBC*, no. 46.
9. *OBC*, nos. 71 and 70 (see note 13 below).
10. James R. Anthony (1973) *French Baroque Music from Beaujoyeulx to Rameau*, London: Batsford, p. 221.
11. Franz Ziska and Julius Max Schottky (eds) (1819) *Oesterreichische Volkslieder mit ihren Singeweisen*, Pest: Hartleben, pp. 44–61.
12. For a summary of the origins of this carol and a discussion of some of the myths associated with it, see *NOBC*, pp. 304–5.
13. Percy Dearmer, R. Vaughan Williams and Martin Shaw (eds) (1928) *The Oxford Book of Carols [OBC]*, London: Oxford University Press.
14. *OBC*, pp. v, xiv.
15. *OBC*, nos. 33 and 138 respectively.
16. See *NOBC*, p. 469.
17. *OBC*, p. 482.
18. Oxford: Oxford University Press.

CHAPTER 6

Christmas Songs – Sentiments and Subjectivities

Sheila Whiteley

It is somewhat of a paradox to think that the popularity of the Christian feast of the Nativity, not least the sentiments now associated with Christmas, is largely due to the enduring relevance of a Victorian morality tale concerned primarily with the twin evils of social injustice and poverty. Haunted by spirits which appear at the 'witching hour' of midnight, there is also a hint of the Gothic, but as Christmas combines the celebration of the birth of Jesus Christ with traditions and customs that draw on the winter solstice feasts of Saturnalia, Yule and Mithras, this is not so unlikely as it might at first seem. What is, perhaps, more surprising is that *A Christmas Carol* (1843), with its five stanzas reflecting the title's musical connotations, was also politically radical, an attack on the accumulation of wealth which, in the burgeoning years of the British Empire, was central to its ideology of power. Equally resonant in the 'satanic mills' of the Industrial Revolution, it seemed that the social and charitable observances earlier associated with Christmas were under threat as Darwinian evolutionary theory and the problems accompanying industrialisation increasingly undermined the concept of an omnipotent and caring God.

As early as 1823, Lord Shaftesbury had warned that the changing work patterns of men, women and children were causing instability, and that the values on which social and economic equilibrium depended were under threat:

> Domestic life and domestic discipline must soon be at an end; society will consist of individuals no longer grouped into families; so early is the separation of husband and wife, of parents and children. (Hodder 1923: 234)

The significance of his observations was not lost on an emerging middle class that was experiencing both economic prosperity and an enhanced social standing. As discussed in John Storey's chapter, the Victorian Christmas celebrated commercialism, capitalism and prosperity, even though any self-congratulatory pleasure was tainted with guilt and fear that the Industrial Revolution had also brought with it poverty, disease and social unrest. Salvation, it seemed, lay in the family, an axiom central to Victorian belief that a good home life would produce a stable and worthy population. The increasing importance attached to Christmas Day, which was given the timely status of a bank holiday in 1834, can thus be interpreted as 'a deliberate attempt to impose middle-class family values upon a mass working population which, at a time of rapid industrial growth and upheaval, was both feared and distrusted' (Golby 1981: 19). Further, the story of Scrooge reads as a clear warning to the class he represents: share prosperity or face destruction (Storey, p. 26) timely advice in a period of revolution,[1] when the publication of the *Manifesto of the Communist Party* (Marx and Engels 1848) argued that the conditions of modern industrial societies invariably resulted in the estrangement of workers from their own labour, thus precipitating social revolution.

As such, Christmas – the feast of the Nativity – provides an interesting ideological model, drawing into association the Holy Family, the nuclear family, the extended family, the family of the state, the family of the church, and the family of the empire. It is also interesting to note that, unlike the extreme patriarchal hierarchy of Victorian England, the model situates the feminine as central to the underlying discourse of birth, nurturance and family values. The central relationship is between Mary and Jesus and, as such, there is an interesting parallel with the maternal role of Queen Victoria as head of the Church of England, the state and the empire – her own extended family, which by the end of the nineteenth century occupied one-third of the world. The familial ideology continues, with certain modifications, in Queen Elizabeth II's Christmas Message; the emphasis is on a nation composed of small family groups – including the Royal Family – counterposed to the large-scale impersonal forces of war, famine and environmental change which dominate everyday news. It is a message that combines the credo of redeeming love underpinning the birth of Christ, the philosophy of 'goodwill to all men' of *A Christmas Carol*, and a romanticised vision of family and community, albeit tempered by a recognition that this is not always easy to achieve.

It is arguably this emphasis on the utopian of shared values that situates Christmas within an ideological discourse that centres on romantic idealism: a visionary, imaginative, descriptive expression of love which mobilises fantasy, myth and Christian belief through the production of cultural activities, rituals, customs and texts. It is also argued that the effectiveness of such ideologies depends on their passing unnoticed: 'to reveal the formal means and mechanisms by which [they] work is, at the same time, to loosen, to some degree, [their] hold on us' (Bennett 1981: 70). With music playing such a central role in the production and mediation of Christmas as a 'lived culture', the aim of my chapter is to explore the extent to which seasonal songs foster a romantic idealism which influences and informs the practices and rituals of Christmas (our thoughts, feelings and behaviour) in ways that are socially, ideologically and politically consequential.

The association of music with Christian worship is, as Barry Cooper writes, long-standing, but with the Reformation and the spread of Puritanism in Northern Europe in the late sixteenth century, festivals and holidays with 'superstitious' connections and/or Catholic associations were increasingly under attack. By the 1650s no church services were allowed and legislation prevented Christmas from being solemnised in any way. While laws against Christmas were relaxed with the 1660 Restoration, the festival had lost its popular appeal, and apart from the aristocracy and gentry continuing to celebrate the birth of Christ by going to church, partaking of a special dinner and giving presents of clothing, blankets or coals to their tenants, there is little to suggest that Christmas was regarded in any way as a special holiday or as a day to be spent with the family (Golby 1981: 4). It is also evident that before the mid-nineteenth century 'no publisher saw much potential for sales of songs espousing Roman Catholic sentiment, however attractive the music, and despite the Catholic Emancipation Act of 1829' (Scott 1989: 118).

The growth in new publications of old carols began, as Derek Scott observes, in the 1840s and was aimed largely at the family, reflecting the need to organise and control the leisure activities of a large and growing urban population. *Songs of Christmas for Family Choirs*, selected and adapted by 'a Clergyman of the Church of England', was published in London in 1847, and new carols, such as Henry John Gauntlett's 'Once in Royal David's City' (a setting of verse by Mrs C. F. Alexander), were published in *Christmas Carols Old and New* (1850). 'God Rest Ye Merry Gentlemen', a wait's carol dating from the seventeenth century, featured in *A Christmas Carol*, and by 'the last quarter of the century, the Christmas theme was just one more option open to songwriters' (Scott 1989: 119), with drawing-room ballads such as Brinley Richard's 'Christmas Chimes' (1854) and Stephen Adams's setting of 'The Star of Bethlehem' (1887) providing early examples of the centrality of the home in Christmas Day activities. It was, however, the introduction of the gramophone and the development of the radio in the 1920s and of television in the 1960s and 1970s that most affected the importance of music as a central focus of Christmas entertainment, not least its mediating role in developing and evolving the traditional associations and sentiments associated with the

Victorian Christmas, in particular those emphasising the centrality of the family, benevolence and charitable giving. Even so, 'it is important to appreciate that this is not what Christmas means or is about in some essential and timeless way, but is rather what it has been *made* to *mean*, living in a particular culture at a particular moment in its historical development' (Bennett 1981: 49; emphasis original).

Bennett's observation is particularly relevant to the heady concoction of religious belief and popular music that has become a major component of contemporary Christmas and which is exemplified in Elvis Presley's 1957 cover version of the Rev. Phillips Brooks' carol, 'O Little Town of Bethlehem'. Written in 1868 after the clergyman's visit to the Holy Land, with music by Lewis H. Redner, the carol was first performed in the Christmas service of the Sunday School of the Church of the Holy Trinity, Philadelphia, in 1868. For many children, the singing of carols, either at church or at school, has been a way of learning the Christmas story, reminding the listener – often subconsciously – of what we should be doing and what we should be feeling. By taking the carol into the popular domain, via *Elvis's Christmas Album* – which also included 'White Christmas' and 'Santa Bring My Baby Back To Me' – the centrality of the Christian message is taken into a secular context. In effect, the alignment of a carol describing the quiet beauty of Christ's birthplace with a song situating Christmas within a nostalgic winter landscape effects a shared romantic discourse, which is heightened by Presley's mellow crooning baritone. The inclusion of a prayer to Santa to return his 'baby' adds myth to the vernacular of a pop love song and, as such, it is not difficult to see why Bible belt America attacked the album as amoral, profaning both Christmas and Christianity. It is also interesting to note that songwriter Irving Berlin mounted a campaign to prevent radio play of Elvis's cover of 'White Christmas' and that DJs were actually fired for playing the track.

While Joan Baez's 1966 album, *Noël*, which included such carols as 'O Come, O Come Emmanuel', 'The Coventry Carol' and 'Good King Wenceslas', was less controversial, the interpretation of carols as folk music again problematises their original status as church music. In effect, both Presley and Baez have moved 'carols' into the domain of 'romantic nostalgia'. Their status, as iconic figures within pop and folk respectively, also brings into focus the implicit ideological tension inherent in popular music's relationship to Christmas: namely, that of family and community versus the star who is, by definition, conspicuously individual. Presley's Christmas albums were sandwiched between otherwise highly sexual rock 'n' roll LPs and, in common with the Christmas 1968 Special, which was stage-managed by Colonel Tom Parker to re-establish the star's singing career after years of formula movies, were overtly commercial, confirming his role as a celebrity singer. Elvis's original *Christmas Album* sold more than any other of his LPs, with 'Blue Christmas' ('You'll be doing alright, with your Christmas of white, but I'll have a blue blue Christmas') accounting for 22 million sales.[2] In contrast, *Noël*, with its songs of peace, was a dedicated protest against the war in Vietnam. Already committed to social and political protest when *Noël* was released, Baez had founded the Institute for the Study of Non-Violence in Carmel, California, in 1963, subsequently joining Amnesty International.

While there are numerous ballads from the Boer War, World Wars I and II, and Vietnam, 'Happy Christmas (War is Over)' is one of the very few songs specifically composed to focus on the ideological gap between Christmas and war: 'Let's stop all the fight.' Like Joan Baez, both John Lennon and Yoko Ono were committed to peace, and their campaigning slogan, 'WAR IS OVER! (If You Want It) Happy Christmas from John and Yoko,' was posted on billboards in eleven cities including New York, Tokyo, Rome, Amsterdam and London in late 1969. The war in Vietnam was then in its eighth year[3] and television coverage had brought the atrocities into the family living room. Horrifying self-immolations[4] and breaking news of a massacre in My Lai (16 March 1968) led to an escalation of student demonstrations across American campuses and a protest by 3,000 Vietnam Solidarity Campaign (VSC) militants who charged the US Embassy in London's Grosvenor Square (July 1968), the demonstration turning into a riot after an eighteen-year-old girl became trapped underneath a police horse. The anti-war movement swept across Europe with uprisings in Paris, Rome, Berlin and Czechoslovakia. In the USA a unit of the Ohio State National Guard shot dead four students, wounding nine others, during a peaceful protest at Kent State University (4 May 1970). The gulf between those who wanted to change America and its foreign policies and those who believed in the maintenance of the status quo ('My country, right or wrong') deepened, culminating in the infamous Operation Linebacker II (1972), a massive surprise air bombing of Hanoi and Haiphong, which extended over Christmas Day. As Christine Agius notes, 'Despite claims that military facilities were targeted, the Nixon administration faced accusations that hospitals and civilian targets were attacked (National Security Archive 1973)' (p. 139); civilian casualties, including children, were estimated at 1,624.

'Happy Christmas (War Is Over)' was released on 6 December 1971 and became significant both as a protest against the war in Vietnam and subsequently as a peace anthem, most recently on the demonstrations against the war in Iraq. Starting with a barely audible 'Happy Christmas, Kyoko' from

Yoko Ono and 'Happy Christmas, Julian' from Lennon, the identification of their young children draws them into association with the lyrics' appeal to young and old, weak and strong, rich and poor, black, white, yellow and red, to reflect on 'what we have done' in an anthemic ballad, replete with the Harlem Community Choir and the Christmas essentials of sleigh bells, chimes and glockenspiel. The lyrics are repetitive, stepping up with each reprise, with vocals by Lennon, Ono and choir, supported by the Plastic Ono Band, with a dense musical texture typical of co-producer, Phil Spector. The effectiveness of the song, lies in the simplicity of its repetitive structure. The 16-bar stanza (4×4 bar phrases, 'And so this is Christmas . . . A new one just begun', with slight changes in the lyric line) repeats nine times. Opening with Lennon's effected vocals over an acoustic guitar and a mandolin-like accompaniment, the chugging waltz and simple lyrics are repeated, so cementing the words and melody in the listener's memory. Sleigh bells accent the second and fourth bars, with the third reprise heralded by a drum fill as Yoko and the children's choir lift the refrain before the fourth repeat where John takes over the lyrics and the choir sing in counterpoint: 'War is over . . .'. The build in dynamics and musical texture across the song is enhanced by increasingly heavy drum fills, and strings which lift into the final repeats. Initially fronted by Lennon over the children's chorus of 'War is Over', the penultimate stanza is given additional lift as Yoko and the choir take over the lead vocals before a final unison 'War is Over if you want it', where the instrumental fade effects a dramatic space for the children's voices on 'Now' and the final spoken exchanges: 'Happy Christmas'.

It is, perhaps, appropriate that 'Happy Christmas . . .' was re-issued on 8 December 1980, immediately following John Lennon's murder, a reminder that it is not only war that takes lives and that the fight for peace and freedom should continue. Its invitation to stop what you are doing and join in – 'And so this is Christmas . . .' – to reflect on the past and the present, to hope for a future 'without any fear' is, it seems, eternally relevant; yet while Christmas provides a particular space for reflecting on the inhumanity of war, it is also evident that the ensuing devastation – not least in relation to disease and malnutrition – is equally a cause for concern, as evidenced most recently in Iraq and Afganistan. In Africa, where emerging warlords continue to sabotage peaceful intervention by the United Nations in, for example, the Congo and Sudan, the immediate need for medical supplies and food highlights the problems of refugees fleeing from the brutalities of tribal conflict and corrupt leadership. As such, the ideology of charity and benevolence, whereby 'Christmas becomes a bridge between the world as it is and the world as it should be' (Golby and Purdue

2000: 45) is both idealistic and problematic. Charity may relieve suffering, 'but what it does not do is change the causes of suffering' (Storey, p. 26), a concern that is highlighted by Band Aid's 1984 single, 'Do They Know It's Christmas?'

Written by Bob Geldof to raise money to support famine relief in Ethiopia and sung by a community of stars including David Bowie, Paul McCartney, Bono and Sting, its message of 'feed the world' had an immediacy of appeal, grafting the concept of community spirit on to the ideals of benevolence. In essence, it combines the preacher-like qualities of contemporary church songs with a 'sing-along' chorus, appropriately spiced by a musical arrangement replete with uplifting chimes and bells. The opening line sets the scene, 'It's Christmas time', establishing a narrative which contrasts the Western world of 'plenty' with a 'world of dread and fear', the specifics of drought-ridden Africa, hunger and the promise of relief. Religious connotations – 'Pray for the other ones' – are blended with the bonhomie traditionally associated with Christmas festivities – 'Here's to you. Raise a glass to everyone'. The song is thus moved into the secular of the largely unison chorus, signifying a unanimous agreement to the solution of 'feed the world', fortified musically by a dramatic shift to the major against a peal of Christmas bells.

'Do They Know It's Christmas?' debuted at Number One in Great Britain on its release in November 1984 and was Number One in the United States two weeks later. Geldof had promised that every penny raised would go to famine relief and it seemed that the public were behind him. The Government, however, were less willing to comply and refused to waive VAT on the sale of the single. Geldof again made the headlines, this time by publicly standing up to Prime Minister Margaret Thatcher; sensing the strength of public feeling, the Government backed down and donated the tax back to the charity. The single sold over 50 million copies, 3 million in the UK alone, and Midge Ure, as co-producer, personally accompanied the first relief shipment of over $70,000 worth of food and medical supplies to Ethiopia on 11 March 1985.

As discussed earlier, while the ideals of generosity and kindness are particularly acute at Christmas, charitable intervention is problematic and criticism was voiced that famine relief should be the concern of the British Government rather than pop stars, and that the publicity surrounding Band Aid undermined the real political causes of world hunger. As such, Band Aid's revamped anniversary performance in 2004 met with a mixed response; 69 per cent of Britons interviewed by *The Guardian* newspaper stated that they were 'fed up with charity records' (William Cederwell, 9 November 2004). Further, the Mengistu dictatorship,[5] which had earlier used food as a political weapon in its dealings with the Western world, had been replaced by an elected government and, despite a severe drought in 2003, the new infrastructure allowed for a better distribution of food and aid.

'I haven't met anybody in the business sector in Ethiopia – whether in tourism or any other type of business – that welcomes the 20th anniversary,' said Tony Hickey, who runs tour company Village Ethiopia. 'What Ethiopia needs now is foreign investment and a flourishing private sector . . . So this 20th anniversary is very bad news for us . . . Band Aid and Live Aid project an image of Ethiopia which doesn't help Ethiopia or the Ethiopians:' (http://news.bbc.co.uk/1/hi/entertainment/music/3982243.stm, 5 November 2004)

Even so, the CD sold over 200,000 copies during the first week and became the fastest-selling single of the year. It is now but one of many such Christmas singles and albums sold in support of charity, drawing both on the ideological model of how you should behave to those less fortunate than yourselves earlier established in *A Christmas Carol*, and on the relationship between folk/rock and political protest which originated in the mid-1960s with such artists as Bob Dylan and Joan Baez.

While Band Aid provides one contemporary example of the charitable intervention prescribed in *A Christmas Carol*, the Pogues' 'Fairytale of New York' (composed by Shane MacGowan and Ronan Keating) also has curious parallels in its reflection on past, present and future, albeit within the context of alcohol and its relationship to poverty – another favourite with Victorian moralists and abstinence groups, including the Salvation Army. Underpinned by two distinctive musical styles which relate to the structure of the song and its two distinct moods, the slow piano melody and string introduction is a typical arrangement for a love song, but the sentiments of the lyrics ('Christmas Eve in the drunk tank') and the rough grain of the voice create an immediate tension with its 'romantic' connotations. Sung by Shane MacGowan, his fairytale situates Christmas within a world dominated by drunks, gamblers, junkies and lost opportunities: 'I turned my face away and dreamed of you.' Past and present are then reconciled in thoughts of a better future, 'when all our dreams come true', as the reflective of the ballad, with its mood of introspection, moves to an upbeat Irish feel, appropriate to the personality of singer, Kirsty MacColl. It is, it seems, a shared romantic discourse ('you were handsome', 'you were pretty'), a reflection on the optimism of young love, which dissolves into a barrage of insults – 'You scumbag, you maggot, you cheap lousy faggot' – and a rejection of the romantic charade of Christmas as a time of togetherness – 'Happy Christmas your arse, I pray God it's our last.' The conflict between past and present is heightened by the sentimentality of the chorus, which pulls into association New York's Christmas Day bells with memories of Galway Bay, evoking the appropriate feel of a boozy pub sing-along, reconciling conflict through an alcohol-inflected dream of a brighter future: 'I love you baby, I can see a better time, when all our dreams come true.'

The association of Shane MacGowan with alcohol abuse gave 'Fairytale of New York' an underlying sense of authenticity, the blend of punk realism with Irish sentimentality situating MacGowan as an iconic spokesman for the disadvantaged at Christmas – a time which traditionally draws attention to the less fortunate, including the homeless, the out-of-work and low-income families. Appearing on the cover page of *The Big Issue* (28 November–4 December 2004), he focused attention on the re-release of the single, reflecting on the death of Kirsty MacColl who had been killed in a boating accident in Mexico on 18 December 2000. Five years on, no one had been made accountable and the proceeds of the record were shared between the Justice for Kirsty campaign and the homeless charity, Crisis at Christmas, so highlighting the centrality of home and the problems confronting a family fractured by the death of the mother. To have a home, to be at home with the family, is central to Christmas ideology and whether it is the death of a mother or, as in the countless Victorian morality tales, the death of a child, the message is simple: it can't be Christmas if you're not with your loved ones.

The ideal of being together at Christmas is given a particular focus by Joni Mitchell in her 1972 album, *Blue*. Prefaced by songs which highlight homesickness ('California', 'This Flight Tonight'), 'River' constructs an introspective vision of the tensions inherent in the romantic ideology surrounding Christmas. Opening with a moody and resolutely minor 'Jingle Bells', the 'out of tuneness' of the piano intro provides a musical metaphor for not belonging within the context of Christmas, a time when the awareness of being alone is particularly acute: 'cutting down trees', 'putting up reindeer', 'singing songs of joy and peace'. The mood of nostalgia, of looking back over the past, is focused by an all-pervading sense of absence: of snow, of money and of her lover. The bleakness of the narrative is underpinned by the repetitiveness of the vocal line to create a musical alignment between the 'what he did for me' and the 'why' of loss. The introspection of the lyrics, the underlying pain, is thus heightened by the formal tensions of the music. The narrative of loss is rooted in repetition, creating a musical metaphor for the introspection accompanying a failed romance, 'he tried hard to help me . . . he loved me so naughty'; the need to escape ('I would teach my feet to fly') by upward melodic movement and chord colouring;

the desolation inherent in being alone, by the lack of harmonic resolution in the final chorus ('I wish I had a river I could skate away on') and the reprise of 'Jingle Bells', twisted harmonically as a musical metaphor for self-reproach ('I made my baby cry'), ending with a stark perfect fifth over D (D7 omitting the F#) to provide a final and reflective coding of emptiness. There is no going back and the next song, 'A case of you', creates a mood of even deeper introspection and aloneness: 'I could drink a case of you, darling, and I would still be on my feet.'

While Mitchell's sentiments are less extreme than those of MacGowan, they nevertheless share a common association with the season's emphasis on being with the one you love, the potential for extremes of loneliness and 'drowning your sorrows in drink'. Similar sentiments are expressed in 'Blue Christmas' (Elvis Presley), 'Lonely This Christmas' (Elvis Presley, Mudd), 'Lonely Christmas' and 'It Isn't Christmas When You're Not Here' (Three Degrees), and, despite its upbeat mood and determination to 'find someone better', 'Last Christmas' (Wham!, Whigfield), all of which play on the tensions generated by the ideological framing of Christmas as a season of heightened romantic expectations. As Chris Rea joyfully exclaims, what we should be doing is 'Driving Home for Christmas . . . get my feet on holy ground'. The chuntering rhythmic motif propels the melody, sustains the momentum, and makes for a good Christmas drive-time song when traffic jams and tailbacks are an added frustration for the countless people undertaking journeys in order to be with their families: 'the driver next to me / he's just the same.' While such Christmas songs have the appropriate feel-good factor, the expectations generated by 'Driving Home for Christmas', while rooted in the reality of the festive season, nevertheless perpetuate a highly idealised image of the family which is often at odds with the tensions generated by family gatherings. By glossing over complexities and contradictions, such songs nevertheless exert a tendential pressure on the listener, reinforcing the deeply organic theme of family-centredness: 'I can't wait to see those faces.'

It is evident that songs organised around a romantic discourse can teeter dangerously close to sentimentality which, because of the established rituals and customs associated with Christmas, nevertheless comes across as 'this is what it's all about.' The trick, it seems, is to provide evocative images which have an immediate impact on the imagination, conjuring up the necessary contrast between inside warmth and outside cold that characterises the northern hemisphere's Christmas. At worst they come across as cloying schmaltz; at best they become Christmas classics, as exemplified in 'The Christmas Song'. Written by Mel Torme and Bob Wells, and originally recorded by Nat King Cole in 1946, the lyrics are simple and direct, establishing a mini-narrative which starts by setting the scene, 'chestnuts roasting on an open fire', and ends with the traditional greeting, 'Merry Christmas to you', so establishing a rapport between singer and listener. The song was re-recorded in 1953, with an arrangement by Nelson Riddle (known for his big band arrangements for, among others, Frank Sinatra, Dean Martin, Peggy Lee and Judy Garland); the fourth and final version was recorded in 1961, this time with Charles Grean and Peter Rugolo's orchestration, and is considered to be the most popular of the versions, the one most frequently played on radio stations today. The mood is suitably relaxed and is warmed by strings which colour and inflect the tried and trusted imagery associated with the Christmas season. This is as the song reminds us, what 'everybody knows' and as such, there is a feeling of tradition which binds the listener to an imaginatively constructed sense of the past through established customs (the Dickensian roasted chestnuts, the celebratory turkey, mistletoe and yuletide carols) and myths (Santa with flying reindeer pulling his sleigh, Jack Frost nipping at noses). While the lyrics and musical arrangement clearly contribute to the effectiveness of the song, it is the understated vocal style of Nat King Cole that impacts most on the listener. Characterised by its warmth, clarity of diction and smoothness of phrasing – which owed much to his experience with the Nat King Cole (Jazz) Trio – his delivery impacts on the mood of the lyrics, creating a feel of relaxed well-being that invites the listener to chill out and enjoy his promise of 'a Merry Christmas'.

While the sentiments associated with Christmas songs can be taken with a pinch of salt, they are interesting in that they offer an 'abbreviated ideal model of the festive season, a highly condensed checklist of ideological themes in relation to which we are invited to assess our performances as Christmas subjects'.[6] They remind us of what we should be doing (celebrating with the family and loved ones, singing carols, decorating the tree, giving to those less fortunate than ourselves) and what we should be feeling. In effect, there is an ideological discourse that governs the construction of the lyrics and the feel and arrangement of the music, which draws on the sentiments engendered by the religious basis of Christmas and such familiar texts as *A Christmas Carol*. Given the centrality of children to Christmas, the question thus arises as to why there are so few contemporary songs aimed specifically at the tots and tweenies who still believe in the magic of Christmas – not least the promise of parties and presents.

The child-centredness of Christmas, legitimated by the theme of the Nativity, is both unchallenged and supported by non-stop commercials offering a super-abundance of toys and goodies – which today include such expensive items as personal computers, mobile phones and i-pods. For many parents Christmas has become a season of dread rather than good cheer, as present lists are drawn up and compared with those of school friends. Then there are the pantomimes, Christmas plays and films and, in the tradition of Dickens's 'middling classes', visits to the ballet to see Tchaikovsky's *Nutcracker* or the local theatre's offering of *A Christmas Carol*. But what is wrong with contemporary popular music and its engagement with the children's market? Having been brought up on a diet of Uncle Mac and his supposed insights into *Children's Favourites*,[7] I was sufficiently motivated by 'Sparky's Magic Piano' to end up as Chair of Popular Music at the University of Salford, and sufficiently sickened by the essentialism inherent in 'I'm a Pink Toothbrush, You're a Blue Toothbrush' to become an ardent feminist. While the nostalgia surrounding my career development is somewhat rose-tinted(!) there is no doubt that what did inspire was John Masefield's *The Box of Delights*, where the cry 'The wolves are running' and the 'Adeste Fideles' theme from Vaughan Williams's *Christmas Music* had me clinging to my chair when it was serialised on *Children's Hour* in the lead-up to Christmas. What inspired was fantasy – the juxtaposition of real and imaginary worlds. Current writers such as Philip Pullman and J. K. Rowling offer just this access to the imagination, and for the younger reader there are, for example, such Christmas classics as Charles Tazewell's *The Littlest Angel* with illustrations by Guy Porfirio, *A Snowy Day*, written and illustrated by Ezra Jack Keats, and, more recently, Mary Engelbreit's *Queen of Christmas*. In addition there are countless other books which provide an introduction to the myths and legends surrounding Christmas and, of course, the Nativity itself. In contrast, children are given decidedly second-best options when it comes to contemporary Christmas music, even though CDs/DVDs such as Gustafer Yellowgold's 'Wide Wild World', Peter Himmelman's 'My Green Kite' and Stevie on the Street (Stevie Wonder on *Sesame Street*) offer exciting stocking fillers (see Warren Truitt, Children's Librarian, New York Central Library, whose informative blog 'Children's Music that Rocks' provides some up-to-date recommendations).

For teenagers, the connection between Christmas and romance remains an enticing proposition, not least when it is fronted by winners of the *X-Factor*, which attracted (UK) viewing figures of around 10 million (series 2); over 3 million votes were cast in the semi-final and 6 million in the final. Series 3 figures were even higher, attracting 8 million votes and 12.6 million viewers. It is not too surprising, then, that while Band Aid topped the 2004 charts, Shayne Ward (winner of the UK *X-Factor* on 17 December 2005) took the Number One spot in 2005 with 'That's My Goal', which was rush-released on 21 December. The following year, 'A

Moment Like This' was released in the UK as a debut CD on 20 December 2006. Sung by Leona Lewes, winner of the 2006 American *X-Factor*, it topped the British Christmas charts in 2006.

'That's My Goal', while not specifically Christmas-centred, nevertheless carries many of its romantic themes; 'I'm here to say I'm ready / That I've finally thought it through' creates a mood of reconciliation as past and present are drawn into association with the possibility of future togetherness. The promise of 'happily ever after', the 'I can't believe it's happening to me', is also central to the romantic discourse of 'A Moment Like This'. Predicated on that 'one special kiss', the lyrics hint at both the fairytale magic of the sleeping beauty, and the promise of Christmas as a special time when dreams can come true. What is evident is that such songs do not have to be written specifically for the Christmas season. Provided they have the right ingredients, they have the power to convey the appropriate codes of romance, those 'big moments' when developing relationships suddenly become 'the real thing'.

Traditionally, 'the ideology of romantic love is . . . defined by its deflection of the adolescent girl's experience of sexuality on to the terrain of romance . . . neatly wrapped in the gift package of the ideology of femininity' – if she knows how to play her cards right, then Christmas, as a season of heightened romantic expectations, will bring her closer to the next stage of her feminine career: marriage (Bennett 1981: 65[8]). The combination of a romantic song with a celebrity performer is thus a winning one, but evidence suggests that the codes of romance have shifted significantly over the last decade, that while the expectations generated by 'what to wear' continue to dominate teenage pre-Christmas fashion pages, parties have now become the link between heavy drinking and casual sex. As *Newsnight* (BBC2, 7 February 2007) reported, 6,000 abortions took place in nine clinics in January 2007, 13 per cent up on the previous year, a testimony to the contemporary adage that 'if you can't pull a fella, you're no good.'

It would seem that for many teenagers, the ideology of romance, 'the one special kiss' ('A Moment Like This') that presages true love and a future committed relationship, no longer equates with their experience of the rituals associated with Christmas parties. It is also apparent, as my analysis so far suggests, that the customs and rituals associated with Christmas – including Christmas music, films and television – are themselves part of an imaginary landscape, and that the expectations generated by the ideology of romance and its inscription within Christmas songs is as misleading as the happy ever after of fairytale and myth. In effect, the romantic discourse blurs into a nostalgic sentimentality that is far removed from the social reality of contemporary urban society, which resonates more with the festivities associated with Yule and Saturnalia in their emphasis on drinking, sex and general feasting.

The question thus arises as to whether the songs discussed continue to have relevance to contemporary society. At a common sense level, the belief that Christmas can unite the world through a promise of peace, love and understanding is as remote from reality as wishing on a star. Yet the thought of a world without war, without famine, without religious conflict, where the devastation promised by environmental change can be reversed by charitable goodwill, and where famine, AIDS and family breakdowns are no more, continues to inform an ideology which taps into the Christmas *Zeitgeist*. It is also suggested that while the meaning of Christmas is what it has been made to mean – it is historical, cultural and social – it continues to provide a space for both romantic nostalgia and idealistic action. Moving between sentimentality and cynicism, the cultural forms associated with Christmas, not least Christmas songs, provide a particular insight into the problems associated with meaning; they can challenge or maintain existing conventions. In a period of uncertainty and world-wide conflict, optimism, however framed, is surely worth preserving.

Notes

1. The European revolutions of 1848 were a revolutionary wave which erupted in Sicily and then, further triggered by the revolutions of 1848 in France, soon spread to the rest of Europe and as far afield as Brazil. They were the consequence of technological change, new values such as liberalism, nationalism and socialism, and a series of economic downturns and crop failures. The UK, Russia and the Ottoman Empire were the only countries not to be affected.
2. See also Jarman-Ivens's discussion of *Elvis's Christmas Album* (pp. 123–5).
3. The US involvement in Vietnam goes back to the 1950s, but President J. F. Kennedy's 1961 despatch of 400 Special Operations Forces-trained (Green Beret) soldiers to teach the South Vietnamese how to fight what was called a counter-insurgency war against Communist guerrillas in South Vietnam provides one starting date (John Whiteclay Chambers II (ed.) (1999) *The Oxford Companion to American Military History*, New York: Oxford University Press).
4. These included Alice Herz, an 82-year-old survivor of Nazi terror, who set herself on fire in Detroit shortly after President Johnson announced major troop increases and the bombing of North Vietnam (15 March 1965); Quaker Norman Morrison, setting himself on fire and dying outside Secretary of Defense Robert McNamara's Pentagon office (2 November 1965); and Catholic worker Roger Laporte, self-immolating opposite the United Nations building.

5. Colonel Haile Mariam Mengistu overthrew Haile Selassie as ruler of Ethiopia in 1974 (and later executed him).
6. This point was made originally with reference to Christmas quizzes and its relevance to, for example, Christmas music makes it a useful observation (Bennett 1981: 54).
7. Uncle Mac (Derek McCulloch) was the presenter of the BBC Light Programme's Saturday morning request programme, *Childrens' Favourites*. 'Sparky's Magic Piano' told the story of a young boy with a magic piano that played all the big piano concertos, Chopin and so on, but ends with Sparky having to practise so he might, one day, be able to do this himself.
8. Bennett's discussion of romantic love relates to his analysis of McRobbie's 1978 paper on '*Jackie*: an ideology of adolescent femininity' (Birmingham: Centre for Contemporary Cultural Studies).

CHAPTER 7

The Musical Underbelly of Christmas

Freya Jarman-Ivens

In the perennial Yuletide preparations, the great media machine launches its most impressive marketing event of the year. Shortly after the summer sales (at the latest) and with little heed to the increasingly multi-cultural nature of societies, stores across the capitalist world pull out all the stops in an attempt to remind consumers of the 'values' of Christmas. 'Traditional' 'family' Christmases are the primary image being sold: children clad in tartan pyjamas running excitedly downstairs to a living room decked with the finest trees, garlands, candles and baubles; opening a pile of beautiful hand-made wooden toys in front of an open fire with their adoring, attractive biological parents looking on; and basking in the glow of their family's love. This is the Christmas reserved for catalogues published by expensive department stores, of course, and to a certain extent the consumer knows this. Thus, a few of these details can be changed by us mere mortals, as we strive for the closest we can get to that 'perfect' Christmas. The wooden toys may be plastic electronic goods; the open fire is most likely a gas simulation; and the prefix 'step-' can be inserted in front of the moniker of either parent without substantially affecting the overall Christmas vision. The intended atmosphere, however, persists: a happy, family-centred occasion, a time of comfort and contentment, accompanied by good food and good company, and preferably marked with snow.

A rather more pessimistic expectation of the reality of Christmas exists in parallel with this hyper-perfect version. Here, extended family members argue and fall out following too much alcohol, chefs-for-the-day verge on the homicidal while preparing the food, and children squabble over what film to watch or complain about their gifts. This cynical 'worst-case scenario' is something of an exaggerated version of what the most likely reality of Christmas is for many: namely, something in between the catalogue and the disaster. The 'worst-case scenario' in turn is often featured in comedic responses to the Yuletide season, quite possibly in an attempt to guard against the possibility of 'festive failure'. Less family-centred versions of Christmas also appear annually without fail, both as marketed ideals and comedic stereotyped scenarios. 'The office party', for instance, provides an ideal opportunity for fashion magazines to suggest the 'ideal outfit' in which to capture the romantic attentions of him-on-the-first-floor or her-in-accounts, and style magazines advise the reader on how to retain a modicum of respect during the potentially disastrous festive mixing of business and pleasure.

Yet, among all the disparate, coexisting versions of Christmas, whether they be ideals or gloomily stereotyped 'realities', certain values are common across the board. Heterosexual union – desired or achieved – is central. Comfort and cheer are at the heart of the ideal Christmases, while the lack thereof is crucial to scenarios in the mind of the cynic or comedian. And, crucially, behind all of these underlying values runs a soundtrack that further promotes these values; throughout the month of December (and probably earlier, even as early as September) a vast proportion of popular music (or, more specifically, music in popular culture) is required by marketers of all varieties to 'mean' Christmas, to add to the expectations and atmosphere, and to help persuade the consumer of the importance of the values on which so much of their marketing depends. The music that underpins the festive season can be roughly categorised into a handful of themes or concepts, and various songs with Christmas at their centre can be associated with those ideas. (For examples, see Table 7.1.)

One significant point to arise from this kind of systematisation of Christmas popular music is the sheer variety of genres that can give voice to Christmas spirits, ranging from easy listening (Carpenters), through classic rock (Darkness), classic pop (Wham!) and disco (Elton John), into glam rock (Wizzard), soul (James Brown) or rap (The Waitresses). Taking this observation as a starting point, what is interesting about 'Christmas music' as a putative genre is the potential for almost any Western popular genre to sound out in honour of this particular festival.[1] Consequently, 'Christmas music' is not always something that carries with it musical generic rules. A vast number of 'Christmas albums' exist and many of these are characterised by a particular musical genre or, more broadly, a mood which they intend to evoke: *Crooners at Christmas* (2003), *Merry Christmas from Motown* (2001), *A Rock and Roll Christmas* (1995) and *The Ultimate Christmas Party Album* (2005), as examples, make quite clear musical statements simply by their titles. The overriding musical factors in these albums tend to be of the underlying genre (Motown, rock and roll and so on), as opposed to the gestures that would typically be used to signify Christmas.

Concepts	Songs
Traditional; Religious[2]	'Mistletoe and Wine'
	'Do You Hear What I Hear?'
	'Mary's Boy Child'
Nostalgia	'White Christmas'
	'The Christmas Song'
	'Winter Wonderland'
Children	'Santa Claus Is Coming To Town'
	'Rudolph the Red–Nosed Reindeer'
	'Frosty the Snowman'
Romance; Desire for heterosexual union	'Merry Christmas Darling'
	'It'll Be Lonely This Christmas'
	'Last Christmas'
	'All I Want For Christmas Is You'
Friends; Party	'I Wish It Could Be Christmas Every Day'
	'Step Into Christmas'
	'Rocking Around the Christmas Tree'
Goodwill to all men	'Do They Know It's Christmas?'
	'Happy Christmas (War Is Over)'
	'A New York City Christmas'
	'Let's Unite the Whole World at Christmas'

Table 7.1 Christmas songs and their relation to Christmas-associated concepts[3]

However, it is true that there is a range of such gestures, many of which can be traced in some way to the Victorian era, which, as John Storey explains in his contribution to this volume, is when Christmas as it operates today found many of its roots. It was during that time that many of the most enduring carols (and other hymns) were written, and it also fostered the bourgeois song tradition that has left a significant musical mark on much twentieth- and twenty-first-century popular song (Middleton 2000: 113). So, many of the popular songs that serve most explicitly the dominant ideologies of Christmas (family, home, charity, romance) commonly feature many of the same musical characteristics found in Victorian songs (sacred or secular): major tonalities; regular phrase lengths; moderate tempi; and a certain 'sing-along' quality generated by a range of around an *octave*,[4] melodies built mostly from consecutive notes and a few 'easy' *intervals*. The orchestration of Christmas pop songs often incorporates at least one metallic instrument, usually located in a treble range – a glockenspiel, celeste, hand-held bells or the obviously significant sleigh bells, all of which function rather like musical tinsel. Choirs are another common feature, possibly implying a religious element or more generally a sense of community, and certainly intended to conjure up images of carol singers at the door such as those found on traditional Christmas cards. These are commonly children's choirs or a less trained children's chorus, both of which point towards the centrality of children to the Christmas picture, and the latter of which particularly suggests that the season is 'for everyone', 'even' untrained singers. What is clear from most of those albums cited above is that these various signifiers are often used (to a greater or lesser extent) to provide some musical justification for the festive lyrics, even if another more coherent genre overrides the musical 'Christmas factor'. So, for example, 'Father Christmas' by the Kinks (from *A Rock and Roll Christmas*) is in many ways typical of the Kinks' general output: heavy on the drums and electric rhythm guitar, and having a mildly distorted lead guitar bending blue notes in a post-chorus solo. Yet, the chorus features a glockenspiel and moments of close, quasi-choral harmonies, musical hints towards the Christmassy content of the lyrics.

Where are you, Christmas?

The songs used as illustrations in Table 7.1 are all very obviously 'pro-Christmas'. That is to say, their lyrical content espouses the dominant ideologies of Christmas (which is why they can feature in that table), and in most instances there are at least some musical gestures to support the obviously pro-Christmas message in the lyrics. As will become clear, those ideologies are in fact rather amorphous and blur dangerously quickly into concepts and values antithetical to the so-called Christmas values. What I want to explore in this chapter, then, is not so much the musical construction of those versions of Christmas deemed acceptable, those versions that somehow endorse the catalogue version of the festive season. Rather, I want to delve into what I call the 'musical underbelly' of Christmas and explore the relations between musical signifiers and some of the 'alternative' versions of Christmas that occupy positions on the outskirts of the festivities.

To illustrate the extent to which the concepts involved blur and merge, I want to draw on a model developed by Douglas Hofstadter in his work on metaphorical and analogical thinking (1986).[5] His target diagram offers a way of thinking about the extent to which a given categorisation is applicable to a given object, how suitable a given analogy is for a topic or idea; the closer the example is to the centre of the target, the more appropriate the categorisation and, hence, the more appropriate a given analogy is to the example that is being offered. If we are thinking about applying an analogy, Hofstadter informs us: 'There are absurd answers, there are good answers, and there are in-between ones.' Here, he draws his own analogy, by continuing, 'just as there are degrees of edibility of food. Some foods lead to no survival, some to bare survival, and others to comfortable survival; the same

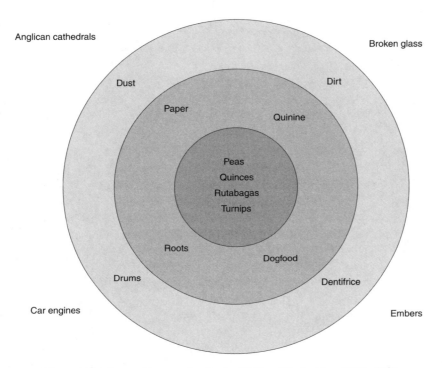

Figure 7.1 Target diagram for food edibility (Hofstadter 1986: 578).

is true of analogies' (Hofstadter 1986: 577). So, in his target diagram for
food edibility (see Figure 7.1), general foodstuffs can be placed at the centre
of the diagram, as they are all perfectly edible (taste and cultural differences
notwithstanding). In the second level are things that provide some nutritional value, but whose status as human food is less conventional; paper and
dogfood are among Hofstadter's examples. Further from the centre again
are substances such as dirt and drums, that have very little nutritional value
but that could be physically eaten. Outside of the target are potentially
harmful objects (broken glass) or physically inedible objects like Anglican
cathedrals.

To think in these terms about Christmas ideologies might generate a
diagram such as Figure 7.2. The levels of 'unsuitability' as one moves out-
wards from the centre are not as quickly and strikingly obvious as in
Hofstadter's food edibility example, but the underlying principle can still
be seen to apply. So, at the centre we might place 'Christian worship',
'Goodwill to all in the name of Christ' and 'Holy family'. Further out, but
still related, are situated 'Charity', the general 'Brotherhood of man' and

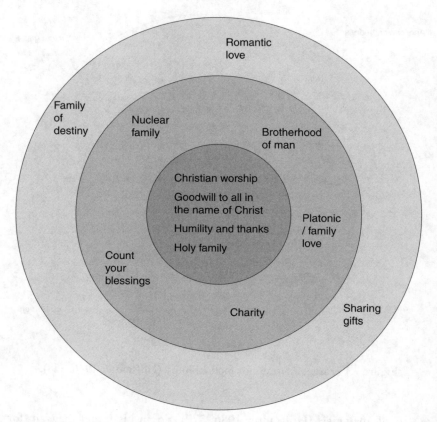

Figure 7.2 Target diagram for Christmas ideologies.

'Nuclear family'. Still further out we find 'Sharing gifts', 'Family of destiny' and 'Romantic love', but these are still contained within the ideological target of Christmas.

Some of these concepts progress easily from one to another, and patterns begin to emerge (see Figure 7.3). When these are taken to their logical conclusions, we very quickly find those notions that would be situated on the borders of, or altogether outside of, the target diagram verging on the 'absurd answers'. 'Sharing gifts' quickly blurs into 'Capitalism', an economic system that obviously enables and supports the circulation of gift objects but that sits uneasily aside 'Charity'; 'Family of destiny', which leads initially to 'Romance', moves through 'Finding someone' to 'Sex'; and 'Sex' and 'Capitalism' might in turn be considered (in the framework of the target diagram) forms of 'Self-indulgence' – as far away from 'Christmas spirit' as one might conceive (see Figure 7.4).

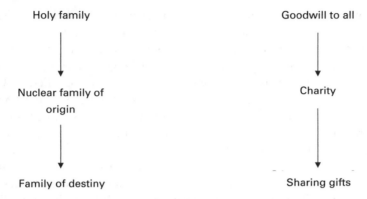

Figure 7.3 Progression of Christmas concepts.

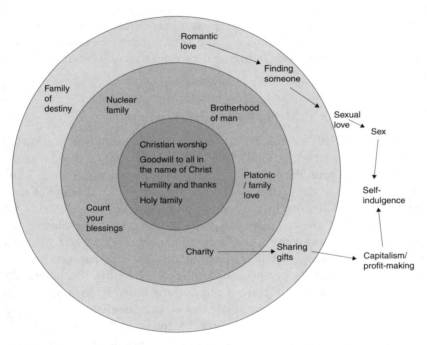

Figure 7.4 Extended target diagram for Christmas ideologies.

Sex is not totally absent from the Christmas picture, of course. Many a department store display showcases 'naughty' goods for Him or Her, and stores such as Ann Summers still manage to capitalise on the Yuletide atmosphere. Yet I would argue that this is firmly situated within two over-riding discourses: heterosexuality and commitment. That is to say, the notion of sex that is 'permitted' at the boundaries of the Christmas vision is that contained within ideas like 'Romance' and 'Family of destiny', within the hetero-normative family unit. Sexual practices outside of this acceptable formulation – queer practices, sexual objectification, casual sex and so on – are almost entirely excluded from the Christmas picture. One 'acceptable' incursion of sex into popular music has been 'Santa Baby', often sung with a girlish sexual charm in the voice. It is worth pausing to notice that this song is, in a sense, a flirtation with Santa in an attempt to acquire a series of expensive gifts: a '54 convertible, a yacht, the deed to a platinum mine and so on. The narrator is clearly a serial flirt, and sings, 'think of all the guys I haven't kissed', before looking forward to 'checking Santa off her list' too. Considering the extent to which both materialism and sexuality merge in this song, it is surprising that it has endured with such success. Perhaps the 'little girl' charm associated with the song goes some way to explaining this, in so far as it may defuse the sexual 'threat' implicit in the lyrics. Ultimately, the song comes across as harmless coquetry more than seedy desire, and therefore saves itself from festive exile.

Merry Christmas, Darling

Let us focus briefly on this theme of love, which is implicit in the very bull's-eye of the target, as God's love for mankind: 'For God so loved the world, that He gave His only son' (John 3:16), the son whose birth is the ostensible focus of the Christmas festival. We can see a continuum of sorts emerging, with Christian love at one end and sexual desire at the other. Of course, as with Table 7.1, these categories are not mutually exclusive, but any one of them may come to the foreground over others; 'I Saw Mommy Kissing Santa Claus' is a tale of romantic love between parents, but it is sung from the child's perspective, implicitly excluding the potentially sexual nature of the adults' contact and drawing the scene in more familial terms. This is, therefore, a simplistic model, but one that offers a way of extracting some of the relations between music and the ideologies of Christmas. We might start, then, by imagining where along this continuum different Christmas songs might be placed, given their musical and lyrical relationship to the pictures of love being painted (see Figure 7.5).

Because of the sheer volume of Christmas popular music, it is impossible to make any reliable musical generalisations about positions on this continuum, and each song must be taken largely on its own merits. That said, a few interesting points arise from some of the examples in Figure 7.5, and some patterns do emerge. For instance, Cliff Richard's 'Mistletoe and

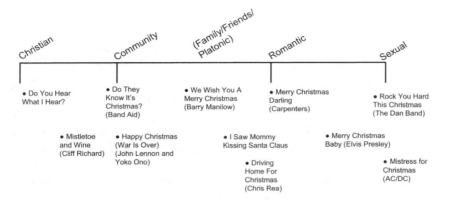

Figure 7.5 Continuum of love in Christmas songs.

Wine' arguably sets the standard, containing everything that Christmas music demands. The lyrics describe 'logs on the fire' and 'dreams of Santa', but this is situated firmly (although not too evangelistically) within a Christian discourse. Christ is not named specifically, and when the song starts with the words 'The child is a king', the explanation immediately follows, 'the carollers sing'. Nonetheless, the song continues, love and eternal joy are available to us all if we only 'follow the master', and the chorus drives home the image of 'children singing Christian rhyme'. A children's choir features, a boy treble sings one chorus and a counter-melody, and sleigh bells abound. When compared with this, then, can it be said to be accidental that AC/DC can be situated at the far right, most sexual end of the spectrum? The lyrics to their 'Mistress for Christmas' (2003) are just as one might imagine from the title. They articulate the nar-rator's desire for the 'female form in minimum dress' and to 'be in heaven with three in a bed'. There is nothing here about love, respect or commit-ment – only a tirade of alcohol-fuelled sexual desire ('with a bottle of my beer'). Moreover, the song is musically everything one would expect from this hard rock band – very much focused on distorted electric guitar and drums, and sung with a gritty, often screechy voice – with only the token addition of some sleigh bells in the introduction. The chorus is anthemic in a very simplistic way, with the refrain nearly shouted out and mostly confined to the *tonic* note (preceded simply by a three-note *anacrusis* on 'I want a' descending from the *mediant*). And although the song uses simple chord progressions, it does not generally perform the predictable (and, indeed, required) pattern of *tonic-dominant tension* characteristic of carols or songs more earnestly in the service of Christmas ideologies. Rather, it circles around the tonic and flattened seventh, and despite a *modulation* up a tone at 1:48 and back to the original tonic at 2:22, the overall sense is of tonic stability.

It is important to guard against any hint of a generalisation here that 'less Christmassy music' always accompanies a 'less Christmassy sentiment', and indeed Greg Lake's 'I Believe In Father Christmas' (1974) is proof that the converse is not always true either; the lyrics of disillusionment are set to one of the most exemplary cases of 'Christmassy' music. The Dan Band's 'Rock You Hard This Christmas' (2003) provides a particularly interesting example of an attempt to resolve romantic love and sexual desire through the vehicle of Yuletide musical signifiers. The song's lyrics are laden with language inappropriate for the season ('Have a very merry motherfucking Christmas'), and with euphemism and humorous metaphor; the narrator declares that he wants to 'rock you hard this Christmas', to 'fill your stocking with [his] candy cane of joy', and to 'drive [his] love train down Santa Claus lane'. He anticipates 'slushing like snow angels till the morning' and the 'seven pipers piping the eight maids a-milking in the snow'. Yet these mockingly anti-Christmas-spirit lyrics are framed in a musical context that in many ways certainly befits the seasonal context. The basic instrumentation is of the rock group that the Dan Band is: drums, distorted guitar lines, keyboard, bass and a generally gruff vocal. Added to this are sleigh bells in the quieter moments and for the final rousing chorus, and violins that swell the texture at strategic moments. There is effective use of dynamics too, that brings the song firmly into that of a soft-rock ballad-style song. The song builds from almost nothing (only sleigh bells and piano) in the introduction, until increased drum action leads into an anthemic chorus filled with cymbals, distorted rhythm guitar and screeching solo interjections. The pattern repeats through the second verse and chorus, and the dynamics build through the first bridge (from 1:51, 'We'll be slushing like snow angels'). During the bridge, a sub-plot emerges in the lyrics, in which Santa and the narrator's grandma make 'hot ass cookie love'. At this revelation (2:20), everything falls away but the piano and a cello, and Santa is tenderly voiced by the singer at the top of his range: 'Granny, I rocked you hard this Christmas'. Sleigh bells re-enter (2:34), a single bell sounds (2:38), the dynamics build again through the second bridge ('And the world will start rejoicing'), and a *modulation* up a tone (at 'Merry Christmas, Ho ho ho!') heralds an inspiring finale. Melodically, the song confines itself mostly to stepwise motion, with an occasional jump of a perfect fourth up to the tonic to start a line. It is melodically repetitive, but its patterns are infectious and the chorus at least is easily memorable.

However, amongst all this appropriately cheery musical setting that is typical of many a classic Christmas pop song, certain darker aspects lurk that destabilise the festive mood. From the introduction, as sweet as the simple and Christmassy instrumentation may be, the piano circles around the three chromatic notes of C#, C and B, while the vocal melody enters in E flat. At first, the E flat is quite clearly established by a stepwise descent to the tonic from the mediant (G), but the second line of each verse brings with it a sharpened fifth (B) that unsettles the harmony on the final syllable: 'While the jingle bells are jingling / And the snow begins to <u>fall</u>'. Through the song, this discord recurs, as the B sounds quite subtly in the piano in the first verse, and a distorted guitar leads screechingly into the second verse with the same pitch. Furthermore, the vocal line repeatedly sounds this note in the second bridge (from 2:40. Listen out for the 'choir' of 'choir-boys', 'five' of 'five ass golden rings', and the 'milk-' of 'eight maids a-milking'.) Taken as a whole, 'Rock You Hard' seems openly to navigate, and to a certain extent resolve, a tension between the lyrical content and some of the dominant ideologies of Christmas. The hard-rock surface and discordant harmonies give way to the tenderness of Santa for the grandma, and – unlike the seediness of the AC/DC song – there is an implicit sense of a relationship between the narrator and his love object. The final chorus is a triumph of music over lyrical content, and the jarring harmonies of earlier in the song are shunned in favour of a classic soft-rock pro-Christmas musical text. So, despite some significant initial unease (both lyrically and musically) the final effect – as much as it is a parody of the soft-rock codes of Christmas, or perhaps partly *because* it is this parody – also gestures towards an acceptance of the lyrics' sentiment within the Christmas context.

Blue(s) Christmas

Another interesting case study arises by considering two versions of one Christmas song, 'Blue Christmas'. Elvis Presley was not the first to record the song, but almost certainly his recording, on *Elvis's Christmas Album* (1957), is one of the most well-known versions of this song. Several years later, Jim Reeves recorded the song for his own Christmas compilation album, *Twelve Songs of Christmas* (1963). The differences between the two recordings are striking, and ultimately, despite the songs presenting the same lyrics, they offer very different effects in relation to the Christmas value systems.

The two recordings are taken at roughly the same tempo (Reeves at about 100 dotted crotchet beats per minute and Presley at about 96), and both chunter along in a *compound triple time*. Yet the rhythmic styling in Presley's recording makes his version feel rather slower than it is, as it is so heavily laden with slight delays and anticipations of beats, and because of Presley's own intense 'boogification'[6] on the track, which contributes to these jerky rhythmic patterns. In contrast, Reeves places the majority of his notes more precisely on the beat, and although he does introduce several interpretive gestures with strategically placed anticipations and delays, even these feel more predictable and somehow more containable within the rhythmic boundaries. His *anacruses* ('I'll have a . . .', 'I'll be so . . .', 'You'll be . . .') are almost all very evenly sung. In addition, when he starts to sing in unison with his all-female backing choir, which he does at the beginning and end of the second and third verses, the entire group sings together precisely on each beat. Presley's recording features a male vocal backing group[7] that provides a similarly stabilising rhythmic effect, but this is definitely a temporary stability in a very 'swung' rhythmic environment. And, if Reeves's female backers help to ensure rhythmic solidity, Presley's men do quite the opposite, as their repeated motif works roughly on a crotchet/quaver pattern that maintains the swinging rhythms and thus propels the temporal motion. Melodically too they disrupt, as their floating 'oohs' slide between notes, starting on the already unsteady leading note and slipping upwards to the tonic. Presley himself uses *portamento* tactically, sometimes shifting almost imperceptibly by only a fraction of a semitone at the beginning or end of a note, and often sliding more noticeably across notes. Reeves's diction, furthermore, is far more precise than Presley's, partly because of the lack of 'boogification' that added to Presley's general tendency to slur his words slightly. These various vocal factors are superimposed in Presley's recording over a blues-based arrangement that draws attention to rhythm and a bassy guitar, while Reeves's more controlled and contained vocals are aligned with lush strings, bells and a choral backing.

Overall, Presley's recording hints at a certain raunchiness bubbling beneath this heartfelt comment on Christmastime solitude, a sexual nature that is also enhanced by Presley's own star text at this early stage in his career. The spectre of sexual desire draws this recording to the right of the 'continuum of love'. Reeves's tamer and more melodically and rhythmically predictable recording is comparatively lacking in a sense of sexuality, presenting a much more romantically oriented recording and even pulling the song towards an almost platonic effect. Presley's 'Merry Christmas Baby' is even more sexualised in its delivery and makes a useful point of comparison. Here, a very casual compound triple time (approximately 76 dotted crotchet beats per minute) lays the foundation for piano, guitar, harmonica and vocals to extemporise over a twelve-bar blues. The rhythmic pulse in Presley's track adds to the stereotypically bluesy rendition, and the song is more easily associable with sexually oriented blues numbers than with Christmas tunes. When Presley sings that his loved one 'sure did treat me nice', the field is left wide open as to precisely what that involved. Thus, 'Merry Christmas Baby' becomes less about the festive season that these two people have enjoyed than about the relationship between them. It is easy to sense, then, how production and vocal delivery contribute to or detract from an overall Christmas effect in any given song. It is not that these songs of Presley's endorse positions entirely outside of our target diagram for Christmas ideologies, and they may be superseded in this sense by 'Rock You Hard', but they certainly are closer to the edge than many other Christmas-oriented songs. 'Rock You Hard' may contain more sexually explicit lyrics than Presley's songs, but in many ways it adheres more traditionally to the musical codes associated with Christmas; ultimately, both the Dan Band and Presley negotiate tensions between Christmas ideologies and sexual desire.

Come to Cover the Muck Up

Another song that is ostensibly a Christmas song, but that can be seen to work in ways not obviously in keeping with 'Christmas values', is Kate Bush's 'December Will Be Magic Again'. The song was released as a single in November 1980, and has only found its way into album formats as part of compilations, either of Bush's work or of Christmas popular music. There are multiple versions circulating in parallel: the original single from 1980; a remix of that version for the CD single release of 'Moments of Pleasure' in 1993; and one known as 'the bongos version', performed by Bush on Abba's UK-aired *Snowtime Special* television show in December 1979.[8] Although the bongos and original single versions display many similarities, the earlier version presents a very different version of Christmas to that offered by the 1980 release, and a comparison of these two recordings raises some interesting points about Christmas values in popular music.

The different moods are set immediately in the introduction. The opening 19 seconds of the single release establish a very relaxed, softly undulating atmosphere. The bass pulses slowly on each minim, falling a major third (C–A flat), and then a perfect fourth (B flat–F) to an ostensible tonic in F minor. Meanwhile a piano circles in quavers (that is, four notes for every note in the bass) around A flat, G and F. Four seconds in, high female voices enter singing wordlessly and providing a somewhat ethereal mood quickly enhanced by shimmering cymbals. The bongos version, however, is so called precisely because of the percussion that opens the earlier recording, with no other instrumentation, and provides a rhythmic

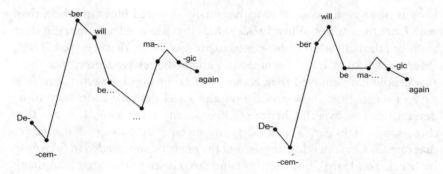

Figure 7.6 Melodic contours in 'December Will Be Magic Again': 1980 (left) and 1979 (right).

foundation for the rest of the track. Four seconds into this version, a chorus of male voices enters, singing 'ooh' to a G minor chord. This is built up slowly with a whispered female breath interjecting 'hah hah', and female voices gradually supplement the male chorus. The breathing and singing are themselves interplaying rhythmically, and together work in *counterpoint* to the awkward rhythms of the bongos. At 0:08, a piano starts playing a high-octave interval on what is felt to be the tonic, at first on every fourth beat and then at twice the rate, on every other beat. The tension and volume build until Bush enters at 0:16. The first line of the song ('December will be magic again') also reveals an important difference between the two recordings, as Bush's melodic line has been altered. On the official release, Bush leaps during the first word, 'December', from a C on '-cem-' to an F a *compound perfect fourth* above on '-ber', and drops to the F an octave lower by the end of the word 'be'. The 1979 version features a different climb to the high F, as Bush slides up to a D (just below the highest point) on the way, pausing there before hitting and sustaining the F on the word 'will' (see Figure 7.6). This difference in ascent means that the earlier recording draws more attention to the quality and high pitch of Bush's voice in this phrase and, more importantly, builds a greater melodic tension. The greater tension, in turn, means that the descent over 'magic again' – almost identical in each version – sounds more dramatic a release in the bongos version. The tense mood is sustained throughout the bongos version of 'December Will Be Magic Again', and there is a distinct unease in this recording not present in the single release. However, both versions somehow manage to keep the music in a state of instability, and as such the musical effect underpins the lyrics' rather unconventional approach to Christmas. Even the 'tamer' 1980 version – that does not unsettle the listener as explicitly as the 1979 bongos version – is never entirely stable

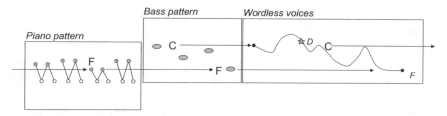

Figure 7.7 Harmonic patterns in 'December Will Be Magic Again'.[10]

harmonically. The single release hints at an F minor tonic in the slowly pulsing bass line, but the entry of the high female voices also pulls the ear towards C minor, as they introduce a D natural (see Figure 7.7).[9] Towards the end of this introduction, both F and C are shunned, and the vocals enter in what emerges as G minor. This too remains unstable, though, and throughout the song are moments of brief and false resolutions amid constant harmonic fluctuations. Indeed, it is only near the end of the first verse that the sense of G minor becomes clear, in no small part because Bush's vocal line seems to carve out B flat major. In the harmonic sense, the bongos version is initially more stable, as the drone of the male hums in the introduction grounds the piece clearly in G minor from the start. After this initial stability, though, the 1979 recording is as fluid as the 1980 release in its harmonic shifts, and a secure tonic is eluded in both.

Over the harmonic fluctuations, Bush's melodic lines are extremely angular, and the *pitch range* – hard to identify exactly because of the half-pitched nature of many notes – is somewhere close to two octaves. There are wide leaps between distantly related notes, repeated melodic hiccups, and the melody is neither easily predictable nor easily imitated. This is quite the opposite of the qualities of most Christmas popular songs, and carols before them, with largely stepwise motion and triad-based intervals, and a range of around a ninth or tenth. Moreover, this bizarre and jumpy melody is the vehicle for some quite unorthodox Christmas lyrics. In a sense, the lyrics paint a picture of happy festive hopes and memories: 'Bing Crosby sings "White Christmas" / He makes you feel nice'; 'the snow / Come to cover the lovers / Come to sparkle the dark up'; 'Kiss under mistletoe / Don't let the mystery go'. Yet there is also talk of 'conjuring Mr Wilde into the Silent Night' and the comment 'Ooh it's quiet inside . . . Oscar's mind'. There is no Santa Claus here, only 'old Saint Nicholas' 'popping up' in the narrator's memory, and the lyrics overall give an impression of a dark psychological drama. A rather cynical take on the Christmas sparkle is revealed in the final line of the chorus, where the snow – after 'covering the lovers' and 'sparkling the dark up' – is said to 'cover the muck up'. The question immediately arises: what is this muck? Arguably, this is a comment on the annual ritual repetition of nostalgic elements such as Bing Crosby, 'feeling nice', Saint Nicholas and the 'beautiful white city'; they are cultural patches over our darker and less 'perfect' day-to-day existence. Ultimately, the effect is not of a song about happy childhood Christmas memories or of a simple and innocent hope for a winter wonderland. Rather, the slightly icy quality of Bush's voice places jagged melodies over unsettled harmonies, and the picture is more one of a sinister Jack Frost than of a cuddly Frosty the Snowman. It unsettles and discomforts, and this is far from what we ask of our Christmas popular songs.

Happy Christmas . . . War is Over?

The final song that I want to explore briefly is one that, in itself, is not connected to Christmas: 'Mad World', as recorded by Michael Andrews and Gary Jules for the soundtrack to *Donnie Darko* (dir. Richard Kelly) in 2001. The song was not released in the UK until December 2003, after the film had developed something of a cult following. Neither the song nor the film has a Christmas content, and yet 'Mad World' achieved the coveted Christmas Number One spot in the UK charts in 2003. This is certainly not the first time that an ostensibly non-Christmas song has succeeded in this way; 'Stay Another Day', a typical love ballad, gave Christmas Number Ones to East 17 in 1994 (on its first release) and to Girls Aloud (as a double A-side) in 2002 for their debut single. Some bells repeating descending scales in East 17's recording added a festive edge, and the video featured the group in white winter coats beneath falling fake snow. The song conforms to the generic conventions of the love ballad, and in many ways it is hardly surprising that it was a success for East 17. Once the festive association had been established by East 17, it was then easily possible for Girls Aloud to have their own Yuletide success with the song, particularly because they were the subject of a highly publicised competition for the Christmas Number One, as part of the television show *Popstars: The Rivals*.

'Mad World', however, does not so easily yield explanation for its Christmas success. The songs against which it was pitted included the Darkness's soft-rock anthem 'Christmastime (Don't Let The Bells End)', Shane Richie's charity release 'I'm Your Man', and a cover of 'Happy Christmas (War Is Over)'[11] by the finalists of the television show *Pop Idol 2*. Any one of these songs would have been more likely contenders for the top of the charts over Christmas. The Darkness seemed to hark back to a

All ar-ound me are fam-iliar fa-ces, worn out pla-ces, worn out fa-ces... ... ...

And I   find it   kinda   fun-   ny I   find it   kinda   sad

Figure 7.8 Melodic patterns in 'Mad World': tonic in black, highest note in gray.

golden age of Christmas popular music, with hints of Lennon's original 'Happy Christmas' or 'Do They Know It's Christmas?'; Richie's single for Children In Need would certainly tug at the charitable heart strings; and the *Pop Idol* finalists had the hype of the television show and a standard Christmas success song in their favour. 'Mad World', on the other hand, is an extremely dark and melancholy song, that has an emphatically minor tonality and a pitch range of only a major sixth; the pitches seem to circle around themselves and each other, always arcing back to the tonic note (see Figure 7.8).[12] The lyrics are cheerless, speaking of the banality and bleakness of everything, concluding that 'when people run in circles it's a very very / Mad world'.

Placing 'Mad World' in its historical and cultural context might help to explain how such a gloomy and uninviting song managed to make Number One with such promising competition, and the story could well go back to two years before the song had its Christmas success. September 2001 had infamously seen the World Trade Center's twin towers reduced to rubble by an attack blamed on Middle Eastern terrorists. The US sought Osama bin Laden, whom they held responsible for the attacks and believed to be hiding in Afghanistan. When the Taliban refused to hand bin Laden over, America led air strikes on Afghanistan in October 2001. In January 2002, Iraq was declared part of an 'axis of evil' by President Bush, and tension mounted over a period of several months while UN inspectors searched for weapons of mass destruction in Iraq. Despite a serious lack of evidence, Iraq was held by the US and the UK to be hiding illegal weapons and providing a haven for key al-Qaeda operatives. In March 2003, amid extreme international controversy, the US declared war on Iraq, and in April of the same year, US forces took Baghdad with military support from the UK. Although major combat operations in Iraq were declared over by the Pentagon by May 2003, the rest of the year saw sustained fighting in the country. Over the summer, both Bush and UK Prime Minister Tony Blair were facing serious criticism over the intelligence that led to the initial invasion. November 2003 became the bloodiest month in Iraq since the war had begun eight months previously (Chevallot 2004), and 'Mad World' was released the following month.

Clearly, there are very many factors to consider in evaluating the success of any song, but it must be of some significance that late 2003 was a time of great political strife, military action and a sense of there being little end in sight. Nine months after war had been declared and eight after the symbolic toppling of a statue of Saddam Hussein in Baghdad, the fighting looked set to continue. Meanwhile, the politicians who had led their countries into battle had very much lost the trust of their countries, and to an extent of other nations, and it was within this atmosphere of increasing dissatisfaction and sustained unease that the bleak message of 'Mad World' hit the UK charts. While I am keen not to imply any firm links between the political situation and the success of this song, there is certainly cause to speculate that 'Mad World' spoke clearly to Britain's national mood at the time. One cannot help but feel that the unity and hope in the lyrics of 'Happy Christmas (War Is Over)' and the idyllic community feel of the song were less appropriate for the moment than the hopeless pessimism of Jules and Andrews's release.[13]

We Need a Little Christmas

Christmas as a festival has an indelible association with Christianity and Christian values. Underneath the fairy lights and wrapping paper, it is all supposed to be a time of rejoicing: 'Gaudete, Christus est natus!' However, it is increasingly pitched as less religiously specific than this, as sellers of goods and services appeal to the consumer's sense of what a 'perfect Christmas' looks like,[14] a Christmas that is more about a secular fantasy of possible social perfection than it is a religious celebration. Indeed, this may be part of a social pattern in Britain of increasing secularisation despite Christianity being claimed by the vast majority of Britons. The UK Census in 2001 revealed that 71.8 per cent of respondents described themselves as

Christian (Office for National Statistics 2001), yet in 1999 only 32.5 per cent said they believed in God (Voas and Crockett 2005), a figure that had been steadily falling over previous years. Each December seems to see 'Christmas values' superseding Christian values, and even absorbing some along the way. 'Charity' and 'Goodwill', 'Family' and 'Peace' remain central tenets of the hegemonic Christmas message, while the story of Jesus's birth is relegated to a sideshow. The festivities are sold on the basis of being about 'something meaningful', but increasingly that 'something' cannot be religiously explicit, for fear of alienating the high numbers of non-believers. Even the most hard-core atheist risks being drawn into the media-manufactured Christmas, and the Christmas period is seen as an immensely important time by millions of people who may not even believe in God.

Behind the Yuletide celebrations runs a soundtrack that, for the most part, confirms what we believe about the season. The perennial favourites sing of friendship, love, peace and happiness, but generally much less of the Nativity. Yet, hidden amongst these banal vehicles of propaganda are occasional gems that confront both lyrically and musically the dominant Christmas values. These songs often do not find their way to the Christmas surface, but lurk beneath as a musical underbelly. By achieving a Christmas Number One and partly because it is so un-Christmassy a song, 'Mad World' may even have heralded the end of a golden age of Christmas pop. With that song, it was no longer a case of 'Joy To The World', but rather one of resigning oneself: 'So This Is Christmas'.

Notes

1. Genres difficult to square with 'Christmas spirit' include heavy rock, punk rock, heavy metal and so on. The relations between some of the musical signifiers of those genres and Christmas are explored briefly below.
2. This category is not intended to include carols, but songs written for or subject to a more secular circulation that contain a significant religious element.
3. The categories here are clearly not mutually exclusive. 'The Little Drummer Boy', for instance, has an unavoidable religious theme, but might also be associated with the 'Children' category by virtue of the subject position of the song's narrator and the nursery-rhyme style refrain 'pa rum pum pum pum'.
4. Musical terms appear in italics in the main body of the chapter and are explained in the glossary.
5. My thanks go to Dr Bethany Lowe (University of Newcastle) for bringing this model to my attention. Dr Lowe has used the model herself to very good effect as a way of thinking about Sibelius and sonata form (Lowe 2003).

6. See Middleton 1983.
7. Another track on the album is credited as featuring The Imperials and The Jordanaires, two groups who recorded frequently with Presley. It is possible, but not clear, that one or both of these groups provided the backing for 'Blue Christmas'.
8. According to evidence from Bush fans, the recording of this 'bongos version' was not ready in time for a Christmas release in 1979. The track was rearranged significantly and released for Christmas in 1980. See http://gaffa. org/dreaming/1st3_bsi.html. Accessed June 2007.
9. An F minor tonality would require a D flat.
10. The crucial D in the voices is marked with a star. The piano pattern establishes an F tonic and the bass pattern also hints at this. The continuity is marked here with arrows. The bass line starts on C and is marked as continuing to the voices, who start on a C and hint towards a C tonic.
11. Originally recorded by John Lennon and Yoko Ono, and released in the US in 1971 and in the UK in 1972.
12. 'Pitch range' refers to the distance between the highest and lowest notes used in a song or piece of music. This interval, a major sixth, is small for a song. A typical pitch range is just over an octave. A major sixth is the interval between the first two words of 'The Lord's My Shepherd'.
13. Intriguingly, Lennon and Ono's protest song 'Happy Christmas (War Is Over)' had reached great heights in the charts on either side of the Atlantic in the winters of 1971 and 1972, amid the controversial American action in Vietnam. It is notable that neither the original release nor the *Pop Idol 2* cover made Number One.
14. For an amusing take on the commercialism of Christmas, see Tom Lehrer's 'A Christmas Carol': 'Angels we have heard on high / Tell us to go out and buy'.

Glossary and Discussion of Terms Used

The notes in a scale are often given Roman numerals. Within Western musical notation the following terms are also used:

I	II	III	IV	V	VI	VII
Tonic	Supertonic	Mediant	Sub-dominant	Dominant	Submediant	Leading Note

The *tonic* is also less technically known as the 'home note'; it is that note on which a melody can end with a sense of closure, according to Western musical values. As an example, in 'God Save the Queen', the first 'God' is on the tonic, as are the second and third 'Queen's. The second half of the song propels the listener precisely by avoiding that tonic note for the most part, and the ear is satisfied by the final 'Queen' landing on the tonic. The term also refers to a chord, the main note of which is the tonic note. This chord is crucial to the resolution offered by the tonic note: several chords can accompany the tonic note, but only the tonic chord will leave a musical phrase satisfactorily 'finished'.

Tonic-dominant tension. If the tonic is note 1 in a scale, the dominant is note 5. Playing in the key of C, the dominant would be G. Within Western musical systems, the dominant chord – especially the dominant seventh, e.g. G^7 – creates a kind of harmonic tension that demands to be resolved by the tonic. As an example, think of 'Silent Night'. The first line, 'Silent night, Holy night', is accompanied by the tonic chord. The following phrase, 'All is calm', is on the dominant chord, and the listener is drawn towards the next phrase ('All is bright'), back on the tonic. 'Away in a Manger' offers a different example. In the first verse, the line 'The little Lord Jesus lays down his sweet head' demonstrates this tension, because the word 'head' lands on the dominant chord. This is a momentary reso-lution, in that the tonic note has been temporarily moved to what was the dominant note (for example, starting with a tonic of C, the tonic is now G). Yet the harmonies also require some resolution and the next phrase starts again on the original tonic chord.

The *seventh note* (also called the 'leading note') is an essential part of tonic-dominant tension, as it forms part of the dominant chord, and is the note that most leads the Western ear back 'home' to the tonic. It is the note immediately below the tonic note (for example, the 'gra-' of 'gracious' in 'God save our gracious Queen', or 'the' in the third line 'God save the Queen'). When the seventh note is altered (in this case flattened – that is, played as the next note down), the tension is defused.

An *octave* is the distance between two notes with the same name but of different pitches. Think of the 'Somewhere' at the beginning of 'Somewhere Over the Rainbow'; this interval is an octave. In 'December Will Be Magic Again', the piano is playing two notes one octave apart at the same time.

Interval refers to the distance between two notes. *Compound perfect fourth* is a description of an interval (a gap between notes). It is the same as a perfect fourth but with the second note up an octave.

Pitch range refers to the highest and lowest notes used in a piece of music.

Modulation describes a change of tonic note. A tone is a single whole note: for example, from C to D. (A semitone would be from C to C#, the note in between C and D.)

In music, *anacrusis* describes a usually small number of notes that start a phrase (perhaps a lyric line) but that fall before the first beat of the bar: that is, on an upbeat. The term is also used in prosody to indicate an unstressed syllable or syllables that begin a line of verse but that is not counted as part of the first foot.

Compound triple time has a rhythmic pattern made up of multiple groups of three and is similar to a 'swung' rhythm. In 12/8, there are four main beats to each bar, and one can count in groups of four slowly while listening to the song. However, each of those four beats has three subdivisions, and the pattern to count is [**1** 2 3] [**2** 2 3] [**3** 2 3] [**4** 2 3], where each bold number is a main beat.

Portamento is the technical musical term for sliding between notes.

Counterpoint is a term usually describing melodies. Two or more melodic lines that are independent in rhythm and/or contour (direction, shape) but that work over the same harmonies are described as contrapuntal. Contrapuntal composition was developed extensively in the Renaissance period but many of its best examples can be found in Baroque writing. For an example, listen to Pachelbel's Canon and Gigue in D Major. In Kate Bush's song, I am describing as contrapuntal the various rhythmic layers in the introduction.

Part III

PEACE ON EARTH, GOODWILL TO ALL MEN

CHAPTER 8

Christmas and War

Christine Agius

Introduction

At first glance, the relationship between Christmas and war appears to be in juxtaposition. Christmas, with its celebration of the birth of Christ, is normally the season of goodwill, imbued with religious meaning as a time for moral reflection. Christmas celebrations are family-centred, and the holiday of Christmas suggests a break from the everyday business of life and the impersonal forces that exist outside of our control. War, on the other hand, is the business of politics, conflict and destruction, and the absence of peace. Its meaning and practice seem divorced from the positive notions of humanity and (in most instances) it takes place externally, beyond the contours of civility and the home front. When we think of Christmas and war (or more precisely, Christmas at times of war), we envisage stories of soldiers fighting on our behalf in far-off places, away from the comforts of home; or at home, the sacrifices we make as a community or nation in the interests of 'our troops abroad' or the war effort. As McGreevy notes, 'At no other time of year is absence from home considered more poignantly tragic than at Christmas' (1990: 33).

By exploring the juxtaposition between Christmas and war, this chapter aims to accomplish a number of tasks. It considers, first and foremost, how the celebration and meaning of Christmas become intertwined politically and socially with societies engaged in war. It is concerned with how Christmas has been celebrated and used during times of war and conflict to bolster ideas about community and shared values. From the ideology of Nazi Germany to the ways in which Christmas has been merged with themes of war (as will be discussed below in the case of the first Gulf War and the post-September 11 'war on terror'), this chapter aims to show how the celebration of shared ideas about community and moral values is intermingled with war and conflict to create, for example, the tempering or restraining of dissent. As such, the ways in which the Christmas themes of family and community are used in times of war and conflict arguably involve a political dimension.

I begin by drawing on two examples of Christmas and war that have been most prominent in popular imagination. The Christmas truce of 1914 represents the positive message of Christmas – where infantrymen famously ceased fighting on Christmas Eve to venture into no man's land to exchange gifts, sing carols and play football on Christmas Day. In contrast, Nixon's Christmas bombing of Vietnam, which forced negotiations to bring about the end of the Vietnam War, was mired in negative connotations – inhumanity in war. The loss of civilian lives in this incident confirmed to the protest movements of the time that US intervention in far-off places was neither moral nor worthwhile.

The second section turns to the build-up to the Second World War and investigates how Christmas was appropriated by the Nazi movement for ideological purposes. Here we see a unique merging of nationalism and a reinvention of festivities to adhere to the ideological position of National Socialism, with Christmas becoming both a private and a public form of allegiance to Hitler.

The third section moves to the first Gulf War of the early 1990s, where Americans adopted a less critical view of war and expressed their support for the troops through the assemblage and tying of themes Christmas into the safe return of US forces. Support for troops and the melding of Christmas themes thus show how protest and dissent can be modified in line with certain understandings of place and national identity. Finally, I examine post-9/11 America, arguing that consumerism, emotion and symbolism have been incorporated into the celebration of Christmas.

Christmas and War

The Christmas Armistice of 1914 is a story that is part of the popular imagination. The cessation of fighting in the trenches during the First World War, and the celebration of Christmas and fraternising of the troops have served as a potent example of how humanity can overcome conflict, however briefly. Goodwill and shared understandings of what it means to be human underscore this extraordinary example in history, and offer a tenuous bridge between the seemingly opposing relationship of a religious/festive celebration and the ugly business of war. The Christmas Armistice therefore tells us that even in the direst of conditions humanity can exist, albeit for a short period of time. In the popular imagination, the story of the Christmas truce is one of comradeship amongst soldiers, but a more defiant angle to the story exists; the fraternisation with the enemy was condemned by high commanders, and infantrymen were punished for engaging in friendly relations with those they were meant to consider the enemy. The act of the truce and the fraternisation that took place produced, according to some descriptions, a different attitude and understanding – that the 'enemy' was just like them. As Weintraub explains, this had political implications: 'The impromptu truce seemed dangerously akin to the populist politics of the streets, the spontaneous movements that topple tyrants and autocrats. For that reason alone, high commands could not permit it to gain any momentum to expand in time and in space, or to capture broad appeal back home' (2001: xv; see also Noll 2004). Furthermore, Ashworth suggests the act of fraternisation prompted a more dangerous change in attitude amongst the infantrymen who, after the truce, avoided aggression and 'played' at being at war in order to avoid further deaths and casualties (Ashworth 1980).

In direct contrast to the example of hope in times of war illustrated above, the Christmas bombings of Vietnam serve as a more critical tale. Nixon's 'Christmas bombings' of Hanoi and Haiphong in 1972 (under Operation Linebacker II) were widely perceived to have brought an end to the conflict and forced the North Vietnamese to the negotiating table. However, US involvement in Vietnam was coming under severe domestic and international criticism, and the decision to bomb cities was broadly seen as problematic in moral as well as political terms. Despite claims that military facilities were targeted, the Nixon administration faced accusations that hospitals and civilian targets were attacked (National Security Archive 1973). Sweden's Olof Palme famously likened the bombings to the atrocities of Nazi Germany in his 'Christmas speech', and by the 1970s the protest movement against US policy and military action had become significant. According to Laderman, 'Some members of the Air Force Security Service were even said to have cheered when B-52s were shot down during the infamously destructive Christmas bombing of 1972' (Laderman 2002).

Both of the examples of the Christmas truce and Nixon's Christmas bombings represent the best and worst aspects, respectively, of joining the themes of war and Christmas together. The former shows a side of humanity that many argue is inherent in us all. The latter draws our attention to the inhumanity engaged by the necessities of war. One of the most basic questions about human relations is that of human nature – whether as human beings we live in a 'state of nature' where war and conflict are natural and inevitable, a necessary part of existence and survival; or, conversely, whether we have the ability to cooperate to secure our interests without recourse to violence. The realist view of human nature – that war is inevitable – is pitched against a more utopian view of human nature that imagines peaceful cooperation in the pursuit of mutual goals. Christmas at times of war brings these two positions together in an unusual manner, the message of goodwill across humanity seemingly in stark contrast with fighting and destruction.

But the relationship between Christmas and war or conflict is deeper than this dichotomy. In times of war, ritual and symbolism take on a different meaning. For Etzioni, holidays and rituals perform certain functions in society. They serve to reaffirm communal bonds and values, and underscore a normative understanding of society. They employ narratives and performance in order to articulate these shared beliefs and values to the wider community (2004: 7). The celebration of Christmas certainly stands as a major example of such ritualised practices, with its emphasis on goodwill and giving. Furthermore, Christmas represents a festival of both inward (family-oriented, traditional) and outward (referring to the public nature of its celebration) dimensions, where the public/private divide takes on a different meaning. If one of the purposes of Christmas is to anchor values and practices and celebrate particular shared notions of community and goodwill, then Durkheim's contention that rituals represent an attempt to reaffirm common beliefs and shared practices that may be weakened by the routine of everyday life (Etzioni 2004: 7) provides some context in which to understand such celebrations. In other conceptualisations, festivals perform a necessary social and cultural function. According to Max Gluckman, festivals are the cathartic outlet for hostility which strengthens the established order, but for Mikhail Bakhtin, the festival is a subversive rejection of the prevailing structure, a sign of distrust in official truth and a challenge to authority. There is, then, a certain ambiguity when conceptualising the role of festivities and the functions they perform in relation to society and ideology (McGreevy 1990: 36), not least at times of war.

The relationship between Christmas and war provides an interesting (and troubling) juxtaposition. Christmas is normally associated with notions of goodwill, generosity and empathy for those less fortunate. It is a time of family gatherings, with a shared understanding of returning to a particular tradition that is celebrated within the family unit (be that nuclear or extended) whilst others do the same. War, on the other hand, represents the chaos and anarchy of the outside world. War separates families, and is not normally associated with the themes with which we endow the celebrations or rituals that unite a community. The next section examines how the celebration of Christmas becomes enmeshed in political and symbolic practices that affirm notions of identity and who we are.

'Volksweihnachten' (the 'peoples' Christmas'): Merging Nazism with Christmas

Under Hitler's National Socialism, propaganda played a central role in disseminating Nazi ideology to the masses prior to 1933 when Hitler came to power. The National Socialist use of festivals was created and adapted to inspire an emotional attachment to Nazi ideology. Gajek notes that Nazi festivals spanned the whole of a year: for example, the 'Day of National Socialist Assumption of Power (30 January); Hitler's birthday (20 April); and the 'National Festival of the German People' (1 May). Also, there was 'German Mothers' Day', the German Summer Solstice party congresses, days in honour of the German peasantry and Remembrance Day for those who had died in the name of the movement. These festivals were based on existing traditions, but were recast in line with Nazi ideology and propaganda; they were promoted to the masses by various ministries, institutions and functionaries (Gajek 1990: 3; see also Taylor 1981). Taylor observes that key events and celebrations, be they Christian in origin or representative of the labour movement, 'were taken over by the propaganda machine of the party, emptied of their original content, and transformed into public expressions of the new National Socialist *Weltanschauung*' (Taylor 1981: 506). Christmas was no exception – Perry claims that Christmas was the 'most German' of German holidays (2005: 572) and took on a powerful ideological role; the celebration of Christmas was transformed and absorbed into the ideological arm of National Socialism.

As Perry explains, the Nazification of Christmas involved redefining the celebration in neo-pagan terms, emphasising winter solstice rituals that had their roots in ancient Germanic tribes. Under this reading, Christmas was reworked to refer to a specifically German nationalism and to a particular celebration that referred to inwardness. Even the Christmas tree was seen to be of Germanic origin, and this idea dated back to the nineteenth century (Perry 2005: 575–6; Tille 1892).[1] Reclaiming pagan rituals as a way of bringing the nation together soon merged with the use of Christmas as a political tool in the ideological arms of National Socialism. In the 1920s and early 1930s, Hitler attacked the materialism of Christmas, attributing this to the Jews, and proclaimed Communists, Jews and socialists responsible for eroding the sanctity of Christmas, in an effort to appeal to an authentic German community (Perry 2005: 578).

In the early 1930s, Christmas still retained some of its more familiar themes and aspects, although there were attempts to meld the festival with Nazi ideals. Perry (2005: 577) argues that attempts to merge notions of the *Volk* with the celebration of Christmas had already been made by leading Nazis (although differences existed amongst the leading paganists in the Nazi movement over Christianity and attempts to refashion Christmas as a pagan festival, as Steigmann-Gall (2003) observes). In the late 1930s, however, guidelines began to be issued, instructing citizens on the correct way to celebrate Christmas under National Socialism; around 1937, Christmas, as Gajek suggests, became institutionalised. Publications were issued to all Nazi officers, who were obliged to subscribe to the New Community series that produced guidelines for celebrating Christmas. Christmas books published by the Ministry of Propaganda from 1938 onwards were lavishly illustrated and aimed at families, including recipes, poems, fairytales, stories and songs (Gajek 1990: 4). This was quite different to the way in which Nazism was merged with the festival in the early 1930s, whereby some films and Nativity plays featured Nazi figures or members. Throughout the 1930s, the people's Christmas involved efforts at elite and grass roots level that incorporated the public and private celebration of Christmas according to Nazi precepts and ideology. By 1937, outdoor festivities connected to the winter solstice and celebrations leading up to Christmas involved the Hitler Youth and the SS, and spread to other sectors, such as education. Events were highly organised and coordinated: 'Even the reactions of the participants were orchestrated; individual, let alone spontaneous expression was no longer possible in these events, which were organized from start to finish' (Gajek 1990: 4). 'Fire and light' festivals, parades and radio broadcasts were popular methods of creating a sense of unity around the notion of an 'authentic' German Christmas, and public decorations, Christmas markets and parties were geared towards the population. Citizens could play their part by refusing to shop at Jewish-owned department stores, turning instead to National Socialist-led and organised forms of mass consumption that were arranged through work, education and schools, and more familial settings. On the home front, women had a particularly important part to play as the role of mothers took centre-stage in family celebrations of Christmas (baking and decoration, for instance, being linked to pagan ideals and fertility symbols) (Perry 2005: 579–80, 596–7). Perry argues that rather than a wholly elite-led process that merged political culture, popular celebration and identity production under National Socialism, the rewards of participation (handouts from the Winter Relief charity drives, for example) meant the public were generally receptive towards celebrating Christmas under the terms recast by the Nazi elites (2005: 574). The aestheticisation of familiar settings and ideas, as Edelman observes, 'serve a function to exercise a form of control of populations that may be subtle . . . or blatant'. Celebrations of Nazi power celebrated mythical figures to distract from everyday struggles (Edelman 1995: 47).

Relations between church and state were under some level of strain, as Protestant and Catholic officials resisted the de-Christianisation of Christmas celebrations, although Perry notes that despite the concerns of the church, little was done to challenge the regime, especially from the start of the Second World War on (Perry 2005: 594). With the outbreak of war in 1939, the Ministry of Propaganda recognised that the celebration and 'emotional impact of Christmas Eve could no longer be left to the Church, with its message of "Peace on Earth", which was particularly dangerous in times of war, but should rather be exploited for the Ministry's own purposes' (Gajek 1990: 4) What is interesting in the Nazi case is the blending of public and private forms of control, and the celebration of Christmas was geared towards this end. The 'peoples' Christmas', or *Volksweihnachten*, was not simply the Nazi appropriation of a festival. Rather it melded 'the twinned forms of the Führer and the Son of God, who promised national resurrection rooted in the primeval Germanic forest and the "blood and soil" of the authentic *Volk*' (Perry 2005: 572). After 1941, with the tide of war beginning to turn against Germany, the regime promoted a more politicised and dogmatic form of Christmas celebration as consumer shortages and personal and military losses began to take their toll on the population. Christmas markets were cancelled, the economy suffered and the Winter Relief drives were in decline. After the Battle of Stalingrad, efforts to promote a 'war Christmas' were regarded as the final attempt to keep the population enamoured of the paganistic reading of Christmas. After the war, Christmas was celebrated in a different way in West Germany, where Christianity and consumption became the norm. In East Germany, Christmas celebrations reflected the socialist traditions of decades before (Perry 2005: 602–4).

In the examination of the Nazi uses of Christmas (and to a lesser extent below, how Christmas has merged with themes of loss and community in the case of September 11), ritual or the celebration of particular rituals has a deeper meaning politically. Ross observes that rituals shore up or construct political reality, and therefore the power to control ritual is vital, as it influences ideas about events, policies, political systems and leaders. Furthermore, rituals (although Ross refers to political rituals, I am more interested in the merging of rituals with the political or ideological) 'offer meaning in ambiguous, uncertain situations, and are crucial to the dynamics of identity construction and maintenance, particularly in periods of change' (Ross 2000: 54).

Christmas post–September 11, 2001

The attacks on US soil in 2001 heralded a new age in international affairs. In the post–September 11 international environment, war has taken on a different meaning; the 'war on terror' has come to mean the securitisation of states against non-state actors, and the terrorist threat has been interpreted by many leaders in the West as a 'new type of war' and an 'existential' threat (Blair 2004). International terrorism has become part of the language of everyday life. Daily news reports feature stories of terrorist threats, and in the current age it is difficult to separate the 'war on terror' from everyday practices and forms of existence; from airport security to identity theft, our personal lives have become embedded into the fabric of the new threat, and subsequently this implies that the rituals we normally observe take on a different meaning. In post-9/11 America, the celebration of Christmas has been influenced by the events of September 11, 2001, in commemorative terms (remembering lives lost) and consumerist terms (reflected in the merging of the themes of Christmas with identity and nationalism). Post-9/11 Christmases in America have also invoked a more emotional response from the public. A multitude of websites and blogs commemorating the dead usually mention the loss of loved ones at Christmas. George W. Bush's Christmas radio messages to the nation since 2001 have never failed to mention troops serving the country abroad and the gratitude of the American people for their efforts (Bush 2001–6).

The attacks on American soil invoked a sense of déjà vu in the collective memory – 9/11 as the modern–day Pearl Harbor (although Weber (2002) argues that this correlation is deeply misplaced). In 2001, at the lighting of the national Christmas tree during the Pageant of Peace ceremony, Bush invoked the memory of Pearl Harbor and Churchill's presence to bring together past and present (White House 2001). The shock occasioned by the attack on the only remaining superpower of the post-Cold War era reinforced a particular sense of place and nation. The symbolism of the attacks was also important in this regard – the Twin Towers of the World Trade Center represented American prosperity and capitalism, and the Pentagon America's strength as a nation in terms of defence. The pulling together of the nation after the events of 9/11 was as important as confronting the terrorist threat.

In this sense, the idea of place took on an interesting role during the holiday season. Traditionally, public celebrations of Christmas have been community-based. The practice of community Christmas celebrations began in the US in the 1920s, to bolster community bonding; it is carried on to this day in the form of the Pageant of Peace, which stems from the

National Tree Lighting Ceremony of 1923. As Waits explains, the ceremony began at a time when alienation was a threat to civic unity (as demographic shift occurred with people moving from rural to urban communities to find work) and festivals were a popular comfort at times of heightened anxiety. Christmas was also a time for sombre reflection in times of war, so celebration had a dual nature – first, to embrace a notion of shared community and a fostering of civic identity; and, second, as a '[r]eaffirmation of the nation during the war as a duty, not as entertainment'. From expressions of celebration and festivities to reflect community and household, the public celebration of Christmas, especially at times of war, also reflected shifts in values – at certain times emphasising thrift and identification with the larger community of mankind, when leaders encouraged citizens to use Christmas to express brotherhood (Waits 1993: 156–62).

Christmas celebrations continued as families spent billions on holiday decorations and ornamentation in 2001, and 'gave some sense of normalcy to consumers that was critically needed after the terrible shock of September 11'. According to one market research report, Americans spent around $6.4 billion purchasing decorations, trees and lights (*Christmas and Seasonal Decorations Market Report* 2002). Christmas is a crucial festivity in US culture: 'The power of both the marketplace and the family is mobilized to support the celebration' (McGreevy 1990: 32). Bush's call to the American people soon after the 9/11 attacks was to carry on as normal – to go to work, to shop, to 'buy, buy, buy' – and in the lead-up to Christmas 2001, retailers merged Christmas themes with those of solidarity with those affected by the 9/11 attacks and the reinforcement of American values and identity.[2] The most popular Christmas presents in 2001 were GI Joe dolls, soldiers and 'America's Finest' action figures (featuring firemen and policemen) (Lorber 2002: 382; LoBaido 2001). A year after September 11, 2001, the trend migrated to clothing, with fashion designers including 'fire fighting-style' coats in their collections (Collins 2004: 58). At a time when the US economy was slowing down and welfare was being cut even further, the message of sacrifice and spending was presented as the best way Americans could show their support in the aftermath of the attacks (Davidson 2001; Reid Mandell 2002). Church attendance was reported to be high at Christmas time, and Ground Zero was considered by some to be an important site for the remembrance of lost ones during the holiday season (Gould 2001).

Consumers could also remember September 11 in their Christmas decorating. The White House-issued Christmas decorations merged patriotic symbols with commemoration of those who lost their lives in the 9/11 attacks, and other Christmas tree decorations commemorated troops serving abroad. Such examples include the 2006 White House 'Air Force One' ornament, depicting the plane flying under the Presidential Seal and an American bald eagle with a ribbon displaying the motto of the USA. This was a particularly potent merging of Christmas and war – the eagle clutches an olive branch (to symbolise peace) and arrows (representing the original colonies and 'the acceptance of the need to go to war to protect the country'). The public can also buy ornaments to commemorate the September 11 tragedy (called 'United in Memory') which '[honor] the courage and compassion of the thousands of surviving families, those who risked their lives to save others, and those who supported the United States of America in its darkest hours'.[3] The Christmas 2005 'Support our Troops' ornament shores up the notion of honouring military personnel at home and abroad in Afghanistan and Iraq. All of these ornaments merge the symbols of the US – the White House, the bald eagle and the Pentagon – with the Christmas message. Collins notes, however, that although patriotic items were prominent during the Christmas season of 2001, it was not visibly observed that Americans were displaying these emblems (clothing and jewellery) at this time; rather these emblems made an appearance on the anniversary of September 11 one year later (Collins 2004: 58). Retailers, already aware of the slowing economy and a less cheerful spending public in 2001, pushed the patriotic theme in an effort to persuade consumers to purchase gifts for the holiday season, noting a 'renewed focus on family and nesting instincts' (Clark 2001).

The merging of patriotic themes with Christmas celebrations is not a new phenomenon. According to Santino, during the first Gulf War of the early 1990s, Americans expressed their support for the troops and the war through public outdoor decorations that resembled those of Christmas and other holidays or festivities. Christmas decorations augmented the yellow ribbons and flags that were traditional symbols of patriotism and support. The custom of 'folk assemblage', of decorating inside and outside the home during the holiday period, merged with support for the Gulf War, 'allowing people to deal with, if not resolve, certain contradictory cultural values while still demonstrating support for their country at a difficult time' (Santino 1992: 19–20) This was in stark contrast to the Vietnam era, when mass protest signified widespread public criticism of American involvement in Vietnam. As Santino observes, the protest of the 1960s was 'personalised' and part of a particular lifestyle that was broadly perceived as antithetical to American values. In the case of the Gulf War, Americans returned to a more family-based form of support for the war, a less critical stance. Nearly all public statements about the war gave support to the troops, which seemed to be understood as a more ambiguous and less value-laden concept than supporting the war; a socially agreed-upon middle point between full support of the war effort and the policies and perspectives that informed it, and total opposition to it. To identify oneself as supporting the troops allowed people to avoid declaring a more extreme, and possibly controversial, position. (Santino 1992: 26)

The merging of Christmas with this show of support could be seen in assemblages (for example, snow soldiers and snow tanks in front yards, snowmen clasping American flags, or even 'seasonal flags' which merged American symbols with Christmas ones). Santino finds the merging of folk assemblages of war and holiday motifs as 'jarring', representing an interruption to the seasonal holiday with the outbreak of war as 'an interruption of regular life' (1993: 23–9). In the context of the 'war on terror', it can be argued that everyday life has been interrupted by insecurity. As the US government issues daily alert levels, warning citizens of the risk of attack, there appears to be little chance of separating the holiday celebrations from the problems of insecurity. Christmas 2003, in the year of the war in Iraq, saw the US government raise the national threat level from yellow to orange alert, citing 'increased chatter' picked up by the intelligence community, which suggested 'the possibility of attacks against the homeland around the holiday season and beyond' that 'will either rival, or exceed, the attacks' of 2001 (Department of Homeland Security 2003).

The earlier criticism of war during Christmas as seen in the Vietnam bombings was replaced in the 1990s and beyond with a less critical and more patriotic approach to the celebration of Christmas. Christmas in the post-9/11 world, and particularly in America, is a reinforcement of certain ideas about the nation, its people and its beliefs. Citizens can support ideas about identity and being American, but they do so through decoration and consumerism. In the 'war on terror', ideas of patriotism, consumerism and sacrifice have become melded at times of traditional celebration and merged into a particular standard relating to American identity and definition as a nation. The powerful imagery of the collapsed towers of the World Trade Center was still imprinted on the nation's mindset in the preparations for Christmas, and the direction of sentiment was one of support – support for troops, support for rescue services and support for ideas of liberty and freedom. To do otherwise would be 'un-American'. At Christmas in 2006, Associated Press reported that the number of American troops killed in Iraq had exceeded the death toll of the attacks in Washington, in Pennsylvania and at the World Trade Center in New York (McShane 2006). More and more, support for the Bush administration's policy on Iraq has been decreasing, with polls indicating a preference for withdrawal of the troops from that country.[4]

Conclusion

From the Christmas truce to the 'war on terror', the uses (and abuses) of Christmas are underscored by specific readings or understandings of how easily cultural references and ideas about community and universal humanitarian principles can be subverted as a way to manage dissent and blend themes of identity into a specific idea of 'who we are'. The Christmas Armistice of 1914 works in the popular imagination to tell us that, despite the harsh reality of war and survival, there is something inherent in humankind that appeals to a more positive reading of humans as social and peaceable beings. The Nazi appropriation of Christmas was part of a wider phenomenon of National Socialist ideology that aimed to ensure public and private adherence to the Nazi creed, and the post-9/11 celebration of Christmas has largely been dominated by memory and consumerism. Rather than two opposing themes, the celebration of Christmas and its relationship to war offer a unique way of understanding how rituals and festivities can become an important tool both ideologically and politically.

Notes

1. Berlin Dadaist John Heartfield's photomontage of the Nazi Christmas tree (1934), which depicts a sparse, macabre tree with branches forming the swastika, represents the more politically critical views associated with Nazi Germany. Heartfield's work was banned under the Third Reich.
2. The advice George W. Bush gave to his mother, Barbara Bush, according to the *Sunday Herald* (Scotland). See Davidson 2001; Bush 2001a.
3. See White House, Official White House Christmas Ornament, www. whitehousechristmasornament.com/United_In_Memory_September_11th. html; and also www.whitehousechristmasornament.com, www.whitehouse-christmasornament.com/2006-Air-Force-One-Christmas-Ornament.html, www.whitehousechristmasornament.com/September_11_5th_Anniversary. html, and www.whitehousechristmasornament.com/2005_SS_Support_Our_ Troops.html.
4. In March 2007, 58 per cent of Americans wanted to see troop withdrawal either immediately (21 per cent) or within a year (37 per cent), according to a CNN poll. See poll results collated by US-Iraq ProCon.org; www.usiraqprocon.org/ pop/Resources-Polls.html#*.

CHAPTER 9

Christmas and the Media

Tara Brabazon

I don't know what a happy ending is. Life isn't about endings, is it? It's a series of moments and it's like if you turn the camera off, it's not an ending, is it? I'm still here. My life's not over. Come back here in ten years and see how I'm doing then. I could be married with kids. You don't know. Life just goes on. (Tim Canterbury (Gervais and Merchant 2003))

A pretty usual Australian Christmas concluded 2004: too much food, too much grog and an endless tapestry of heat. Barbecue-burnt sausages were followed by wine, garlic bread and cheesecake. Steve Hawke remarked of such baked Christmases that 'you have to be in the mood for warm beer at nine in the morning' (1998: 116). Families – in all their complexity and difficulties – enfolded us. Once more, I heard too much Abba and talked to (too many) relatives about shoe shopping and Christmas tree decorations. This banality and repetition has a comfort to it. On returning home on Boxing Day and expecting a lazy day watching Gillie and the lads dominate the Second Cricket Test, by mid-afternoon my benign channel switching became more urgent. It appeared that enormous waves – named first a seaquake and then a tsunami – had destroyed the coastlines of Southeast Asia. Loss of life was indeterminate at the start, but slowly – over two weeks – built to 150,000 deaths.

The mid-afternoon television uptake in Western Australian on that Boxing Day was startling. The first of the pay television news channels to commence reportage was BBC World. Their wide radio network of global journalists began submitting stories. Within thirty minutes, CNN activated its mesh of reporters with satellite phones, sending grainy and jolted images back to a shocked audience. Sky News followed. Fox News did not bother cutting into its pre-programmed Christmas footage about brave soldiers, patriotic civilians and the distribution of American flags to the military forces in Iraq.

In subsequent days, this news story changed modes of coverage, from crisis reporting to the shadowing of terrorist narratives. CNN generated subtle and emotionally attuned investigative journalism. Mike Chinoy, the channel's (now former) senior Asia correspondent, coordinated an integrated coverage within the region. Fox News moved very little from its patriotic coverage of Iraq. The metaphors from the inked well of terrorism had little clear application in this new environment of deluge and death. The South-east Asian region features many religions, languages and markers of social differences. George Bush's pronouncement to Congress that 'either you are with us or you are with the terrorists' (2001a) did not salve the grief, mourning and disease. President Bush did not speak on the disaster for three days after the event. In such a context, what could Fox News offer? The answer was continued coverage of Iraq where – supposedly – the ideological order was clear and predictable.

The odd and awkward convergence of terrorism, the second Iraq War and the tsunami in the immediate media coverage was uncomfortable. 'Ground Zero' and 'waves of mass destruction' were used too often to describe the passage of the seaquake. There were concrete journalistic and political reasons for this overlay of ideas and events. Community borders of otherness and difference have calcified after the events of September 11. The emotional responses to those burning buildings mean that it has subsequently been difficult to and evaluate critically how these events have been represented. Three thousand people lost their lives on that day. But 250,000 lost their lives in the Bosnia conflict, and up to one million people were killed in 1994 during the genocide in Rwanda. Every day, 24,000 people die from malnutrition and 30,000 children under five die from preventable causes. Such a scale of death places the tsunami into a context beyond the Twin Towers.

The tsunami that sliced through 'the festive season' questions the positioning of Christmas in the media, particularly within broadcast television. Even when an event the size of a tsunami kills hundreds of thousands of people and damages millions of homes, Christmas television is preprogrammed not to manage news, change, crisis or deviation from a celebration of family, shopping and 'spirit'. This mediation and masking of grief during a time of joy triggers the core problem of this chapter. How have Christmas specials transformed since September 11 – indeed, have they been transformed? With conflicts from Basra to Baghdad punctuating the news, has light entertainment reinforced or questioned a war on fundamentalisms? Through case studies of *The Office*, *The Catherine Tate Show* and *Doctor Who*, I investigate the costs of terrorism and war on Christmas media. In establishing the discourse and history of the

Christmas special, it is possible to track how this genre has moderated and managed conflict, terror and xenophobia.

Putting the Light into Entertainment

Popular culture generally, and the popular media specifically, configure a secular Christmas that circulates meanings and interpretations of goodwill, family, love, peace and generosity that are disconnected from religion. From *It's a Wonderful Life* to the multiple re-presentations of *A Christmas Carol*, new definitions of Christmas overwrite and mediate religious discourses. News programming, soap opera, current affairs and drama naturalise highly ideological renderings of family, friendship, the home and consumerism under the comforting blanket of Christmas. While acknowledging this wider function in popular culture, this chapter has a more precise focus on light entertainment, exploring the remaking of 'the special' for the twenty-first century. In the fight over fundamentalisms, Christmas is the pivot of change.

Through an era of the 'post' – postmodern, postcolonial, postindustrial and post-Fordist – the certainties of origins and endpoints, narratives and their resolutions, disappear as rapidly as weapons of mass destruction. After September 11, the televisual domination of cooking, shopping, gardening and makeover programmes is implicated in a political system where the United Nations is sidelined and news journalism is conflated with infotainment and the configuration of celebrity. While citizens are occupied with sundried tomatoes, bargain hunting, water features and plastic surgery blunders, there has been an acidic corrosion of thinking, questioning and critique. From this space of denial and displacement, remarkable doco/mocko/facto-fictional screen programming has emerged. Michael Winterbottom's *24 Hour Party People* darted around the shiny surfaces of pop, playing with punk, acid house, time and narrative. Peter Kay became a leader in comic ethnography, creating humour from recognisable situations in family life: the difficulty of finding a working pen when writing a telephone message, the grubby uncle lurking at weddings with ever-ready sleazy comments, and grandmothers obsessed with home security and funerals of people they hardly know. Concurrently, *The Office* offered a critique of reality television which demonstrates what media and cultural studies theorists should have been writing about the genre in the last few years, rather than celebrating the pseudo-democracy of voting off housemates.[1] This programme has captured and enmeshed the futility of post-work culture (Aronowitz et al. 1998) with the banality of reality television. Leaving the workplace, Catherine Tate was able to track a post-identity politics, where a fear of difference results in clichés of indifference. Like her most famous character, Lauren Cooper, Tate shows the social and political consequences of not being 'bovvered'. The cringe of recognition comedy is beyond humour; it transgresses the boundaries of self and society, identification and identity. Similarly, the rebirth of *Doctor Who* in 2005 created a savvy, modern and honest reassessment of humanity from the omniscience of the last timelord. As an explanation for our investment in both the banal and the image, *The Office*, *The Catherine Tate Show* and *Doctor Who* provide a more subtle interpretation of (under)employment and power distribution in our era than most daily newspapers. Within these three programmes, Christmas was a hub of challenge and an opportunity to unravel assumptions about the confluence of tradition, family and television.

Compared to North America and Europe, broadcasting in the United Kingdom was restricted to three – and then four – channels through much of television history, ensuring a wide audience for the most popular programmes. Christmas specials from *Morecambe and Wise* (1969–83), *The Two Ronnies* (1973–87) and *Top of the Pops* (1964–2006) were the backbone of family entertainment. Yet from these celebrated examples, a range of other programmes featured famous Christmas episodes. *Dad's Army* specials were broadcast between 1969 and 1976, with *Only Fools and Horses* episodes commencing with 'Christmas Crackers' in 1981 and continuing until 2003. *One Foot in the Grave* featured specials from 1991 until 1997, with the *Keeping up Appearances* episodes in 1991, 1993, 1994 and 1995. Many examples parallel this history in the United States; *The Andy Griffith Show* broadcast its 'Christmas Story' in 1960, with the *Andy Williams Christmas Show* showing episodes from 1962 to 1971. The palette of programmes from *The Beverly Hillbillies* to *The Munsters*, *Mork and Mindy* to *Bing Crosby* and *The Brady Bunch* all featured the festive season as a context or plot device.

Most of these Christmas specials are – tellingly – comedic. Televisual comedy is complex and subtle. The more culturally specific the comedy, the less likely it is to move into other national markets and continue to be popular through time. Through the use of Christmas, however, a shared sweep of experiences can be summoned and the comedy can travel. The British programmes that were successfully exported – such as *Absolutely Fabulous*, *Mr Bean* and *Benny Hill* – were the least tied to a particular context. Yet in the United Kingdom and through much of the Commonwealth, it was *Morecambe and Wise* that arched beyond television and the media to become a Christmas institution. Partly caused through the longevity of the programme's run, spanning from 1969 until 1983, the scale of their popular cultural impact is difficult to grasp in retrospect, or beyond the reaches of the former British Empire. For example, the 1977 Christmas episode attracted 28 million viewers in Britain alone: that is, half the population ('Morecambe and Wise' 2007). The scale of such a domination of televisual schedules will not be repeated. Derek Kompare confirmed that 'television is currently engaged in an array of changes that affect how it is financed, produced, distributed, experienced, and linked with the rest of culture' (2006: 335). This shift from analogue low-definition to digital high-definition masks other changes in legal and regulatory structures, and the consequential transformations to programming and content management. Christmas media has also morphed in this new social, political and economic environment, being recreated, represented and resold through DVD and subscription television services. Christmas can be delayed, paused, replayed or stopped to suit the individual viewer. The key with these new media options is that texts are moved through both time and space, raising issues of 'how new technologies intersect with existing practices' (Kompare 2006: 243). While the Christmas special was 'special' because of its intense temporal distinctiveness, DVDs allow the reorganisation and disconnection of programmes from a broadcasting schedule.[2] The consequences of this audience plurality – often reified into clichés of marketing to 'the long tail' (Anderson 2006), user-generated content/context or socially networked digital 'communities' – are that a shared popular cultural Christmas has been fragmented, marginalised and displaced. Perhaps this loss of the analogue – the specific, the distinctive and the unique – is one justification for the rise of reality television formats at the cost of other genres. Lawrence Hill and Robyn Quin stated that:

> Reality programming is clearly not 'live' in any technical sense. However, these programmes offer the same enticements as live television. They promise unpredictability, spontaneity (through a supposed lack of editorial control), and audiences which choose to consume them do so as if they were indeed live. (2002: 50)

The notion of a shared, specific Christmas has similarly been lost, only to be re-imaged through pervasive possibilities of a 'special' being replayed every day of the year. Through social networking sites such as YouTube, My Space and Flickr along with reality television, new mediations of 'the real' are being summoned. John Schwartz, in evaluating the transformations of visual communication in news, described the effect of this media transformation as 'the paradox of plenty' (2003: 57). Therefore the gentle humour of a shared Christmas television moment with a nuclear family no longer has a televisual context or social environment in which to operate.

The gendering of home entertainment technologies is part of this frag-
mentation (Keightley 2003), but so is the need to understand and live
within a culture of crisis. Kirby Farrell termed this environment 'post-
trauma culture' (1998). Farrell mobilised this phrase before the 'war' on
terrorism as a way to understand the 1990s as a decade of upheaval, disappointment and denial, including the movement from industrialisation to
post-industrialisation, the decline of the union movement, the management of post-feminism, the rise of the men's movement and the increasing
economic disparity both globally and within nations. In a post-traumatic
millennialism, the banality of light entertainment and the concurrent
rise of the cruel and ruthless comedic programmes like *The Office*, *Little
Britain* and *The Catherine Tate Show* enact a critique of liberalism and
acknowledgement of the failures within progressive 'projects' like multi-
culturalism, universal health care, unemployment protection and care for
the elderly.

Some trace of this post-religious Christmas even emerges within *The
Vicar of Dibley*, which broadcast its final episode as part of Comic Relief in
March 2007. Not surprisingly for a sitcom set in an Anglican parish, five
Christmas episodes were made during the season's run. 'Merry Christmas'
was broadcast in 2005 and celebrated Geraldine's ten years in the village.
In reviewing her decade, she saw many changes. While 'the churches are
filled with chicks', she questioned prejudice against gay clergy. She also
asks whether or not she has 'wasted' her life in the village. The complex
spirituality of *The Vicar of Dibley* ensures that humour does not emerge
through mocking God or formal religion as is often the case in *Father Ted*,
but rather is based on the behaviour of the vicar and the parishioners. The
programme allows their views, values and behaviour to appear outside
modernity and urbanity, creating a nostalgic vision of community. Yet
in this Christmas episode, Geraldine is embarrassed in front of the
Archbishop of Canterbury after dipping her head and shoulders into a
fountain of chocolate. Then, after drinking heavily to mask embarrassment, she forgets about the midnight mass and delivers the sermon heavily
inebriated, to offer a warning about the dangers of binge drinking. The
'political' commentary of the programme was limited to the institutions of
religion: women and the gay community, rather than offering wider discussions of oppression and prejudice beyond the village. Even the follow-
up episode – the tortured 'New Year's Day' – discussed the need to 'Make
Poverty History'. The overworked message left the European colonisation
of Africa, civil war and militarism outside of the discussion. Therefore *The
Vicar of Dibley*'s Christmas is the basis of laughter, drinking and sentiments of goodwill, but not an opportunity to revalue structures or history.

In choosing more marginal and confrontational programmes in this chapter, such as *The Office*, *The Catherine Tate Show* and *Doctor Who*, the notions of enemies within and without are more precisely drawn.

Redemption of the Prat

Stitch up. It was a stitch up. They filmed hours of material, most of it showing a good bloke doing a good day's work, and the one time I actually head butted an interviewee makes it to the programme, you're gonna look a prat. So you head butt a girl on the telly and you're labelled a prat. That's the game . . . We want a scapegoat. We wanna dumb down. We want to give them the biggest plonker of the year, you know. I'm not a plonker. (David Brent (Gervais and Merchant 2003))

The Office is set in Wernham Hogg, a paper mill in Slough, Berkshire. Before the programme was broadcast, the city's only claim to fame was a mocking poem by Sir John Betjeman. Swindon is sophisticated in comparison. Like fingernails down a blackboard, *The Office* is an observational comedy that is so close to the ruthless boredom of contemporary labour that it is almost unwatchable. Just as *The Royle Family* rewrote family life, revealing the comfortable silences and dinner-on-the-knees-before-the-television archetypes, so did *The Office* reinscribe the micro-traumas punctuating the open plan. The programme continues the British comedy tradition of appalling men directing the narrative: from Basil Fawlty in the 1970s through to Alan Partridge in the 1990s and David Brent in the 2000s. Brent and Fawlty have much in common; both are dreamers, aspirational men who use frustration, humiliation and sarcasm to understand a world where their lived experience does not match their hopes. Brent, unlike Fawlty, is unable to mask his embarrassment with anger.

 The Office has translated the boredom, banality and pettiness of office life into comedy. The first episode was shown on BBC2 on 30 August 2001. Few watched it. It was a show without stars, without plot and lacking a laughter-infused backing track. Slough paper merchants were unable to capture an early, intrigued audience. Slowly it built a following. In early 2002, the first series was repeated, and went on to win two BAFTA awards, for best comedy series and best comedy actor. By September 2002, an innovative DVD was released, with value-added context and detail of the programme. In that same month, the second series was broadcast – after great promotion. On 26 January 2004, *The Office* won two Golden Globes, for the best programme and best comedic actor, the first time that a British comedy had received such acclaim. Significantly, the final two episodes of the programme would be Christmas specials, deploying one of the few workplace archetypes unaddressed by the programme: the office Christmas party.

Before the screening of two Christmas episodes of *The Office* in December 2003, there was much concern that there was no way to match the quality of the landmark twelve shows. Critics wanted it to be like *Fawlty Towers*: finishing on a high. However, the best moments of the programme were saved until this 'new' ending. While the first series tracked the life and disasters of David Brent, creating more cringes per minute than any previous British comedy, the second series – brilliantly – shifted narrative focus, recognising that Brent had almost become too appalling to watch. A focus on Tim Canterbury and Dawn Tinsley allowed overt and poignant commentary on life, love, work and masculinity. The final two Christmas episodes summoned a new imperative: working through the problems of reality television. David Brent – no longer in the office or the boss – was 'managing' the consequences of his (mock) reality television celebrity. He was continually humiliated in nightclubs, by grocers and by women in a desire to stretch out micro-fame, while simultaneously being critical of the format that granted him minor notoriety. In a brilliant inversion, he passionately craved celebrity but criticised how he received it. Like countless (post)-reality television 'stars', he was unable to understand how fame can be so quickly delivered and even more rapidly removed. The mourning for a loss of pseudo-celebrity triggers brilliant black comedy. In a nightclub, and after a truly appalling copy-cat performance as Austin Powers (an already existing facsimile of Bond), he is labelled a 'beardy twat' by one of the punters. He can only reply, 'What have you ever done on telly?' (Gervais and Merchant 2003). There is no way to dismiss such a rejoinder in an era where television is in fact reality, and the role of a minor celebrity has become both a worthwhile aspiration and a full-time job.

Slicing through this overwhelming conformity and ruthless craving for celebrity, *The Office* provides viewers with a final surprise and gift. In the final few moments of the last episode, David Brent – the archetypal boss from hell – is redeemed, not by Finchy, Gareth or even Tim. The other – a black woman – is one of the three free introductions sent to Brent via a dating agency. He used the introduction service in his desperate attempt to appear popular with 'the chicks' and find a date for the party. Carol is intelligent, beautiful, funny and understanding of Brent. In short, she is his redeemer, transforming a small white man in an irrelevant job into a person with depth, consciousness and empathy. After all the (reflexive) sexism and racism of the programme, David Brent expresses pride in his meeting with Carol, describing her as intelligent, beautiful and sensual. Redemption is complete when David defends her from hyper-heterosexual abuse. When Finchy calls Carol 'a dog', David Brent does not snicker or laugh at the insult, as he had done in the thirteen preceding episodes. Instead, he takes a breath, pauses, and tells 'Chris' – rather than the matey label of 'Finchy' – to 'fuck off'. He then walks away from the masculine circle of innuendo and sleaze.

The function of this Christmas special was clear. While using the frame of the banal office Christmas party, with Secret Santa gift-giving and George Michael on the stereo, the religious tropes of salvation and rebirth also found a space for expression. In other words, Stephen Merchant and Ricky Gervais exfoliated Christmas as signifier of family, tradition and institutionalised religion. They then used this empty signifier as the sensitive skin for an authentic and emotional ending to a programme that picked the scab off the simulacrum. In a comedic knight's move, Christmas offered the possibility of redemption and renewal through the displacement of religion. Stephen Moss describes both David Brent and Basil Fawlty as 'essentially tragic figures' (2003: 130). Yet Fawlty was never redeemed. He remained lost in his self-created rage at the world. *Fawlty Towers* never produced a Christmas episode. There was no birth, rebirth, hope or salvation. Yet Brent was saved: not by a messiah, but by a black woman who allowed him to express authentic emotions and offered the potential of intimate relationships.

The Office presents a visual, political history of the 2000s that few have talked about and fewer have addressed in refereed scholarship. Petty hierarchies pepper the scripts, like our workplaces. As with the best comedies, *The Office* is punctuated by tragedy. Just as *The Goon Show* rewrote the Second World War and *Monty Python* reframed the swinging sixties, *The Office* attacked the blandness and mediocrity of Blair's Britain. Neither television nor work could provide the patch for masculine identity. Formal religion offered no hope. Through *The Office*, a first view is offered beyond tropes of masculine crisis and post-Fordism and towards negotiating and addressing more important social injustices. If David Brent can be saved by an intelligent and beautiful black woman at a Christmas office party, then indeed anything is possible.

Am I bovvered? Christmas and Catherine Tate

Catherine Tate, like *Little Britain*'s Matt Lucas and David Walliams, has built on the courage of *The Office* to produce one of the most startling and disturbing commentaries on Blair's Britain. While *Shameless* captured what happened to a working class that no longer works, Catherine Tate was able to understand identity post-identity politics. Her characters range from Derek, the gay man who at the slightest mention of his gayness takes offence and hisses 'How very dare you?', to the Yorkshire couple who complain about everything south of the Pennines and Lauren – one of the most stunning comedic creations of a postfeminist 'yoof' culture – blanking all emotion with the catchphrase of the 2000s, 'Am I bovvered?', Tate has offered a representational palette of a population headed by a Labour government that has displaced the working class from the priority of their interests.

Perhaps the closest comedic archetype to *The Catherine Tate Show* is *Absolutely Fabulous*. Commencing in 1992 and concluding in 2001, the latter was a satire that jutted from the drab self-righteousness of the John Major years and travelled through to the pseudo-meritocracy of Tony Blair. While Eddy was a public relations consultant and Patsy a fashion writer, Catherine Tate has domesticated their interests into the excesses of the suburbs and repetitive workplace disappointments. However, both programmes confront the insecurities of being a woman managing patriarchy without actual men filling roles of leadership, power or domination.

For her 2005 Christmas special, Tate assembled her most popular characters for an aggressive poke at suburban banality. The Yorkshire couple complained about food – again. Upon visiting a food court, their displeasure was obvious.

> *Yorkshire woman*: They're not doing Christmas dinner, are they? Seventeenth of November and they're not doing Christmas dinner. Signs up saying the council won't let 'em do Christmas dinner 'til December.
> *Yorkshire man*: It's political correctness gone mad, innit?
>
> (Tate 2005)

Similarly, Derek was also offended, but not by the food. Once more, 'assumptions' were drawn about his sexuality when he was made the Christmas fairy for the pantomime. He denied these suppositions, along with his desire to be 'parking his bike up the dirt track'.

Lauren auditions for *Fame Academy* accompanied by Lisa and 'MC' Perkins, featuring the chorus of 'shu-u-up just shu-u-up shu-u-up'. Their aim to 'keep it real' results in Lauren being attacked as possessing no talent, about which she was 'not bovvered'. Similarly, Margaret – the woman of an extremely delicate disposition – screams every time the Christmas trees flicker. Finally, Nan attends her local hall's Christmas party to complain about the food, the people, the smell of the elderly and Charlotte Church's social life. She prefers the sounds of Chaz and Dave to the soprano's carols.

For Catherine Tate, Christmas is merely another excuse to complain. Her cast of characters assembles a catalogue of grievances that do not subside through the festive season. As with *The Office*, religion is simply ignored or – in the case of Nan's treatment of a vicar and volunteers – dismissed as a 'fucking liberty'. The Christmas trees, family gatherings, shopping, gift-giving and food are merely variables added to a grievance culture where 'someone' (else) – the government, employers, friends or family – must take responsibility for personal unhappiness. This displacement of emotion and responsibility is one explanation for the popular cultural fame and survival of Tate's provocative comedic invention, Lauren. When deeply offended – and commanded by her friends to 'take the shame' – her face is removed of all emotion. A pensive pause is only ended through her – and Blair's Britain's – catchphrase: 'Am I bovvered? Does this face look bovvered? Face? Bovvered?' (Tate 2005). The simulacrum reached its full effectiveness when Tony Blair agreed to participate in a sketch with Lauren/Catherine Tate for Comic Relief in 2007. Lauren, on work experience in the Prime Minister's office, proceeds to ask banal questions and endlessly interrupts Blair on the telephone. He merely returns the phone to its cradle, looks up at Lauren from his desk and replies, 'Does this face look bovvered?' (Tate 2007). Perhaps there was no greater review of his Prime Ministership.

The Doctoring of Christmas

The Doctor: Christmas Trees. They kill.

('The Runaway Bride' 2007)

Russell T. Davies is – alongside Ricky Gervais, Stephen Merchant and Catherine Tate – the best contemporary writer of original television programming. Further, he is becoming one of the truly significant thinkers about popular culture, using the medium to comment on the medium. When he cast Christopher Eccleston as the ninth Doctor, a revolution in 'family' viewing, script writing, special effects and ideologies of tradition, masculinity, femininity and sexuality followed. With this casting, fans and prospective viewers knew the rebirth of the character would be more expansive than the simple rebooting of a children's series. Fashionable people suddenly stayed at home on Saturday nights to watch these new episodes. Viewers who would never have laughed with Tom Baker's Doctor or screamed with (or at – depending on your perspective) Colin Baker's Doctor, suddenly became born-again Whovians. Great television was being made that was thinking about the nature of television. The two Christmas specials, of 2005 and 2006, continued this trajectory. Titled 'The Christmas Invasion' and 'The Runaway Bride' respectively, the latter also starred Tate in the title role. While British television has a history of

Christmas specials, *Doctor Who* has rarely been part of this tradition. William Hartnell's seventh episode of the Daleks' Master Plan was titled 'The Feast of Steven'. In the conclusion of this show, Hartnell broke the fourth wall and wished his viewers a Merry Christmas.

Davies spent his season with Eccleston's Doctor ensuring the survival and success of the new series. All the popular cultural tricks were pulled; the Daleks returned, a beautiful, young, blonde companion was part of the cast, a dashingly handsome Captain Jack added fighting, humour and ambiguous sexuality to the mix. Davies needed these tricks. Everything was working against the new Doctor. It had been fifteen years since the series was cancelled. Yet the music (dumb dumb dumb – dumb dumb dumb – dumb dumb dumb – dumb dumb dumb – dumb dumb dumb – dumb dumb dumb – whooo eeeee whooo), the enemies and shoddy special efforts remained landmarks in popular culture for Generation X and Baby Boomer viewers. These rose-coloured Ray-Bans did not bode well for the new series. Nothing can compete with childhood myths of fear and fascination.

Then – remarkably – this new series and the new Doctor were so well scripted and acted that science fiction was re-imaged. The Doctor was Northern, the dialogue was whippet-fast, quirky and queer, and Eccleston was light, comedic and Cary Grant-charming. It was the combination of Eccleston and Russell T. Davies's writing that remade a memory. This actor and writer did the Doctor with a difference. 'Bad Wolf', the second-last episode of the first revived season, offered a sharp commentary on reality television that built on the platform established by *The Office*. Davies created a macabre twist to the conventional tale; instead of being expelled from these shows into a life of micro-celebrity, housemates were voted off and killed. The prize was to live. Amid such brutality, the Doctor diagnosed the problems of Earth's future and our present: 'Half the population's too fat. Half the population's too thin and the rest of you just watch television' ('Bad Wolf' 2006).

After twelve episodes of speed, energy and laughter, this first new season concluded. In 'Parting of the Ways', the war of fundamentalisms that punctuates the 2000s also gutted the dystopic future. The Daleks survived genocides and holocausts by discovering religion. Extermination was no longer enough. They quashed all threats of difference with cries of blasphemy. The Doctor was the heathen to be feared and killed. The most evocative and devastating moment at the end of this new *Doctor Who* did not come from the title character but his companion, the weeping Rose. On returning to her home – and our time – she was horrified at the banality of life, work, tasteless food and a quiet night in front of the telly. In remembering the adventure, the challenge and the good fights in the Tardis, Rose remarks that 'The Doctor showed me a better way of living your life. You don't just give up. You make a stand. You say no' ('Parting of the Ways' 2006). The banal acceptance of words and phrases like detention centres, asylum seekers and weapons of mass destruction alongside the exhausted sympathy in response to waves of tragedy from tsunamis to earthquakes and cyclones has created many moments to scream, rage, argue, fight or say no. Instead cooking programmes suggest that viewers pour another glass of wine, become immersed with the fascinations of frittata and feta cheese, and titter endlessly about celebrities rather than debating about how – precisely – a war can be won against fundamentalisms by constructing another set of fundamentalisms.

Significantly, even when Davies had rejuvenated the character and the series, he confronted another challenge. Christopher Eccleston left at the conclusion of thirteen episodes, the first time this rapid turnover of Doctor occurred outside of the failed American telemovie. It was at this point of crisis that Davies deployed the genre of the Christmas special. This was a significant move. At the two points of transition in Davies's reign as executive producer he has wielded the safe and comfortable Christmas format to shape the greatest challenges to *Doctor Who* as a programme and a franchise: the replacement of the Doctor and a change in companion. The former was completed in the Christmas episode of 2005 the latter in the Christmas episode of 2006.

'The Christmas Invasion' was a sixty-minute episode broadcast on 25 December 2005 in the United Kingdom and globally circulated through DVD within two months. It had an important function: to move the viewers from their deep investment in the depressive, dark and paranoid Doctor of Christopher Eccleston and into the breezy, fashionable and confident era of David Tennant. Throughout the episode, the oddity of a regeneration – a different face for the same characters – was probed.

Jackie: Where's the doctor?
Rose: That's him. Right in front of you.

('The Christmas Invasion' 2006)

Doctor: Who am I? I literally don't know.

('The Christmas Invasion' 2006)

Unlike in *The Office* and *The Catherine Tate Show* specials, formal political structures are presented, with Prime Minister Harriet Jones managing the threat of an alien invasion. A nod to Tony Blair's compliant acquiescence to George W. Bush's war in Iraq was presented when Jones stated of the American President that 'He's not my boss, and he's certainly not turning this into a war' ('The Christmas Invasion' 2006). Similarly, her directive to destroy the retreating alien ship at the end of the episode resonates with Thatcher's attack on the General Belgrano during the Falklands War (Pixley 2006: 15). Significantly, this act was made more cowardly because the killing occurred on Christmas Day, a time of forgiveness, peace and birth. Instead of religious iconography, it is masked Santas who are the armed threat to Rose and her occasional boyfriend Mickey while shopping. When they return to her mother's flat, a Christmas tree attacks the family through whirling, sharp branches to the soundtrack of 'Jingle Bells'. Rose's mother could only scream, 'I'm gonna get killed by a Christmas tree' ('The Christmas Invasion' 2006).

The masked Santas returned once more when Catherine Tate made a guest appearance as Doctor Who's companion Donna. Russell T. Davies justified his casting decision by stating that, 'Doctor Who and Catherine Tate is just the most irresistible combination, a genuine treat for Christmas viewing' (2006). As expected from Davies, he provides insight into the rationale for the special: a conventional format with a twist. However, once more, he was managing a threat to the programme. Billie Piper had left the series, along with her character Rose. While preparing the viewers for a new companion, the frame (and shield) of a Christmas special created a rupture and pivot for change. Significantly, Donna was marrying on 24 December because she 'hates Christmas' ('The Runaway Bride' 2007). Needless to say, her wedding day becomes even worse than she could have imagined. Her fiancé is part of an alien plot to cleanse the Earth of humans and is murdered at the conclusion of the episode. Her workplace is destroyed by the Doctor's attempt to counter this scheme. She is left to 'celebrate' a Christmas dinner with her parents, without partner or employment. Even the Doctor deserts her, unable to manage domesticity after the loss of Rose. While using the banter of comedic dialogue between Tennant and Tate and revelling in the camp physical humour of a woman running alongside the Doctor on London streets in a full wedding gown, the final shot of the timelord retracting to his Tardis alone, shunning the humanity that has been his companion through all former regenerations, created movement in the Doctor's character. This is unusual, as it is the companions who change; the title role rarely alters in function or purpose in the plot. Davies has therefore used the Christmas special – and the comedic skill of Tate – to manage the departure of Rose and to create room for a new companion, along with a fresh set of emotional problems for the Doctor to overcome through the next series.

Conclusion

This chapter has investigated the impact of a precise convergence: television, Christmas and a war on terror. Three media case studies have been chosen to probe this relationship: *The Office*, *Catherine Tate* and *Dr Who*. Each took part of the Christmas ritual – an office party, food, pantomime, shopping, Santas and trees – to agitate the generic limitations of comedy, reality television and children's programming. All these episodes confirm that there can never be a happy ending – or even a happy day – without consequences. Tim may hold Dawn for the Christmas party, but can she deny the desire for stability and family that he cannot provide? At what point in her life would Lauren be bovvered about failure, defeat or disrespect? As for the Doctor, after having lost the love of his nine lives, has he buried the capacity to commit or dialogue deeply with others? Christmas in/and the media provides a warm and comfortable place to deny and displace pain, discomfort or problems while hoping for a different and better future life. From such a cultural space, there truly can be no happy endings.

Notes

1. John Hartley, for example, coined the term 'democratainment', in *The Uses of Television* (1999).
2. Mark Poster noted the link between particular technologies, historical change and modes of representation in *The Second Media Age* (1995).

CHAPTER 10

Christmas and the Movies: Frames of Mind

John Mundy

Despite its origins in pagan festivals, modern Christmas is seen as a rein-vention of tradition dating from the mid–Victorian period. Christmas Day only became a public holiday in Britain in 1834 and a national holiday in the United States in 1865. In spite of continuing exhortations by religious authorities to remember its 'true meaning', by the late nineteenth century Christmas was less about Christian spirituality and more about a 'senti-mental humanitarianism [which] saluted and celebrated the family, child-hood and the extended family of the nation' (Golby and Purdue 2000: 80). Charles Dickens's short novel *A Christmas Carol* (1843) is regarded as a seminal text in this modern construction of Christmas, though with its emphasis on ordered social hierarchies, their permissible if temporary inversion, the centrality of the midwinter feast, and visitations from dead souls, it is as much an echo of pagan and early Christian festive priorities as it is a precursor of our contemporary experience of Christmas. Even before Dickens, Columbia College professor and anti-abolitionist Clement Clark Moore had created the modern Santa Claus from an amalgam of European ancestors in his 1823 narrative poem 'A Visit From St. Nicholas', better known as 'The Night Before Christmas'.

Important as these and other literary texts were, the construction of modern Christmas relied as much, if not more, on visual imagery. From the illustrations by Phiz, John Leech and Randolph Caldecott for books by Dickens and Washington Irving, illustrations in magazines such as *Punch* and *The London Illustrated News* in the second half of the nineteenth century, the practice established by the 1880s of sending pictorial Christmas cards, Thomas Nast's series of drawings including the famous 1881 visualisation of 'Merry Old Santa Claus' in *Harper's Weekly*, to Haddon Sundblom's portraits of Santa for Coca Cola beginning in 1931, the construction of Christmas was saturated with images of plenitude, familial conviviality, enchanted children, winter snow and other festive images. The importance of the visual realm to our cultural understanding and engagement with Christmas was maintained throughout the twentieth century by the movies that flowed not just from America, but also from a number of other national film industries. (Austin 2000; Beumers 2000; Evans 2000). However, since the end of the Second World War, Hollywood films have increasingly dominated big-screen representations of Christmas and ensured that movies, including their soundtracks, have become an integral aspect of our contemporary experience of the Christmas festivities, whether at the cinema or on television and DVD.

Quite apart from the commercial importance of Christmas as a major release period for new films, representations of Christmas have become increasingly pervasive in contemporary Hollywood, even in big-budget blockbusters whose generic centre of gravity lies elsewhere. In the comedy *Home Alone* (1990) young Kevin McCallister (Macaulay Culkin) is mistakenly left at home while the rest of his family go to Paris for the Christmas vacation. With the help of his neighbour, the aptly named Marley, Kevin inflicts a malicious, even sadistic, defeat on the two burglars who attempt to ransack what they believe to be an empty house. In the action thriller *Die Hard* (1988), Christmas operates as a coded mechanism by which audiences distinguish between the family-friendly good guys and the anti-festival, anti-family villains. In these and a host of other films, the transformative power of Christmas is co-opted to resolve tension and conflict in ways that are ideally suited for Hollywood's formal requirement for narrative resolution. In doing so, their representations of Christmas work 'to convey a potent, highly condensed expression of American faith and values' (Restad 1993: 171).

However, such values are not without ambiguity; nor is Christmas usually treated as an experience of unalloyed joy. Though Dickens's textual strategies may lead us to condemn Scrooge for regarding Christmas as 'humbug', there are surely few who will disagree with his verdict, at least during those moments when the stress of modern Christmas is at its greatest and when sentiment and sociality lose their attractions in the frenzy of shopping. Christmas movies have always acknowledged the ambiguities enshrined in our experience of the festive season, though the darker, dystopian elements of Christmas have been increasingly evident in movies as different as the slasher film *Silent Night, Deadly Night* (1984), Joe Dante's comedy-horror *Gremlins* (1984), the animated musical *The Nightmare Before Christmas* (1993) and the recent unpretentious slapstick comedy *Deck The Halls* (2006).

In *Silent Night, Deadly Night*, the central character Billy Chapman, having seen his mother and father killed by a man in Santa Claus costume and having been sadistically punished by the nuns in the orphanage he is sent to, comes to associate the character of Santa Claus with the power to punish. As a young adult and dressed as Santa Claus, Billy goes on a killing rampage, making instant judgements between those who have been 'naughty', and sparing those who, like the little girl Cindy, have been 'good'. Though Billy is shot dead by the police, his death is witnessed by his little brother, who addresses the camera with a cold stare and the chilling word 'naughty', a clear implication that the bloodshed will continue. Less controversially, though not without its violent, macabre moments, in *Gremlins* the cute furry mogwai (Cantonese for 'evil spirit') given to young Billy Peltzer as a Christmas present spawns hordes of horrendous offspring that turn into gremlins when the explicit rules not to get him wet and not to feed him after midnight are ignored. Though order is restored, the mogwai's original Chinese owner concludes that Americans are not yet sufficiently mature to be entrusted with powerful gifts.

Both these films are narratives of punishment and both deny the transformative power conventionally associated with Christmas. In Tim Burton's *The Nightmare Before Christmas* punishment is both accidental and temporary, as the attempts by Jack Skellington, the Hallowe'en Pumpkin King, to understand the meaning of Christmas have disastrous results. Bored with the drabness of Hallowe'en Town and mesmerised by his accidental discovery of the Christmas festive period with its colours, lights and spirit of good cheer, Jack arranges for 'Sandy Claws' to be kidnapped with a view to distributing Christmas presents himself. Ignoring warnings from romantically smitten Sally, Jack's well-intended plans go horrendously wrong, the toys produced by the inhabitants of Hallowe'en Town and distributed by Jack only having the effect of traumatising the children. Realising his folly, Jack rescues Santa Claus who miraculously puts things right. For all its formal innovation, *The Nightmare Before Christmas* reinforces the orthodox ideologies associated with the majority of Hollywood Christmas movies, the 'miraculous', 'magical' power of Christmas triumphant over acknowledged dystopian elements of the festive experience. Much the same can be said of *Deck The Halls*, in which the determination of two (male) neighbours to celebrate Christmas through increasingly outlandish exterior decorations threatens not just the family festivities, but family itself. If, as Kris Kringle announces in *Miracle On 34th Street* (1947), 'Christmas isn't just a day, it's a frame of mind,' such films reveal much about our contemporary frame of mind, conjuring visions in which divorce, structural changes in employment patterns and gender power, competitive pressures to acquire and consume, and the problems of being a parent compete with more positive, utopian images of

Christmas. This contrast, the powerfully felt contradiction between the sentimental construct of Christmas as a time of peace, goodwill and family love, and the contemporary realities of divorce, the sense of guilt associated with commodity values and the mad rush to get the shopping done, accounts for much of the special poignancy of Christmas movies.

Christmas, at least the reinvented traditional Christmas that began with Dickens's *A Christmas Carol*, is about tensions, conflicts and ambiguities of the sort that Hollywood, for much of its history, has struggled to represent. This is true for those films produced in the 1940s such as *Holiday Inn* (1942), *It's A Wonderful Life* (1946) and *Miracle On 34th Street* (1947) which both established the commercial viability of the genre and set a pattern for the cinematic treatment of the modern Christmas experience, and continues to be the case. As my examination of these and more recent films such as *All I Want for Christmas* (1991; dir. Robert Lieberman) and *Jingle All The Way* (1996; dir. Brian Levant) suggests, commercial main-stream family entertainment Hollywood movies continue to reflect the paradoxes enshrined in our experiences of contemporary Christmas, centred as they are on our need to negotiate complex relationships that exist between family, wider society and materialism. As both these films show, Hollywood's simultaneous acknowledgement yet containment of the ambiguities that modern Christmas entails are often expressed as much by what we hear on the soundtrack as what we see on screen.

Though the 1901 trick film *Scrooge; or Marley's Ghost* ushered in silent cinema's interest in Christmas, much of it centred on adaptations of Dickens's work (Chapman 2000), the modern Christmas movie originated during and in the years immediately following the Second World War. While the 1944 musical *Meet Me In St Louis* contained a complex rendition by Judy Garland of 'Have Yourself A Merry Little Christmas', which perfectly expressed the extent to which sentiment, nostalgia and wish-fulfilment were already part of Christmas, it was *Holiday Inn* (1942) which did most to establish the Christmas film. Though *Holiday Inn* was a celebration of all fourteen American public holidays including Easter, Independence Day and Thanksgiving, Christmas was given additional prominence through Bing Crosby's double rendition of Irving Berlin's 'White Christmas'. Written for the film on the condition that Crosby sang it, the song became what Berlin himself described as 'a publishing business in itself' (Rosen 2002: 5). Berlin's earlier attempts to capitalise on the Christmas holiday had misfired and he was clearly keen to exploit the success of Crosby's 1935 double-sided hit record 'Silent Night'/'Adeste Fideles', a record which began the association between the festive season and the enduring specialist pop genre of the Christmas song.

Crosby's 'White Christmas' remained the all-time top-selling single until 1997. Recorded by hundreds of artists from Sinatra to U2 by way of Elvis Presley, Berlin's song retains its status as the Christmas anthem par excellence. Yet, with its near-dissonances, chromatic meanderings and nine-line lyrical expression of deep-seated wistfulness and nostalgia, the song perfectly reflects *Holiday Inn*'s ambiguity towards Christmas, wrapped as it is around romantic rivalry and the commercial pressures to transform the 'authentic' Connecticut club into a 'constructed' Hollywood movie version. The personal and professional are eventually reconciled as would be expected in this classically integrated musical and the transformative power of Christmas is confirmed, encoded through a reprise of 'White Christmas' which serves to untangle romantic and narrative confusions. This transformative power is reinforced in the 1954 remake *White Christmas*, which places much greater emphasis on Christmas through both narrative and *mise-en-scène* and where Berlin's song is used as a triumphal extended closing number combining narrative resolution with seasonal spectacle, the vivid VistaVision colour photography exploiting the newly iconic status of Santa Claus's red and white costume.

If 'White Christmas' has become the definitive Christmas anthem, then Frank Capra's *It's A Wonderful Life* (1946) has assumed the status of the definitive Christmas movie, 'the benchmark against which all other Christmas films are judged' (Munby 2000: 55). As in both *Holiday Inn* and *White Christmas* community cohesion remains important, though in Capra's film family cohesion is as, if not more, important. With the help of angelic intervention, the central character George Bailey comes to realise the significance of his life in Bedford Falls, a life which he has come to see as timid, unadventurous and ineffective. Supernatural intervention is invoked at the start of the film by Christmas prayers and, having learnt about George's life and his decision to commit suicide, Clarence the angel leads George around Pottersville, the nightmarish dystopia that would replace Bedford Falls if George's wish that he had never been born was realised. Whereas George had previously regarded his family, his work and his small-town community as a trap preventing him from exploring an imagined wider, more adventurous world, this vision of dystopia restores perspective. With Christmas snow falling, the miraculous, in the form of a guardian angel and the citizens of Bedford Falls who rally round to replace the 'missing' money from the Building and Loan Company while singing 'Hark The Herald Angels', restores family, community and ethical responsibility to central place. In a film that is in many respects dark and troubling, this image of the redemptive, transformative power of Christmas appears to have lost little of its emotional resonance and serves to explain the film's contemporary status as 'an ontological guarantee of Christmas itself' (Munby 2000: 56).

Movie representations of the miraculous power of Christmas to restore normative values and social relations have increasingly depended on the equally miraculous agency of Santa Claus. The descendent of European symbolic figures including Saint Nicholas, Father Christmas and Sinterklaas, the American Santa Claus has become 'first and foremost a symbol of material abundance and hedonistic pleasure' (Belk 2001: 83). Though problematised in films such as *The Santa Clause* (1994), in which divorce and family break-up loom large, and *Bad Santa* (2003), where a conman uses the Santa Claus persona to rob department stores, the image of Santa Claus as a benign materialist deity capable of addressing the contradictions between scarcity and indulgence, between sentimental parental knowingness and innocent childhood expectations, between belief, imagination and their absence, was fixed in the 1947 film *Miracle On 34th Street*. Set within Macy's department store in New York, where Kris Kringle (Edmund Gwenn) 'naturally' agrees to be the store's Santa Claus, since that is who in fact he is, the film sets down a marker for the increasing hegemonic power of the materialist American Christmas, a spatio-temporal zone in which hard-edged mass consumption is softened by sentiment and a sense of the 'magic' of Christmas.

Divorced single mother Doris Walker (Maureen O'Hara) has brought up her daughter Susan (Natalie Wood) to discount silly tales about Santa Claus and other 'fairy stories'; they are, says Kringle, 'two lost souls'. When Susan is befriended by Kringle and becomes convinced that he is the genuine article, Doris's 'silly commonsense' is on trial as much as is Kris Kringle when, affirming that he really is Santa Claus, he is accused of insanity. Of all the adults, only Doris's lawyer neighbour Fred Gailey, who is clearly romantically interested in her and often acts as a surrogate father to Susan, is willing to give credence to Kris Kringle's claims, successfully defending him in court. Having asked Kringle for an 'impossible' gift, Susan's Christmas wish for normative family values, for a proper house with a swing in the garden, is rendered complete when it becomes clear that Doris and Fred will occupy the house 'given' by Kringle as wife and husband, mother and father. With Kris Kringle's walking stick propped against the hearth and 'Jingle Bells' on the soundtrack, it seems that belief in the miracle has been justified. Interestingly, in the 1995 remake of *Miracle On 34th Street*, the desire for normative family values is made more explicit. Here, the miraculous, magical qualities of Kris Kringle are deliberately put to the test when the sceptical mother, now named Dorey Walker (Elizabeth Perkins), deliberately prompts her daughter to ask for an 'impossible' gift, a house, a father and a brother, the first two of which are duly delivered and, as romance blossoms, a new baby brother is promised.

When Kringle's honesty and integrity are co-opted by Macy's management to increase their sales position, *Miracle On 34th Street* suggests that any seeming incompatibility between Kringle's warm humanitarianism and the promotion of material acquisition through consumption can be reconciled through the suspense of adult scepticism. Kringle's present to Susan and her newly completed family is represented less as material commodity, more as a gift that emanates from a desire for social and emotional fulfilment. Not that Kringle himself is unaware of the dangers of the modern Christmas. After all, he only volunteers to help Macy's out because the fake incumbent is inebriated. Later, he expresses his worries that the frenzy of Christmas consumption is in danger of squeezing out the values that he represents.

This post-war concern that Christmas was being taken over by materialist mass consumption driven by commercial interests was not confined to American films. In the 1952 British film *The Holly And The Ivy*, the Vicar complains that '[T]he brewers and the retail traders have got hold of it. It's all about eating and drinking and giving each other knick-knacks' (Richards 2000: 108). However, while such anxieties are recognised, films such as *Holiday Inn*, *It's A Wonderful Life* and *Miracle On 34th Street* established not just the commercial viability of the Christmas film, but also a sentimental format that enabled the ambiguities and contradictions of Christmas to be contained in ways that reinforced its centrality.

Such films also marked the growing hegemony of the American Christmas. Whatever its origins as a syncretic form, Christmas has become increasingly Americanised, not least because of the influence of American popular cultural forms including film, television, advertising and popular music. This 'reverse migration', together with the 'ability of Santa Claus to represent modernity and Western values' (Belk 2001: 82), has meant that, with some acknowledgement of localised customs, Christmas is a global festival largely dedicated to expenditure on, and consumption of, commodities, whatever religious, cultural and spiritual allegiances are ostensibly in operation. In a global economy dedicated to maintaining a precarious balance between the production and consumption of goods, Christmas in America, Europe, Japan and other 'developed' nations serves an important function, enabling shoppers to worship at the shrine of Mammon as they flock to the shops and stores in November and December, their purchasing underscored by the ubiquitous soundtrack of Christmas pop songs. Such is the intensity of this consumption in the United States that it accounts for one-third of annual retail sales there (Carrier 2001: 61).

Though the giving of gifts, along with social fraternisation, the desire to decorate dwellings and the refutation of midwinter scarcity through feasting, all echo festive traditions found in antiquity and the Middle Ages, the increasingly asocial and impersonal aspects of giving commodified Christmas presents can sit uncomfortably with the celebration of family, especially in an age when family life has become increasingly dysfunctional. If, as Miller suggests, modern Christmas needs to be understood in terms of the complex relationship between family and materialism (Miller 2001: 6), the giving of presents can often be a suturing process, an attempt to repair ruptures which can result from modern family life, to provide stability where such stability is too often absent. This suturing process is often represented as being at its most urgent and emotionally powerful with respect to relationships between parents and children. Sometimes, as Hollywood movies are only too keen to emphasise, the greatest gifts are not commodities at all, but are, as we have seen with *Miracle On 34th Street*, much more to do with the restoration of normative family values and structures. Though the emotional resonance of the nuclear family is increasingly beset by the realities of divorce and dystopian family relationships, Hollywood movies continue to construct Christmas as an alternative reality, a world in which the family retains its central presence, whatever the evidence to the contrary. Like their forerunners, contemporary Christmas movies such as *All I Want For Christmas* and *Jingle All The Way*, engage with the conflicts, tensions, frustrations and ambiguities of Christmas. However, these dystopian aspects of the Christmas experience are given much greater prominence, as their plots negotiate that complex relationship between family and materialism. This relationship is expressed not just through the romantic sentimentality of 'Christmas' songs, but also through the increasingly ironic use of traditional Christmas songs on the movie soundtrack.

All I Want For Christmas (1991) was designed for family viewing, though it clearly places narrative agency in the hands of the juvenile protagonists and their plot to reunite their divorced parents. This inversion of established social hierarchies, where children are normally subservient to parental power and authority, clearly resonates with aspects of medieval Christian festivities where 'the lords of misrule' were allowed temporary sway. Though the film's *mise-en-scène* exudes material abundance, not least through the comfortable O'Fallon house nestling at the foot of New York's snow-bound Brooklyn Bridge and the expensive costumes worn by most of the characters, commodities and material possessions are deemed, thematically at least, to be of less value than a loving, united family. As he admits, it was a mid-life crisis that motivated Michael O'Fallon (Jamey Sheridan) to 'drop kick our yuppie lifestyle for something that actually gives us plea-sure.' We learn through the film's back-story that it was this decision to turn his back on a comfortable, lucrative but predictable career and open a down-town diner, his rejection of materialism and its limitations, a decision made without consulting his wife, that led to Michael's divorce from Catherine (Harley Jane Kozak). This central theme, that materialism matters less than family, is consistently reinforced throughout the film, not least in the romantic sub-plot between thirteen-year-old Ethan O'Fallon and attractive out-of-town teenager Stephanie, whose parents are also divorced.

Any expectation of festive perfectionism is punctured in the opening scene where we see an ordered, near-angelic school choir singing 'God Rest Ye Merry Gentlemen'. Gradually, ensemble harmonic purity and visual composure are disrupted by the sounds of hip-hop on a Walkman, shots of a choirboy reading a porn magazine and by Ethan running down corridors, making it just in time to render his dissonant, off-key and, as we discover, ironic solo phrase 'comfort and joy'. Whilst other children expect weird gifts and cash for Christmas presents, Ethan and his younger sister Hallie want the 'miracle' that will reunite their divorced parents. Hallie, young enough still to believe in his miraculous powers, goes to Macy's to ask Santa Claus (played engagingly by Leslie Nielson) to make her mother remarry, having to revisit him later when it appears that she is about to do so, only this time to the deeply unsympathetic Wall Street stockbroker Tony. Ethan, at thirteen too old to believe in Santa Claus, seems to accept that Christmas is about commercialism and commodities when he warns Hallie to ask him for 'toys, hair care products, parakeets', but not anything to do with 'interpersonal relationships', a point reinforced by Santa who tells Hallie that her request represents 'a tall order – I usually specialise in things you can wrap.'

Unlike Hallie, who places her faith in his miraculous powers, Ethan sees Santa Claus as 'a jolly fat guy, not a marriage counsellor' and decides that something more than childish faith might be needed. Catherine's announce-ment that she is going to marry Tony triggers the plot by the children to prevent the marriage and reunite their parents. If Michael represents a rejec-tion of conventional materialism, swopping business suits for homely sweaters, Tony embodies the drive towards its acquisition, much to the barely disguised disdain of Catherine's mother, Lilian Brooks (Lauren Bacall). Tony is more concerned with preventing scratches on his BMW than he is with the children's interest and happiness. As such, he is the one who is pun-ished as a result of Ethan and Hallie's intricate machinations, locked inside a Ben and Jerry's ice-cream delivery van on its way to Jersey City. With Michael and Catherine on the verge of being reunited, a thawed-out Tony bursts into the house, spitting venom towards the 'brats', only to be told by Catherine that 'Christmas is for families' and that she and he are not a family nor ever will be. As he storms out of the house, Lilian remarks that 'holidays can be fairly bloody' and declares that 'now we know all the rats have gone', a reference to the earlier apparent infestation of vermin triggered when Ethan and Hallie let white mice loose in the house.

Ethan's confessional speech in front of the family Christmas tree, explaining that he undertook the plot because he did not realise 'how much I missed us', serves to reunite the family. The depths of Ethan's realisation are grounded in an earlier scene where he watches a family video, tears in his eyes, the soundtrack suffused with the wistful, deeply nostalgic, minor-key song 'All I Want', with its imploringly lyrical desire for family stability. The emotional chill of fractured families is also reinforced musically when grandmother Lilian and Hallie perform Frank Loesser's 'Baby It's Cold Outside' at the Christmas Eve house party. Such nostalgic sentimentality failed to impress critics who condemned the film's 'combination of sugary Christmas fare with cynical New Yorkers and MTV soundtrack' and its supposed lack of dramatic tension (O'Brien 1992: 38).

Arguably, such criticism fails both to address the appeal of the Christmas movie genre and to understand the ideological work it undertakes, not least in its exploration of that complex relationship between family and materialism which is given heightened prominence during the festive season. It has even been suggested that Christmas constructs an alternative reality of a world in which the family retains its central presence, despite evidence to the contrary. Since its importance as a central cultural platform in the fourth century, the nuclear family has become in modern times a 'lost core' as divorce has evolved into a significant factor in 'normal' family life. Understandably, the tensions between idealised family life and the realities lead, at Christmas time, to anxiety, tension and quarrelling (Löfgren 2001: 219). It can be, as Lilian says, 'fairly bloody'. As *All I Want For Christmas* asserts, this particular festive season affords opportunities for people to negotiate and transcend tensions and conflicts, to re-affirm the importance of family in an increasingly commodified, impersonal world. As Miller argues from his anthropological perspective, 'Christmas may be everywhere but the only true Christmas is within one's home' (Miller 2001: 30).

The tension between innocence and experience lies at the heart of *All I Want For Christmas* just as much as it does for many other Christmas movies, including *Miracle On 34th Street*. What makes the film interesting, despite all its limitations, is the unresolved attribution of agency. In the end, ambiguities surround the reunion of Michael and Catherine. At one level, the film's narrative suggests that it happens as a result of Ethan's carefully managed plotting, the literal freezing out of Tony from the family structure. At another level, we cannot dismiss seven-year-old Hallie's belief in the miraculous agency of Santa Claus, particularly when, and defying all realist and narrational logic, he appears at the family home to meet 'his toughest customer' and return Hallie's lost mouse Snowball. Earlier, as Ethan, Stephanie and Hallie celebrate the impending success of their plot, joyously playing in the snow outside the diner, they gaze up to the sky as the light changes momentarily, accompanied by the sound of sleigh bells. Nothing is seen, but then of course it would not be. Like all the best magic, we see the results, not how the trick was performed.

The need to resolve tensions between family and materialism also sits at the heart of *Jingle All The Way*, another of Arnold Schwarzenegger's forays, like *Kindergarten Cop* (1990), into family-orientated territory. Described as a 'vacuous addition to the recent ranks of Christmas movies' (Johnston 1997: 40) and 'the comedy from hell' (Walker 1996), *Jingle All The Way* certainly wants to have its Christmas cake and eat it, simultaneously carping about Christmas exploitation and consumerist pressure whilst celebrating the power of Christmas to reconstitute and reaffirm the nuclear family. Yet, for all the limitations of Schwarzenegger's performance and the intrusive dominance of its pratfall, slapstick, comic-book aesthetic, the film offers some interesting ruminations, not just on the necessary angst involved in the desire to give children the 'right' present, but also on masculinity and fatherhood within contemporary family life. As the double meaning of its title suggests, *Jingle All The Way* acknowledges both the magic of a family Christmas and the ineluctable cacophony of cash machines which are part of modern Christmas.

Schwarzenegger plays Howard Langston, a busy furniture salesman with a track record of not being there at important family occasions. After missing his son Jamie's karate belt presentation, Howard makes clumsy attempts to apologise which only succeed when Jamie is reassured that Santa Claus will bring him this season's must-have toy, Turbo Man, an action doll based on the Turbo Man TV series in which each episode climaxes with the hero's reassuring catchphrase, 'You can always count on me.' The prospect of this material gift erases Jamie's disappointment and enables father and son to express their love for each other. Ironically, unlike Turbo Man, Howard cannot always be relied on and he is forced to lie when his wife Liz asks him whether he already has the present. The following day, Christmas Eve, under the pretence of going to the office to pick up the doll and promising to meet up with Liz and Jamie at the Twin Cities' 'Wintertainment' Parade, Howard begins his increasingly frenetic attempts to buy a Turbo Man, not realising that this Christmas's 'must-have' boys' toy has sold out and is impossible to find. Howard's increasingly desperate attempts to get hold of a Turbo Man involve him in masculine rivalry not only between him and Myron, a postman also searching for a Turbo Man for his son, but also between Howard and his divorced neighbour Ted, who uses his superficially politically correct manner to try to seduce Howard's wife. Howard's paternal angst is only resolved when, by accident, he ends up playing the part of Turbo Man in the parade and when both father and son realise that their love is more important than any material possession.

Though Howard's descent into commodity hell is marred by some 'thudding comic timing' and 'wearisome slapstick overkill' (Johnston 1997: 40), the film offers an intriguing commentary on parental pressures during the Christmas season, as grown men fight to fulfil anticipated expectations. In an ironic inversion of his iconic screen image of indestructible physical masculinity, constructed through movies such as *Conan The Barbarian* (1984) and *Terminator 2: Judgement Day* (1991), Schwarzenegger is here at the mercy of elements he appears unable to control. He attempts to get a Turbo Man by any means, is savaged by mothers in the shopping mall who accuse him of being a pervert, gets involved with a black market Santa Claus factory selling damaged and counterfeit goods, narrowly avoiding arrest, and even nearly goes as far as stealing Ted's son's Turbo Man from beneath the family Christmas tree. With Myron the postman, he is involved in a bomb scare at the local radio station. All of this takes place against a soundtrack that makes ironic use of Christmas songs including 'Most Wonderful Time Of The Year', 'The Little Boy Santa Claus Forgot' and 'I'll Be Home For Christmas'.

Howard's seemingly disorganised, uncaring and forgetful masculinity is also contrasted with Ted's 'new-man' interest in sharing recipes, doing home maintenance and making sure Christmas presents are bought well in advance. When Jamie says he wishes his dad was like Ted, Ted's son reveals that 'divorce did wonders for my dad.' In fact, there is an underlying chauvinism to Ted, a suppressed and rather sleazy sexual desire that finally erupts in his sexual mauling of Liz. Divorce, clearly threatened by Liz and Jamie's exasperation with Howard, heightened by the pressures of Christmas, a time of year when, as Ted tells Howard, 'there's a very heavy incidence of stress-related breakdowns,' is actually shown as deeply corrosive and something to be avoided above all.

Defeated and accused by Jamie of never keeping his promises, condemned by his wife and facing divorce, Howard shares his despair with Myron, who reveals the trauma of being let down by his own father, making the comparison with a neighbour's son who did get what he wanted and is now a billionaire. Such sentiments clearly articulate the pressure that

Christmas places on parents, even though, as Myron has previously pointed out, that pressure emanates from 'the fat cats of the huge toy cartels' who spend 'billions of dollars on TV adverts' in creating demand. This view that Christmas has become overly commercialised appears to be reinforced by the film's opening title sequence, as Jamie is shown watching Turbo Man on TV. When Jamie tells Howard that he wants a Turbo Man, it is in the language of television, ending with 'batteries not included'. As Ted tells Howard at one stage, 'You can never do too much to make a child's Christmas magical.'

Howard's role as man, husband and father in meltdown, it is the comic-book construction of masculinity that leads to resolution of the tensions between family and materialism. Dressed as Turbo Man, Howard unwittingly performs stunts that make him a real hero in his son's eyes. Though Jamie is gifted the last remaining Turbo Man doll, he gives it away to Myron's son, since he now has a real-life Turbo Man at home. What matters is not a plastic, material simulation of an action hero, but the reality of a loving, caring father who is able to demonstrate familial love and responsibility.

Jingle All The Way may appear to be ideologically confused. Yet it suggests that, whilst the anxieties about getting modern Christmas 'right' need to be acknowledged, we can also mark out and overcome the antisocial potential of materialism. As James Carrier argues, 'Christmas shopping is an annual ritual through which we convert commodities into gifts' (Carrier 2001: 63). Unlike Scrooge, who has lost the ability to use his wealth to generate sociality through giving, Howard is swept up in the compulsion to articulate love for his child through the act of shopping, to transform a commodity item into a gift that betokens emotional attachment and engagement. This angst-ridden, compulsive, raged-against but seemingly inescapable experience is one that many parents will recognise only too well. In America and increasingly across the globe, if family is seen to be threatened by an impersonal world of work and commodities, then the appropriation of commodities that are then transmuted into gifts for the people who matter most to us makes complete sense. That the process is hard work, that it appears governed by a growing commercialisation, only makes the contrast between the material world and the world of the family that much sharper. And even if we are frustrated in this desire to reinforce sociality, even love, through commodity appropriation, then as *Jingle All The Way* and a host of other Christmas movies suggest, we can rely on the magic, transformative power of Christmas to make things right.

Part IV

WE WISH YOU A MERRY CHRISTMAS!

CHAPTER 11

Popular Culture and Christmas: A Nomad at Home

Thom Swiss

When you develop an ear for sounds that are musical, it's like developing an ego.

John Cage

Introduction

Like many homes, mine was gendered; it was my mother's sphere. Airless as a snow globe, neat as the wrapping on the family Christmas presents, my parents' suburban home outside of Chicago was orderly and suffocating. Not so the world around us; it was the mid-1960s in America.

As other writers in this volume have suggested, home can be understood as one part of a binary relation in which the private is defined by distinction from the public. This is a story of how the two collided in my own life as a teenager. The chapter is built around both central and peripheral life experiences, mostly during the years 1965–7. I write about a number of specific artifacts, cultural texts, and events as part of my consideration of how the ideologies and customs of Christmas in those years both masked and made painfully evident deep disagreements and family problems. I think of this chapter as a lyric essay so I employ section breaks, digressions, and my own poems in telling this story.

I begin with some material evidence. In the photograph of me at twelve, shown here, taken in the fall of 1964, I am sitting on a chair in our dining room, holding my brand new electric guitar. My shirt is Western-style, a popular fashion prompted by a hit television drama, *Bonanza* (see Figure 11.1). I know why I bought an electric guitar. The Beatles were everywhere that year. It was the first year they visited America, the first year they had multiple hits here. And I know how I bought it – with paper route money I'd been saving from about the time I began taking guitar lessons at the music store downtown. The first song I learned to play that I actually liked

Figure 11.1 Photograph of the author at twelve with his Gibson ES-335 (1964).

(not a 'learning' song like 'Red River Valley') was a novelty tune with French lyrics: The Singing Nun's 'Dominique'. Like the Beatles, the singer, Sister Jeanine Deckers, appeared on *The Ed Sullivan Show* in 1964.

You could play 'Dominique' on an acoustic guitar like the one I had been renting from the music store for three dollars a week. An electric guitar, however, was a whole different business. Along with my 9-volt walkie-talkie and my plastic transistor radio, the guitar was a technology of change, a pedagogy that was teaching me about new ways of knowing, ways of being-in-the world that had little to do with the life I was living at home. For Christmas that year, my parents bought me a box of Fender picks and a guitar case lined with a soft red material that reminded me of a casket. I didn't own an amp, so I hadn't yet 'gone electric', though neither had Dylan at that time.

My parents' complicity in my process of growing away from family through the magic and metaphors invoked by the technology I owned was lost on us all at the time. For Christmas of 1964, they had bought me a single walkie-talkie, a companion to the one my best friend and neighbor David received from his parents that same holiday. A year earlier, in 1963, my Christmas present had been the transistor radio, its one little white bud of an earplug bringing me the transporting sounds of WLS, a station which just a year earlier had moved from a country to a contemporary rock format. I remember its signature jingle. The vocals were by the Anita Kerr singers, whose album, *We Dig Mancini!*, beat out the Beatles' *Help!* for a Grammy award in 1965 – a fact that says a lot about the politics, musical and otherwise, of the times. The singers warbled, 'Wonderful double-youuu elllll esssssss. In Chicago!'

In my Chicago home, though, things were progressively less than wonderful. Through the wireless magic of radio, my thinking and desires were becoming de-territorialized so that when I was home – which I was most of the time – I felt less at *home*. Indeed, within a few years, certainly by 1968, I started to think of myself as 'homeless'. That was naïve, of course, even melodramatic, but I was wishful and possibly frightened at the same time – and it was true that new communication devices (including my electric guitar which was fundamentally a social instrument) routinely transgressed the symbolic boundaries of the private household that my mother had worked so hard to erect and continued to labour to police. The electronic landscapes in which I had begun to dwell were haunted by all manner of anxieties that arose from this destabilizing flux. These anxieties presented themselves almost daily as 1964 passed into '65, '66, '67 and beyond, until I left for college in 1970. Christmases during this time were over-determined but telling. They are among the occasions from which I will now make a few links between ideas of residence, communication, and consumption in the construction of identity – my own.

Chez Moi

Although Christmas arrives only and always in late December, it was on my mother's mind all year. Her holiday shopping started in July. She had a gift for giving; it was her talent, her art. Like my developing ear for music, her sense of exactly who needed what was a blend of the intuitive and the studied. Even when she was riffing – as for a present for a distant relative – things often turned out right. The right costume jewelry, right kind of candy, right fondue set, right book or game, right camera, right shaver or globe . . . right or mostly right. Her intuition ruled; she was the queen of Christmas.

The presents the queen amassed were stacked in her room near my parents' bed in piles that grew taller as the holiday approached. They were not to be fussed with. They were a kind of fortress – like other barriers my mother had erected to protect her notion of 'family'. Christmas was not just a day, not a season for her, but an ongoing process through which in my home, in my life at least, conflict was generated. My identity was taking shape and being shaped by her many and various attempts to expel alterity beyond the boundaries of the life she wanted for herself and her family. The crucial issue for my mother was always deciding who or what 'belonged' in the home and who or what was 'out of place'.

And I was growing more out of place each year – both at home and more generally in the Chicago suburbs which perfectly reflected my parents' impulse towards conflict avoidance. As critics have noted, the suburbs embrace an 'anti-politics' of withdrawal from the public sphere; it is a politics of conformity, self-interest, and exclusion. What did belong in the home at Christmas, however, were the signs of nature without the sloppy realities of the great outdoors. Hence we had artificial mistletoes in the doorways and, in the living room, an artificial tree that was not green but metallic, the kind of tree first introduced in the US around 1958 and popular throughout the 1960s (see Figure 11.2). Made with aluminum-coated paper, which was flammable, our tree was a fire hazard if decorative lights were put on it. WARNING! shouted the sticker on the silver pole. So, like others at the time, my mother illuminated the tree with a floodlight that had a motorized (and very noisy) rotating color wheel in front of it.

I Saw It On TV

I

The television was always on in my house, even on Christmas. If it occasionally presented us with problematic and disturbing events in those days (civil rights beatings, multiple assassinations), nevertheless, by virtue of its predictability and the reliability of its scheduling, it mostly performed a reassuring function. As many critics have noted in recent years, there is an affinity between television and the suburbs. That is, television is not simply the result of the suburbanization of the world, but is itself responsible for the suburbanization of the public sphere, characterized by the ultimate suburban genre, the situation comedy. Like the soap opera, it is largely devoted to the representation and working through of the problems of domestic life.

Bewitched, The Dick Van Dyke Show, My Three Sons, Lassie, The Munsters, Gilligan's Island, My Favorite Martian, Flipper – we watched,

Figure 11.2 The author, finger on the trigger, beneath an 'aluminum'
Christmas tree (1962).

listened, and learned from these situation comedies. I preferred, though, the James Bond-inspired show *Secret Agent* with its hit song by Johnny Rivers (re-titled 'Secret Agent Man'), and shows like *I Spy* and *The Man from U.N.C.L.E.* (I read the spin-off paperback novels from both, too) with their high-tech props and spy equipment, later parodied on the series *Get Smart*. I had my own wireless arsenal with my transistor radio and walkie-talkie and, increasingly, other gadgets, like a wireless toy racing car. After I bought my first amplifier, a small Fender in 1966, I soon added a wah-wah pedal (inspired by Cream's first album) and a fuzzbox which gave my electric guitar the wooly sound of that famous riff that runs through 'Satisfaction'.

My mother liked domestic laugh-track comedies; her favorites were *The Beverly Hillbillies* and the rural *Green Acres*. One dreary night in December '66, the whole family watched the schtick-driven holiday-themed shows from both series ('The Hillbillies Head Home For Christmas!'). Part of the appeal of these two shows for my mother was that they performed what she believed in her heart – that the 'originary' world from which one came was also the best world, the happiest world. Thus it came as no surprise to her that these refugees on television (the Clampetts in Beverly Hills; Eddie Albert and Eva Gabor in fictional 'Hooterville') were doomed to feel out of place, homeless and homesick. My mother believed in geographical monogamy.

II

My mother also believed in *Peanuts*, the popular American comic strip by Charles M. Schulz. For many of my parents' generation, the ritual nature of reading the newspaper's comics (my father still called them the 'funnies') was a key part of their morning routine. Indeed a media research project from the 1940s found that people missed reading the comics during a 1945 newspaper strike as much or more than reading the front-page news (Berelson 1949). In the mid- to late sixties, *Peanuts* was at the peak of its popularity, its lighthearted and light-weight 'philosophical' content perfectly in tune with the ethos of suburban life. And from *Peanuts* sprang the hugely popular TV special, *A Charlie Brown Christmas*, still in seasonal reruns to this day. I watched it every year, although I was not really a *Peanuts* fan. There simply was no escaping the phenomenon – not even in my otherwise saving world of pop music.

The #4 song on the WLS 'Official Play List' dated 23 December 1966 (Christmas week) was 'Snoopy vs. The Red Baron'. It was one slot behind the Monkees' 'Stepping Stone' and one ahead of Donovan's 'Mellow Yellow'. 'Snoopy vs. The Red Baron' was a novelty song released in late 1966 by the Royal Guardsmen, a group not from the UK, as you might suppose from its name, but from Florida. The inspiration for the song came from the Peanuts' storyline that focused on Snoopy dressed as a WW1 airman, fighting the Red Baron. The next year, the Royal Guardsmen had an even bigger hit with 'Snoopy's Christmas' – a follow-up that had Snoopy and the Red Baron fighting on Christmas Eve with a predictable holiday ending: 'The Baron had Snoopy dead in his sights/He reached for the trigger to pull it up tight/Why he didn't shoot, well, we'll never know/Or was it the bells from the village below?' Both Snoopy songs were 'story' songs in the tradition of Johnny Horton's historical epics, popular in the early sixties, like 'Battle Of New Orleans' and 'Sink The Bismarck'. But the Snoopy songs irritated me. In the middle of the Vietnam War, sing-alongs about cartoon wars fought on top of a doghouse seemed shallowly allegorical and depressingly jingoistic.

In theaters that same year was a movie titled *The Bible: In the Beginning*. Expected to be a big hit during the Christmas season, the movie was intended by its Catholic producer as the first in a series of films that would eventually cover the Old and New Testament in their entireties. But the many directors engaged for the project dropped out one by one, leaving only the adventurous John Huston who made the film. Huston played homage to the king of the biblical epic, Cecil B. DeMille, with a 'God-like' narration, an intermission (the film was three hours long), and an expensive 'life-like' Tower of Babel. The movie was a box office bust. But I saw it. In fact my whole family went to see it on a Sunday afternoon during the holidays. It was over the top: bombastic and boring. At intermission I wandered the half-empty lobby, loading up on movie food while my mother shepherded my younger sisters to the bathroom.

As I've said, the times, like my family, were complex, contradictory. While I was hunkered down watching *The Bible*, across town other movie-goers were seeing Michelangelo Antonioni's *Blow-Up*. A dark view of the new world of the 1960s that included both the 'mod' fashion scene in London and a possible murder, the movie was one of the most important films of the decade, a milestone in liberalized attitudes toward film expressions of sexuality.

At the heart of *Blow-Up* is photography itself – a meditation on human identity in an image-saturated age. It's an early postmodern fiction. It was hugely popular. Nobody in my house saw it.

A Tale of Two Devices

#1 (The Walkie-Talkie)

Adorno and many others after him have observed that any kind of language draws a circle around the people to which it belongs. It's a circle from which we can escape only if, at the same time, we have access to other circles of language. Media and new technologies were teaching me new and different ways to listen. And to talk: I felt encouraged to escape my home circle, to try out new languages myself.

Here is an imaginary photograph I want to share with you. It's me at twelve again, some time after Christmas in 1964. I'm in my bed, shortly after supper, in the room I share with my brother. I am clicking my walkie-talkie's power wheel on – and then pushing it up to increase the volume. Now I'm hearing a confusion of beeps, and now my own voice mixing with other voices. Much later I wrote this poem about my experiences:

Walkie-Talkie
That tape-box from a talking doll, the Heath Kit stereo,
Anything with wires,
Tubes or transistors –
We loved and broke them all. But not our walkie-talkies.
Nights, in our rooms,
We played at being deejays,
Singing the Monkees, Beatles, Byrds. That's what
I remember. And talking
Too much: our words spliced
To static, awash with others' in a stratosphere complete
With coded beeps and buzzes. And when
One of us grew sleepy,
Both of us signed off: that's what I remember. And once,
When I woke,
I thought I heard you calling –
But was it *you* calling me across those big back yards?
You, if I had answered then,
Who would have spoken
Back again? Or was it only a local ham, or one from among
The order of truckers
Whose nightly blabbing
I resented? Do you remember, neighbor? Dreamer
Or dreamed one, voice that held me
At the glass: *Dave to Thom*,
It whispered, then hushed. *Dave to Thom*, it repeated.

#2 (The Home Intercom)

Of course, not every new technology in my home was purchased for or by
me. My parents were catching the bug, and in 1967 they bought an inex-
pensive home intercom. I'm guessing it came from one of my mother's
mail-order catalogs; regardless, my mother 'gave' it to my father on
Christmas Eve. The purpose of the intercom was two-fold, they explained;
it would help us kids communicate with my mother from our second-
and third-floor bedrooms (previously we had to shout downstairs to her),
and it would let her summon us when she needed to, without shouting up
to us.

For me, though, the purpose of the thing seemed singular and sinister:
to bug my room. Although shared, my bedroom was nevertheless a 'safe'
place – when my brother wasn't in it – where I brought my friends, talked
on the phone, played my records, and used my walkie-talkie. Now it was to
be monitored, surveilled. I wrote about this later:

1967
And so we find my father,
one bored winter. One winter installing an intercom . . .

Room to room, the whole house webbed – wires half-tacked to floors
and baseboards, all of them leading to the kitchen where my

mother stands pumping
the red call-button. Space-age! my sister declared. Just like

The Jetsons!
But all I heard was the white noise, the bad connections,

and the voices of my parents like static from the moon.

Conclusion

[W]e attempt to construct a viable cartography of the world in which we live.
David Morley

In the introduction to this volume, Sheila Whiteley writes 'Christmas is about wish-fulfilment.' Indeed. My mother's endless Christmas was, I believe, about endlessly trying to fulfill her wish that our home would become an 'ideal' place – free of conflict, free of surprises, free of influences from the troubling world outside. As for me, I had my media, my electronic devices, and my electric guitar. They were agents of change, instruments of unanchored desire. Thus a truce at home was impossible.

Rootedness or exile, connectedness or mobility – my mother saw things in black or white. It would have been helpful, I suppose, if somebody had been able to help her re-imagine the relationship between traditional notions of home and identity and the contemporary experiences of my mobile generation. She might not have seen this relationship in such stark terms; that is, not as a contrast between presence and absence of the experience of 'home-ness', but rather as different modes of the same thing. But that would have been a different story – a postmodern story. The kind my mother would not have liked.

CHAPTER 12

Reflections of a Jewish Childhood during Christmas

Gerry Bloustien

The past is another country; they do things differently there.

(Hartley 1958: 1)

The past is re-used through the agency of social formation, and that interpretation of it can only be made with what people know of a social world and
their place within it.

(Steedman 1986: 5)

Contextualising the Non-Christmas (on the outside looking in)

Last Christmas I received a card that jolted me back to my childhood in a
way that has not happened for at least forty years! I received a card from
Helen, one of my oldest friends and yet one with whom, after years of sep-
aration, I had only relatively recently been reunited through persistent
searching and the miracle of global communication systems. As children,
Helen and I had lived as neighbours. We went to the same school, shared
secrets and family holidays, and played side by side with identical dolls.
Every Christmas time, I was regularly invited into her home to share her
family's rituals and festivities.

As a child of migrant parents growing up in post-war Britain, I lived
between two cultures. Indeed, even today in Australia as an adult, particularly with my heightened insights as a professional anthropologist, I feel that
this is true. Perhaps all auto-ethnographic narratives, along with their veneer
of self-indulgence, are inevitably about a sense of cultural dislocation that
emerges when past worlds and lived experiences are consciously or uncon-
sciously evoked (Okely 1996; Motzafi-Haller 1997; Marcus 1992). I am also
sensitive to the fact that the account I give here of Christmas is deeply sub-
jective, recreating a place where, as L. P. Hartley reminds us, 'they do things
differently' and provoking, in Leigh Gilmore's words, 'fantasies of the real'

(1994: 16). Christine Steedman's warning, also cited at the head of this chapter, reminds us too of the nature and purpose of such selective inter-pretations. For these are my own narrated memories and as such they are my own perspectives inflected with gender, class and culture. They are stories about my childhood, my personal past. As a small slice of an auto-ethnogra-phy, nuanced by social and cultural variables, this story could be seen to fit into 'a broader category of counter-narratives, politicized texts that resist ethnographic representation by outsiders' (Reed-Danahay 1997: 139. See also Driessen 1993 and Pratt 1992). Political, because as a feminist I would argue that accounts of home and family always need to be understood and interpreted within the context of broader cultural and political experiences in which they are embedded. Political, because even on this small scale, I find myself evoking the same associated themes of desire and regret that I have read in other accounts of the 'outsider's' experience, an attraction to and yet a simultaneous call to resist dominant culture. For much of my childhood, this became particularly acute around Christmas time.

The card that lay before me that December seems to me now to be extremely English, almost painfully romantic and old-fashioned, particularly since I have lived in Australia for such a long period of time, away from that culture. Covered in silver glitter, it depicts a Victorian winter street scene – ladies in beribboned bonnets, wide colourful crinolines and cosy muffs, arriv-ing in a horse-drawn sleigh pulled by head-tossing restless black horses. In the picture a dog in the foreground appears to be barking a welcome from the porch while a small child excitedly runs forward, abandoning his half-constructed snowman in his eagerness to greet the family guests.

Behind the carriage is a snow-bound, tree-fringed house, windows glowing with soft yellow light, creating long shadowy fingers to spill out over the snow. From the chimney the softly curling smoke drifting into the night sky promises more camaraderie around a roaring log fire within. Peering more closely through the glowing windows, one can just catch a glimpse of a present-laden Christmas tree, coloured lights and more mer-riment in process. Yes, the scene is about family and friends, warmth, food, presents, gaiety, largesse – a tacit welcome to the imagined delights inside.

Of course, I have never experienced a scene like this in reality. The ide-alised Victorian scene is not representing any world I have ever known in terms of place or time – it only exists in the illusory 'third space' (Soja 1999) of our imagination. In Helen's family Christmas events were all on a much smaller scale, urban-bound and lower middle-class. Yet as I gazed at the card, I still felt the pang of warmth and nostalgia for a fictional world that none of us really knew, a shared collective fantasy that resonates so profoundly with this imaginary scene.

As a Jewish child of European ancestry, all of my childhood memories of Christmas, at one step removed as it were, are primarily sensual and visceral. Like the ghost of Christmas past, a myriad of sights and aromas immediately stirs in my mind as I gaze at the card. I close my eyes and see again the greengrocer's carts in the central city district containing what were then seasonal 'exotic' fruits, such as Jaffa oranges, pineapples and delicate clementine mandarins, each delicately wrapped up in silver foil with just enough of their colourful tops peeking through to tantalise and attract the passers-by. I breathe deeply and recall the fresh tangy smell of the fruit mingling with that of the hot chestnuts, roasted and sold from one of the many street barrows nearby. Behind the barrow displays shine the shop window panes, which, outlined with simulated snow of cotton wool and cut-out paper patterns, frame the contents within. A tantalising stack of Christmas crackers or 'bon-bons' artfully surrounds the heavily scented soaps and perfumes (the scents of lavender and roses predominate!) lying cellophane-wrapped and beribboned for display. In another shop are the new season's collections of children's Christmas books each targeted towards what were then considered appropriate boys' and girls' pursuits and interests – nursing, boarding school, fairy and animal stories for girls and adventure, war and pirate tales for boys. My personal favourites, the collected volumes of some comic books such as *Beano* or *Dennis the Menace*, though, were thankfully considered gender-neutral!

I feel again the coldness of the shop window as, with face and fingers pressed against the glass, my steaming breath would inadvertently obstruct my view of shiny tins of toffee and biscuits amongst coloured boxes and gift-stuffed stockings, their lids depicting more idyllic village scenes with crinoline-clad ladies and horse-drawn carriages.

I hear again the ubiquitous Christmas carols, played in department stores and from loudspeakers in the street; later, as Christmas Day itself drew ever nearer, so would the groups of carol-singers. Adults and small children would go from house to house, their sonic cheer spilling through the walls and letter box until we opened the door to exchange greetings and offer cakes and money. I see again the wonder of the huge verdant Christmas tree in the corner of my friend's living room – nature tamed or at least overlain by the domestic: glass, tinsel, holly, streamers, glitter with flickering lights and topped by a plastic fairy balanced precariously at the very peak, standing guard over the sprawl of gaily wrapped presents underneath. Exciting and exotic. Mesmerising but alien. My own family festivals were equally colourful, brash and aromatic but so different from this. I could admire and partake but I was a tourist. I left behind the festivities at the front door as I departed.

Consuming Christmas (on the outside wanting in)

As a child I found the theatricality of Christmas undoubtedly enviable but equally overwhelming; it was everywhere. I lived in South Manchester where the Jewish community was mainly Ashkenazi[1] and saw itself as progressive and integrated. Had we lived in the northern part of the city where, in the late 1950s, the majority of the migrant families from Europe, India and Pakistan lived, my own cultural world would probably have been more insular and therefore possibly cushioned from these outside influences. In that part of the city, many children went to privately funded ethnic or religious schools, and neighbours spoke across each other in their own languages springing from their original heritage – Yiddish, German, Polish, Russian, Hindi – each one but a slice of the cacophony of languages and dialects mingling around the streets, alleyways and market stalls. The languages complemented an equally vivid array of costumes and rituals, for it was usual to see people maintain their religious customs in dress, food and music, whether they came from Europe, Asia or the Middle East.

But in my part of the city in South Manchester this was not usual. The merchants who prepared and sold pickled cucumbers, spices and herrings from large barrels outside their shops were restricted to a few streets and by the time I was of school age, these shops were rapidly yielding to progress and the new homogenised 'supermarkets'. My government-run school regularly held religious assemblies, but they were Christian and normalised. Hymn practices were daily and compulsory, intensifying in April for Easter and then again in December for Christmas. These Christian narratives and themes metaphorically and materially saturated the school curriculum regardless of any non-Christian children in its constituency. From late November until just before the Christmas break, we were directed to read, draw, dramatise and create personal stories about the Nativity; our days in school would be primarily focused on Christmas themes, a large amount of time being spent in making Christmas decorations, gifts and cards for our classrooms and homes; offered as a treat, the more serious lyrics and melodies of the regular hymns of the morning assembly were exchanged for the lighter Christmas carols; we were encouraged to write long letters to Santa and to exchange gifts with each other. The Christmas present for the teacher was particularly carefully selected (home-made was not considered good enough). I recall agonising for hours with my mother on shopping trips, desperately trying to stretch out my pocket money to afford just the right gift. As a European migrant mother, she seemed to appreciate the importance of this ritual – it was important to show respect to your teacher in whatever way was the custom!

My household was an orthodox Jewish home; at home we celebrated Jewish festivals including Hanukkah not Christmas.[2] While Helen and my other non-Jewish friends decorated their Christmas trees, at home we would light the special 'Menorah', the eight-branched candlestick with coloured candles, over the eight nights of the festival; while they ate mince pies and Christmas pudding, we would enjoy potato *latkes* or pancakes; while they exchanged elaborately wrapped Christmas gifts, we would be offered Hanukkah *gelt* (small coins) or sometimes a new piece of clothing by our families and relatives.

Because it was everywhere and culturally naturalised, Christmas seemed magical and seductive, particularly to a child in between cultures, as it were. By comparison, my own festivals seemed, simultaneously and paradoxically, both banal and bizarre. After all, even the children's books that I was devouring from a young age regularly described the fictional characters going back home from boarding schools to their families for the 'Christmas hols', anticipating turkey, Christmas pudding, bon-bons and gifts. The films at the cinema or on television repeatedly indicated that Christmas was the norm and my world was invisible or 'othered'. Only when I was with my family, in the synagogue or participating in Jewish festivals and events with my own relatives or Jewish friends, did I have a sense that we were not alone in our seeming eccentricities; there were other children who did not talk endlessly about Nativity plays or Santa's lists.

Embodying Christmas (trying it on for size)

Of course, such pressure was impossible to resist for long. As a child one wants desperately to fit in, so the charms of Christmas festivities became increasingly overwhelming and addictive. Now I look back and blush to think about the pressure I put on my family and indeed the parental disputes I must have caused. Against my father's wishes or at least despite his displeasure, my mother would take me to 'visit Santa' in his fairy kingdom in the department stores. As did most children, I assume, I 'played the game', pretending to be 'a believer' although deep down I was actually cynical at quite an early age, doubting that the bearded man could really be simultaneously in all Manchester stores and at the North Pole; if he was really omniscient (his persona became blurred with deity when I was little) and if he had really read my letters, which I dutifully burnt and sent 'up the chimney' as my schoolfriends taught me, then why did he need to ask me what I wanted for Christmas? But I loved the drama and the theatricality, recognising somewhere deep inside that somehow we were all agreeing to play our complementary parts in some kind of agreed narrative for our mutual advantages.

At the same time I was consciously withholding disbelief in the same way I would leave food for the fairies in my dolls' house, convincing myself that all of my toys came alive at night. So I would sit on Santa's knee, having decided ahead of time which Santa, in which of Santa's magic kingdoms located in which store to go to, and readily affirmed to his questions that I had been a good girl and helpful to my parents. I was also astute enough to realise that my Christmas wish list should be modest – there was no point in asking for something I could not imagine being achievable even for a magical figure.

My persistent pleading for a Christmas tree and decorations, even just a small one in my own bedroom, was greeted with anxiety and led to rapid consultations between my mother and her Jewish friends in the neighbourhood. How did these parents deal with such requests? Were they undergoing similar problems? The solution for the families of some of my Jewish friends had been to yield to pressure, allowing their children to have small Christmas trees (diplomatically renamed 'Hanukkah bushes') in their homes out of sight in their own bedrooms. My own parents could not accept this, although I have a vague recollection (is this real or just an imaginary memory?) of my mother finally yielding to allow me to buy a tiny plastic tree, paid for by my own pocket money, to put on the window sill of my bedroom. My memory was that I still felt so guilty and that it was such a poor substitute, I threw it away very quickly!

In many British Jewish homes in this post-war period of growing affluence, under constant pressure from their young children and television advertising, Hanukkah gifts became larger and more in line with what their non-Jewish schoolfriends were receiving. The usual Hanukkah *gelt* underwent a metamorphosis to become the latest board game, dolls or toy fad. These gifts were also often given on Christmas Day, whenever the days of Hanukkah fell that year, so that the Jewish children could share the excitement with their peers.

In my home, the issue of Christmas stockings became another heated one. At first my parents categorically refused to allow me to put up a Christmas stocking or small bag, as I argued most of my non-Jewish friends did on Christmas Eve. I knew that my older, then teenage, sisters had never requested anything so audacious but then as the youngest child (with a large age gap between my arrival and that of my siblings) I could push new boundaries and change the rules. Eventually, I was allowed the stocking which soon became a string shopping bag or small pillow case placed on the back of my bedroom door on Christmas Eve. For a few years I was allowed this indulgence, the bag filled on Christmas Eve when I was asleep, with tiny trinkets, sweets and small toys. The gifts were never big or expensive. We did not have much money anyway but my parents also recognised at this stage that the symbolism was far more important than the quality or quantity of the gifts!

Strangely, even then, I was aware that I had pushed my parents into undertaking something that was alien and inappropriate for us. My excited participation in such rituals was overlaid by a sense of guilt and trespass – I should not really be doing these things but perhaps that was part of the attraction (Stallybrass and White 1986). When I reached the age of eleven and transferred to grammar school, things started to change. My new school, which was still a government-funded institution, had a large enough number of Jewish children to allow our own morning religious service in Hebrew and English. Suddenly my own religious festivals became more prominent and as ethnic and cultural minority children, we could meaningfully share stories about our family festivals within the secular space of school. I became suddenly desperate to learn more about my own religion and voluntarily asked to attend a weekly Sunday school class at my synagogue to learn Hebrew and fill in the gaps of my religious education.

Happy Hanukkah! (on the outside looking back)

Helen's Christmas card has taken me on a nostalgic journey. Now in Australia I do not celebrate Christmas but with my own family I focus on the Jewish festivals instead. As my children grew up they and I found ourselves under similar pressure to conform, as in my own childhood. Well-meaning friends would ask how I was celebrating Christmas Day and what gifts was I purchasing for my children. When I explained that we did not celebrate the festival, I was sometimes berated and told I was depriving my children of a universal pleasure. 'It is not a religious holiday,' my remonstrators would say reproachfully. 'Everybody does it.'

Eventually, I took action. More educated and more confident in the school milieu than my parents had been, I was able to take a different tack from them. I went to my children's primary school and pointed out that such an exclusive concentration on Christmas was inappropriate for multi-cultural Australia and for a state-run education curriculum. Joining forces with an Indonesian mother of Muslim faith and an Indian mother who identified as Hindu, I requested some time for us to talk to the children about some of the other religious customs that were occurring around them in non-Christian homes. The teachers readily agreed and I realised how little they themselves knew and how interested they were to learn of other customs around them. We were encouraged to repeat the intervention every year and as other parents voluntarily offered their knowledge and insights, we were able to add a number of other faiths and cultures to our repertoire. One outcome was that, as his classmates around him drew their Christmas cards, my son voluntarily decided to create Hanukkah cards containing a poem inside to celebrate the 'dancing Hanukkah lights' on the Menorah. Another was that one year my daughter was given a deliberately selected 'seasons greetings' card by a particularly culturally sensitive friend instead of the usual card expressing 'Happy Christmas' or depicting a Nativity scene. We very much appreciated the gesture and told the friend so. It was ultimately recognition that we were different but equal, visible and understood to celebrate in our own ways.

Have I laid too heavy a responsibility on the celebration of Christmas? Have I lost my own pleasure and enjoyment of Christmas completely? Of course not! I find that I still enjoy sending Christmas cards to my non-Jewish friends and exchanging gifts. I still love the smells, sounds and excitement of Christmas time, especially when I am travelling in European and British cities where the snow somehow adds another layer of 'authenticity' to the magical mix. The difference is that I am able to remind myself and others that the rituals of Christmas, however splendid and exciting, are cultural creations and constructions alongside many others and as such are open to deconstruction and rejection. They are no less valuable or significant for that insight but neither are they superior or inevitable. In discussing the debates around blurred cultural identities in the modern era, Dieter Hoffman-Axthelm argued for the necessity of 'intuitive selfness, for residing in the world without being disavowed as an individual – the perceptive being-perceived'. That is exactly why as a an adult I recognise the joy of embracing Hanukkah rather than Christmas, of being able to turn to my dear friends and well-wishers with my own greeting in exchange for theirs. This year I am sending Helen a Hanukkah card, which I know she will appreciate and cherish.

Notes

1. Jewish communities originating from Eastern Europe were known as Ashkenazi. As migrants they particularly brought with them the language, customs and rituals of Poland and Russia into their new countries.

2. Hanukkah celebrates the victory of significant resistance against the Roman occupation of Judea in the first century AD and the rededication of the Temple through what is seen as a miraculous intervention (Zeitlin 1938). Unlike Christmas, which always falls on 25 December in most of the Western world, Hanukkah falls according to the Jewish lunar calendar. This means that while its Jewish date is consistent, its coincidence with particular dates on the Roman calendar varied considerably from year to year. It also lasts for eight days and nights with candles being lit and festivities occurring on each night.

Postscript

I would like to thank the contributors for their insights into Christmas. They have been convivial company and I can think of no better companions with whom to celebrate the festive season – Christmas and Hanukkah alike! To paraphrase Charles Dickens, they are not:

> a mere assemblage . . . got up at a week or two's notice, originating this year, having no . . . precedent in the past, and not likely to be repeated in the next . . . So draw your chair nearer the blazing fire – fill the glass and round the song . . . Our life on it, but your Christmas shall be merry, and your new year a happy one! (1836: 221)

Bibliography

Ackroyd, Peter (1990) *Dickens: A Biography*, London: Sinclair-Stevenson.

Acland, Charles R. (2000) 'Fresh contacts: global culture and the concept of generation', in Neil Campbell (ed.), *The Radiant Hour: Versions of Youth in American Culture*, Exeter: University of Exeter Press, pp. 31–52.

Adbusters (2007) 'Buy Nothing Christmas', www.adbusters.org/metas/eco/bnd/bnxmas/. Accessed 25 March 2007.

Anderson, Chris (2006) *The Long Tail*, New York: Random House.

Anonymous, Rodney (2005) 'Who Shit a Christmas Tree?' posted 27 November 2005. www.rodneyanonymous.com/archives/00000199.htm. Accessed 16 March 2007.

Anthony, James R. (1973) *French Baroque Music from Beaujoyeulx to Rameau*, London: Batsford.

Aronowitz, Stanley et al. (1998) 'The post-work manifesto', in S. Aronowitz and J. Cutler (eds), *Post-work*, London: Routledge, pp. 22–69.

Art Journal (1868) New series. Vol. VII, p. 244.

Art Journal (1869) New series. Vol. VIII, pp. 382–3.

Art Journal (1871) New series. Vol. X. 'Marcus Ward's Christmas Cards', p. 295.

Art Journal (1872) New series. Vol. XI. 'Christmas Cards', p. 313.

Art Journal (1873a) New series. Vol. XII. 'Christmas and New Year Cards, Ward', p. 30.

Art Journal (1873b) New series. Vol. XII. 'Christmas Gifts', p. 379.

Ashworth, T. (1980) *Trench Warfare, 1914–1918: The Live and Let Live System*, New York: Holmes & Meier.

Austin, Guy (2000) 'Christmas in French cinema', in Mark Connelly (ed.), *Christmas at the Movies: Images of Christmas in American, British and European Cinema*, London: I. B. Tauris, pp. 165–84.

Barnett, James H. (1954) *The American Christmas: A Study in National Culture*, New York: Macmillan.

Bede, the Venerable (1965) *A History of the English Church and People*, trans. Leo Sherley-Price, Baltimore, MD: Penguin.

Belk, Russell W. (1993, republished 2001) 'Materialism and the making of the modern American Christmas', in Daniel Miller (ed.), *Unwrapping Christmas*, Oxford: Oxford University Press, pp. 75–104.

Bennett, T. (1981) 'Christmas and ideology', in *Popular Culture: Themes and Issues* 1, Milton Keynes: Open University, pp. 49–74.

Berelson, B. (1949) 'What "missing the newspaper" means', in P. F. Lazarsfeld and F. N. Stanton (eds), *Communications Research, 1948–1949*, New York: Harper, pp. 111–28.

Beumers, Birgit (2000) 'Father Frost on 31 December: Christmas and New Year in Soviet and Russian cinema', in Mark Connelly (ed.), *Christmas at the Movies: Images of Christmas in American, British and European Cinema*, London: I. B. Tauris, pp. 185–210.

Black, Fiona C. (ed.) (2006) *The Recycled Bible: Autobiography, Culture, and the Space Between*. Semeia Studies No. 51, Atlanta: Society of Biblical Literature.

Blair, T. (2004) 'Prime Minister warns of continuing global terror threat', 5 March. www.pm.gov.uk/output/Page5461.asp. Accessed 12 March 2007.

'Boom Town/Bad Wolf/The Parting of the Ways' (2006) *Dr Who Series One Volume Four*, London: BBC Video.

Bowler, Gerry (2005) *The World Encyclopedia of Christmas*, Toronto: McClelland & Stewart.

Bryman, Alan (2004) *The Disneyization of Society*, London: Sage.

Buday, George (1954) *The History of the Christmas Card*, London: Spring.

Bush, George W. (2001a) *Address to a Joint Session of Congress and the American People*, Washington, DC, 20 September. www.whitehouse.gov/news/releases/2001/09/20010920-8.html. Accessed 6 July 2006.

Bush, George W. (2001b) *Christmas Radio Message by the President to the Nation*, 25 December. www.whitehouse.gov/news/releases/2001/12/20011225.html. Accessed 12 January 2007.

Bush, George W. (2002) *Radio Address by the President to the Nation*, 21 December. www.whitehouse.gov/news/releases/2002/12/20021221.html. Accessed 12 January 2007.

Bush, George W. (2003) *President's Radio Address*, 27 December. www.whitehouse.gov/news/releases/2003/12/20031227.html. Accessed 12 January 2007.

Bush, George W. (2004) *President's Radio Address*, 25 December. www.whitehouse.gov/news/releases/2004/12/20041225.html. Accessed 12 January 2007.

Bush, George W. (2005) *President's Radio Address*, 24 December. www.whitehouse.gov/news/releases/2005/12/20051224.html. Accessed 12 January 2007.

Bush, George W. (2006) *President's Radio Address*, 23 December. www.whitehouse.gov/news/releases/2006/12/20061223.html. Accessed 12 January 2007.

Campbell, Neil, Jude Davies and George McKay (eds) (2004) *Issues in Americanisation and Culture*, Edinburgh: Edinburgh University Press.

Carrier, James G. (1993, republished 2001) 'The rituals of Christmas shopping', in Daniel Miller (ed.), *Unwrapping Christmas*, Oxford: Clarendon, pp. 55–74.

Catholic League for Religious and Civil Rights (2005a) 'Wal-Mart Bans Christmas: Boycott Launched', Press Release, 9 November. www.catholicleague.org/05press_releases/quarter%204/051109_Wal-Mart_boycott.htm. Accessed 16 March 2007.

Catholic League for Religious and Civil Rights (2005b) 'Wal-Mart Has Been Put on Notice', Press Release, 10 November. www.catholicleague.org/05press_releases/quarter%204/051110_put_on_notice.htm. Accessed 16 March 2007.

Catholic League for Religious and Civil Rights (2005c) 'Wal-Mart Caves; Boycott Ends', Press Release, 11 November. www.catholicleague.org/05press_releases/quarter%204/051111_boycott_ends.htm. Accessed 16 March 2007.

Chapman, James (2000) 'God bless us, every one: Movie adaptations of *A Christmas Carol*', in Mark Connelly (ed.), *Christmas at the Movies: Images of Christmas in American, British and European Cinema*, London: I. B. Tauris, pp. 9–38.

Chevallot, I. (2004) 'A history of terror and slow progress', *Guardian*, 28 June. www.guardian.co.uk/international/story/0,,1248659,00.html. Accessed June 2007.

Christmas and Seasonal Decorations Market Report (2002). www.researchandmarkets.com/reports/6803/christmas_and_seasonal_decorations_market_2002.htm. Accessed 14 January 2007.

Clark, C. (2001) 'What's in store for holiday shopping?', *CNN*. www.cnn.com/SPECIALS/2001/holidayshopping/stories/overview.htm. Accessed 24 January 2007.

Clauss, Manfred (2000) *The Roman Cult of Mithras*, Edinburgh: Edinburgh University Press.

Cole, G. D. H. and Raymond Postgate (1976) *The Common People 1746–1946*, London: Methuen.

Collins, R. (2004) 'Rituals of solidarity and security in the wake of terrorist attack', *Sociological Theory* 22 (1): 53–87.

Connelly, Mark (1999) *Christmas: A Social History*, London: I. B. Tauris.

Count, Earl W. (1948) *All About Christmas*, New York: Harper.

Crossick, Geoffrey and Serge Jaumain (eds) (1999) *Cathedrals of Consumption: The European Department Store 1850–1939*, Aldershot: Ashgate.

Cunningham, Hugh (1980) *Leisure in the Industrial Revolution*, London: Croom Helm.

Davidson, Ros (2001) 'Shop Til bin Laden Drops', 23 December. http://commondreams.org/headlines01/1223-02.htm. Accessed 26 January 2007.

Davies, Russell (2006) 'Tate to guest star in Doctor Who', *BBC News*. http://newsvote.bbc.co.uk/mpapps/pagetools/print/news.bbc.co.uk/1/hi/entertainment/. Accessed 2 March 2007.

Dearmer, P., R. Vaughan Williams and M. Shaw (eds) (1928) *The Oxford Book of Carols*, Oxford: Oxford University Press.

Department of Homeland Security (2003) 'Remarks by Secretary of Homeland Security Tom Ridge at a Press Conference Announcing the Raising of the

National Threat Level', Washington DC, 21 December. www.dhs.gov/xnews/ releases/press_release_0889.shtm. Accessed 15 February 2007.

Dickens, Charles (1836) *Sketches by Boz*, Oxford: Oxford University Press.

Dickens, Charles (1843a) *A Christmas Carol*, Oxford: Oxford University Press.

Dickens, Charles (1843b) *A Christmas Carol: Being a Ghost Story of Christmas*, illustrated by John Leech, London: Chapman & Hall.

Dickens, Charles (1985) *A Christmas Carol*, in *The Christmas Books*, Vol. 1, Harmondsworth: Penguin.

Digger History website (2007) 'Coca-Cola at war (on BOTH sides)'. www. diggerhistory.info/pages-food/coca_cola.htm. Accessed 29 April 2007.

Douglas, Ann (1977) *The Feminization of American Culture*, New York: Avon.

Driessen, Henk (ed.) (1993) *The Politics of Ethnographic Reading and Writing: Confrontations of Western and Indigenous Views*, Saarbrucken: Breitenbach.

Edelman, M. (1995) *From Art to Politics. How Artistic Creations Shape Political Conceptions*, Chicago, IL: University of Chicago Press.

Engels, Frederick (1979) *The Condition of the Working Class in England*, London: Panther.

Etzioni, A. (2004) 'Holidays and rituals: Neglected seedbeds of virtue', in A. Etzioni and J. Bloom (eds), *We Are What We Celebrate. Understanding Holidays and Rituals*, New York: New York University Press, pp. 1–40.

Evans, Peter William (2000) 'Satirizing the Spanish Christmas: Placido', in Mark Connelly (ed.), *Christmas at the Movies: Images of Christmas in American, British and European Cinema*, London: I. B. Tauris, pp. 211–22.

Falk, Pasi (1997) 'The Benetton-Toscani effect: Testing the limits of conventional advertising', in Mica Nava, Andrew Blake, Iain MacRury and Barry Richards (eds) (2001), *Buy This Book: Studies in Advertising and Consumption*, London: Routledge, pp. 64–83.

Farrell, Kirby (1998) *Post-Trauma Culture: Injury and Interpretation in the Nineties*, Baltimore, MD: Johns Hopkins University Press.

Fowles, Jib (1996) *Advertising and Popular Culture*, London: Sage.

Fox, Richard Wightman (2004) *Jesus in America: Personal Savior, Cultural Hero, National Obsession*, San Francisco, CA: HarperSanFrancisco.

Fox, Selena (1996–2007) 'Celebrating the Seasons: Winter Solstice'. www. circlesanctuary.org/pholidays/wintersolstice.htm. Accessed 14 May 2007.

Gajek, E. (1990) 'Christmas under the Third Reich', *Anthropology Today* 6 (4): 3–8.

Gervais, Ricky and Stephen Merchant (2003) *The Office Christmas Episodes*, 26–27 December, BBC.

Gibson, John (2005) *The War on Christmas: How the Liberal Plot to Ban the Sacred Christian Holiday is Worse than You Thought*, New York: Sentinel.

Gilmore, Leigh (1994) *Autobiographics: a Feminist Theory of Women's Self-Representation*, Ithaca, NY: Cornell University Press.

Glancy, Ruth (1998) 'Introduction', *Charles Dickens Christmas Books*, Oxford: Oxford University Press.

Golby, J. M. (1981) 'A history of Christmas', *Popular Culture: Themes and Issues*, Milton Keynes: Open University Press, pp. 8–26.

Golby, J. M. and A. W. Purdue (1981) 'Christmas', in *Popular Culture* U203, Milton Keynes: Open University Press.

Golby, J. M. and A. W. Purdue (1986) *The Making of the Modern Christmas*, Athens, GA: University of Georgia Press.

Golby, J. M. and A. W. Purdue (2000) *The Making of the Modern Christmas*, Stroud: Sutton.

Gould, P. (2001) 'Christmas in New York', *BBC News*, 21 December. http://news.bbc.co.uk/1/hi/in_depth/americas/2001/nyc_out_of_the_ashes/1721158.stm. Accessed 24 January 2007.

The Graphic (1886) Vol. XXXIII, No. 840. 2 January. 'Rural Notes', p. 11.

Gregory of Nazianzen (date uncertain) Oration 38: On the Manifestation of God in the Birth of the Anointed. www.orthodoxa.org/GB/orthodoxy/patrology/gregoiredenazianzenoelGB.htm. Accessed 5 June 2007.

Hannaford, A. (2005) 'A Christmas fairytale', *The Big Issue in the North*, Manchester, 28 November–4 December, pp. 8–9.

Harrison, Michael (1951) *The Story of Christmas*, London: Odhams.

Hartley, John (1999) *The Uses of Television*, London: Routledge.

Hartley, L. P. (1958) *The Go-Between*, Harmondsworth: Penguin.

Hawke, Steve (1998) 'Kimberley Christmas', in A. B. Facey et al., *Blokes: Stories from Australian Lives*, Fremantle: Fremantle Arts Centre Press, pp. 113–16.

Hearn, Michael Patrick (2004) 'Introduction', *The Annotated Christmas Carol*, Norton: New York.

Hebdige, Dick (1988) *Hiding in the Light: On Images and Things*, London: Routledge.

Hervey, Thomas K. (2000) *The Book of Christmas*, Hertfordshire: Wordsworth.

Hill, Lawrence and Robyn Quin (2002) 'Live from the Ministry of Truth', *Australian Screen Education* 30: 50–5.

Hodder, E. (1923) *Life and Work of the 7th Earl of Shaftesbury*, London: Cassell.

Hoffmann-Axthelm, Dieter (1992) 'Identity and reality: The end of the philosophical immigration officer', in Scott Lash and Jonathan Friedman (eds), *Modernity and Identity*, Oxford: Blackwell, pp. 196–218.

Hofstadter, D. (1986) *Metamagical Themas: Questing for the Essence of Mind and Pattern*, Middlesex: Viking.

Hofstadter, Richard (1962) *Anti-Intellectualism in American Life*, New York: Vintage.

Hosgood, Christopher P. (1999) ' "Doing the shops" at Christmas: Women, men and the department store in England, *c.* 1880–1914', in Geoffrey Crossick and Serge Jaumain (eds), *Cathedrals of Consumption: The European Department Store 1850–1939*, Aldershot: Ashgate, pp. 97–115.

Hudson, John (ed.) (1997) *Dickens' Christmas*, Sutton: Stroud.

Irving, Washington (1876) *The Old English Christmas*, illustrated by Randolph Caldecott, London: Macmillan. (Republished New York: Mayflower, 1980.) The text first appeared in 1819 in Irving's *Sketchbook of Geoffrey Crayon, Gent.*

Jacobs, Meg (2001) 'The politics of plenty in the twentieth-century United States', in Martin Daunton and Matthew Hilton (eds), *The Politics of Consumption: Material Culture and Citizenship in Europe and America*, Oxford: Berg, pp. 223–39.

Jefferson, Thomas (1787) 'Letter to Peter Carr'. www.stephenjaygould.org/ctrl/Jefferson_carr.html. Accessed 23 May 2007.

Jewett, Sarah Orne (1896) 'Betty Leicester's English Christmas', *St. Nicholas*, Vol. XXIII, No. 4 (February), 313–18.

'Jim' (2005) 'The Power of Christian America: You Point out the Existence of Other Traditions, You Get Fired', posted 12 November. http://irregulartimes.com/index.php/archives/2005/11/12/the-power-of-christian-america-you-point-out-the-existence-of-other-traditions-you-get-fired. Accessed 16 March 2007.

Johnson, E. D. H. (1986) *Paintings of the British Social Scene from Hogarth to Sickert*, London: Weidenfeld & Nicolson.

Johnston, Trevor (1997) 'Jingle All The Way', review in *Sight and Sound*, Vol. 7, Issue 1 (NS), January, p. 40.

Keightley, K. (2003) 'Low television, high fidelity: taste and the gendering of home entertainment technologies', *Journal of Broadcasting and Electronic Media*, June, pp. 236–59.

Keyte, H. and A. Parrott (eds) (1992) *The New Oxford Book of Carols*, Oxford: Oxford University Press.

Klein, Naomi (2000) *No Logo: Taking Aim at the Brand Bullies*, London: Flamingo.

Kompare, Derek (2006) 'Publishing flow', *Television and New Media*, 7.4, pp. 333–8.

Kovacs, Joe (2005a) 'Wal-Mart faces boycott for "banning" Christmas', WorldNetDaily, 10 November, posted at 1.00 a.m. EST. www.worldnetdaily.com/news/article.asp?ARTICLE_ID=47330. Accessed 4 June 2007.

Kovacs, Joe (2005b) 'Wal-Mart worker "history" after "origin" of Christmas', WorldNetDaily, 10 November, posted at 11.00 p.m. EST. www.worldnetdaily.com/news/article.asp?ARTICLE_ID=47345. Accessed 4 June 2007.

Krythe, Maymie R. (1954) *All About Christmas*, New York: Harper.

Kuisel, Richard F. (1993) *Seducing the French: The Dilemma of Americanization*, Berkeley, CA: University of California Press.

Laderman, S. (2002) 'Remember resistance to war', *Minnesota Daily*, 19 November. www.mndaily.com/article.php?id=4175&year=2002. Accessed 2 March 2007.

Leech, John (1886) *John Leech's Pictures of Life and Character. From the Collection of 'Mr. Punch'*, London: Bradbury & Agnew.

Leech, John (1887) *John Leech's Pictures of Life and Character. From The Collection of 'Mr Punch', 1842–1864*, London: Bradbury & Agnew.

Lévi-Strauss, Claude [1952] (1993) 'Father Christmas executed', trans. Diana Gittins, in Daniel Miller (ed.), *Unwrapping Christmas*, Oxford: Oxford University Press, pp. 38–51.

LoBaido, A. C. (2001) '9-11 toys popular this Christmas', WorldNet Daily, 20 December. www.worldnetdaily.com/news/article.asp?ARTICLE_ID=25763. Accessed 2 March 2007.

Löfgren, Orvar (1993, republished 2001) 'The great Christmas quarrel and other Swedish traditions', in Daniel Miller (ed.), *Unwrapping Christmas*, Oxford: Oxford University Press.

Lorber, J. (2002) 'Heroes, warriors, and "burqas": A feminist sociologist's reflections on September 11', *Sociological Forum*, 17 (3): 377–96.

Lowe, B. L. (2003) 'The blind men and the elephant? Formal analogy as metaphor in British Sibelius studies, 1935–1965', in V. Murtomäki, Kari Kilpeläinen and Risto Väisänen (eds), *Sibelius Forum II: Proceedings from the Third International Jean Sibelius Conference, Helsinki, December 7–10, 2000*. Helsinki: Sibelius Academy, pp. 217–29.

McGreevy, P. (1990) 'Place in the American Christmas', *Geographical Review*, 80 (1): 3242.

McKay, George (2005) *Circular Breathing: The Cultural Politics of Jazz in Britain*, Durham, NC: Duke University Press.

McShane, L. (2006) 'Military Deaths in Iraq Exceed 9/11 Toll', *ABC News*. 26 December. http://abcnews.go.com/US/wireStory?id=2750784. Accessed 5 March 2007.

Marcus, George (1992) 'Past, present and emergent identities: Requirements for ethnographies of the late twentieth-century modernity', in Scott Lash and Jonathan Friedman (eds), *Modernity and Identity*, Oxford: Blackwell, pp. 309–30.

Marsden, George M. (2006) *Fundamentalism and American Culture*, 2nd edn, New York: Oxford University Press.

Marx, Karl (1848) *The Communist Manifesto*. On-line version at www.anu.edu.au/polsci/marx/classics/manifesto.html.

Marx, K and F. Engels (1983) *Communist Manifesto*, London: Lawrence & Wishart.

Marx, Karl and F. Engels (1998) *The Communist Party Manifesto*, Peking: Foreign Languages Press.

Menendez, Albert J. (1993) *The December Wars: Religious Symbols and Ceremonies in the Public Square*, Buffalo, NY: Prometheus.

'Merry Christmas/Happy New Year' (2005) *The Vicar of Dibley*, London: BBC Video.

Miall, Antony and Peter (1978) *The Victorian Christmas Book*, London: Dent.

Middleton, R. (1983) 'All shook up? Innovation and continuity in Elvis Presley's vocal style', in J. Tharpe (ed.), *Elvis: Images and Fancies*, London: W. H. Allen, pp. 155–66.

Middleton, R. (2000) 'Popular music analysis and musicology: bridging the gap', in R. Middleton (ed.), *Reading Pop: Approaches to Textual Analysis in Popular Music*, Oxford: Oxford University Press, pp. 104–21.

Mikkelson, Barbara and David P. Mikkelson (2004) 'Rudolph the Red-Nosed Reindeer'. www.snopes.com/holidays/christmas/rudolph.asp. Accessed 4 April 2007.

Miller, Daniel (1993, republished 2001) 'A theory of Christmas', in Daniel Miller (ed.), *Unwrapping Christmas*, Oxford: Oxford University Press, pp. 3–37.

Moore, R. Laurence (1994) *Selling God: American Religion in the Marketplace of Culture*, New York: Oxford University Press.

'Morecambe and Wise' (2007) in *Television Heaven*. www.televisionheaven.co.uk/morecambeandwise.htm. Accessed 4 April 2007.

Moss, Stephen (2003) '*The Office*', in A. Merullo and N. Wenborn (eds), *British Comedy Greats*, London: Cassell, pp. 130–3.

Motzafi-Haller, Prina (1997) 'Writing birthright: On native anthropologists and the politics of representation', in Deborah E. Reed-Danahay, *Auto/Ethnography: Rewriting the Self and the Social*, Oxford: Berg, pp. 195–222.

Munby, Jonathan (2000) 'A Hollywood carol's wonderful life', in Mark Connelly (ed.), *Christmas at the Movies: Images of Christmas in American, British and European Cinema*, London: I. B. Tauris, pp. 39–58.

Nabarz, Payam (2005) *The Mysteries of Mithras*, Rochester, VT: Inner Traditions.

National Security Archive, The Kissinger Telcons, National Security Archive Electronic Briefing Book No. 123, in particular Document 6: Kissinger and Secretary of Defense Melvin Laird, 3 January 1973, 4.00 p.m. Source: Nixon Presidential Materials Project, Henry A. Kissinger Telephone Conversations Transcripts, Chronological File, Box 17, 1973 2–6. www.gwu.edu/~nsarchiv/NSAEBB/NSAEBB123/index.htm. Accessed 6 March 2007.

Newton, Alfred Edward (1930) *The Christmas Spirit*, Pennsylvania: privately printed.

Nissenbaum, Stephen (1996) *The Battle for Christmas: A Cultural History of America's Most Cherished Holiday*, New York: Vintage.

No author (2005) 'G as in Good H as in Happy'. www.goodandhappy.typepad.com/g_as_in_good_h_as_in_happ/2005/11/lest_the_babe_i.html. Accessed 16 March 2007.

Noll, A. (2004) 'Class war/Christmas truce', *ZNet Daily Commentaries*, 8 January. www.zmag.org/Sustainers/Content/2004-01/08noll.cfm. Accessed 4 March 2007.

Noll, Mark (2005) *America's God: From Jonathan Edwards to Abraham Lincoln*, New York: Oxford University Press.

Nord, David Paul (1984) *The Evangelical Origins of Mass Media in America, 1815–1835*, Journalism Monographs 88.

O'Brien, Lucy (1992) 'All I Want For Christmas' review, *Sight and Sound*, Vol. 1, Issue 10 (NS), February, p. 38.

O'Leary, Janice (2005) 'It's fall, and in the city's littered wilds, wild mushrooms, of all things, thrive', *Boston Globe*, 6 November. www.boston.com/news/local/massachusetts/articles/2005/11/06/its_fall_and_in_the_citys_littered_wilds_wild_mushrooms_of_all_things_thrive?mode=PF. Accessed 16 March 2007.

Office for National Statistics (2001) *Census*.

Okely, Judith (1996) *Own or Other Culture*, London: Routledge.

Okely, Judith and Helen Callaway (eds) (1992) *Anthropology and Autobiography*, London: Routledge.

Origen (1990) *Homilies on Leviticus 1–16*, trans. Gary Wayne Barkley. The Fathers of the Church, v. 83, Washington, DC: Catholic University of America Press.

Ott, Jonathan (1993) *Pharmacotheon: Entheogenic Drugs, Their Plant Sources and Histories*, Kennewick, WA: Natural Products.

Patella, Michael (2006) *Lord of the Cosmos: Mithras, Paul, and the Gospel of Mark*, New York: T & T Clark International.

Perry, J. (2005) 'Nazifying Christmas: Political culture and popular celebration in the Third Reich', *Central European History*, 38 (4): 572–605.

Pixley, A. (2006) 'The Christmas Invasion', *Doctor Who Special Edition*, 14: 15.

Poster, Mark (1995) *The Second Media Age*, Cambridge: Polity.

Pratt, Mary Louise (1992) *Imperial Eyes: Travel Writing and Transculturation*, London: Routledge.

Reed-Danahay, Deborah E. (ed.) (1997) *Auto / Ethnography: Rewriting the Self and the Social*, Oxford: Berg.

Reid Mandell, B. (2002) 'Welfare Reform after 9/11', *New Politics* 8 (4). www.wpunj.edu/newpol/issue32/mandel32.htm. Accessed 2 April 2007.

Restad, Penne L. (1993, republished 1995) *Christmas in America: A History*, Oxford: Oxford University Press.

Richards, Jeffrey (2000) 'Crisis at Christmas: Turkey time, the holly and the ivy, the cheaters', in Mark Connelly (ed.), *Christmas at the Movies: Images of Christmas in American, British and European Cinema*, London: I. B. Tauris, pp. 97–114.

Ritzer, George (1996) *The McDonaldization of Society: An Investigation into the Changing Character of Contemporary Social Life*, London: Sage.

Rosen, Jody (2002) *White Christmas: The Story of a Song*, London: Fourth Estate.

Ross, Marc Howard (2000) 'Culture and Identity in Comparative Political Analysis', in L. Crothers and C. Lockhart (eds), *Culture and Politics. A Reader*, New York: St Martin's, pp. 39–70.

Roud, Steve (2000) 'Introduction' to *Thomas K. Hervey's The Book of Christmas*, Hertfordshire: Wordsworth.

Rycenga, Jennifer (2000) ' "Dropping in for the holidays": Christmas as commercial and evangelical ritual at the Precious Moments Chapel', in Katherine McCarthy and Eric Mazur (eds), *God in the Details: American Religion in Popular Culture*, New York: Routledge, pp. 139–53.

St. Nicholas (1895) Vol. XXIII, No. 2. December.

Santino, J. (1992) 'Yellow ribbons and seasonal flags: The folk assemblage of war', *Journal of American Folklore* 105 (415): 19–33.

Schmidt, Leigh Eric (1995) *Consumer Rites: The Buying and Selling of American Holidays*, Princeton: Princeton University Press.

Schudson, Michael (1993) *Advertising, The Uneasy Persuasion: Its Dubious Impact on American Society*, London: Routledge.

Schwartz, John (2003) 'A cast of thousands', *Australian Screen Education* 32: 52–7.

Scott, Derek (1989) *Music, Culture and Society*, Cambridge: Cambridge University Press.

Searle-Chatterjee, Mary (1993) 'Christmas cards and the construction of social relations in Britain today', in Daniel Miller (ed.), *Unwrapping Christmas*, Oxford: Oxford University Press, pp. 176–92.

Seddon, Laura (1992) *A Gallery of Greetings*. A Guide to the Seddon Collection of Greetings Cards in Manchester Polytechnic Library. (The colour plates are without pagination; the cards are identified by reference to a particular volume of the collection and their own individual number within that volume.)

Soja, Edward W. (1999) *Third Space*, New York: Routledge.

Stallybrass, Peter and Allon White (1986) *The Politics and Poetics of Transgression*, Ithaca, NY: Cornell University Press.

Steedman, C. (1986) *Landscape for a Good Women: A Story of Two lives*, London: Virago.

Steigmann-Gall, Richard (2003) 'Rethinking Nazism and religion: How anti-Christian were the "pagans"?', *Central European History* 36 (1): 75–105.

Storey, John (1985) 'Matthew Arnold: The politics of an organic intellectual', *Literature and History*, 11: 2.

Storey, John (2003) *Inventing Popular Culture*, Oxford: Blackwell.

Strand Magazine (1891) An Illustrated Monthly, ed. Geo. Newnes. Vol. 1. January to June.

Strand Magazine (1892) Vol. 4. July to December.

Tate, Catherine (2005) 'The Christmas Special', *Catherine Tate Show Series One and Two Box Set*, London: BBC Video.

Tate, Catherine (2007) *The Catherine Tate Comic Relief Special*, London: Tiger Aspect/BBC/Comic Relief, MCPS, Endemol West.

Taylor, S. (1981) 'Symbol and ritual under National Socialism', *British Journal of Sociology* 32 (4): 504–20.

Tenniel, John (1895) *Cartoons (from 'Punch') by Sir John Tenniel*, 2 vols 1871–81, 1882–91, London: Bradbury & Agnew.

'The Christmas Invasion' (2006) *Doctor Who The Complete Series Two Box Set*, London: BBC Video.

'The Runaway Bride' (2007) *Doctor Who Christmas Special*, London: BBC Video.

The Studio (1893) Vol. II. 'Christmas Decorations' Aylmer Vallance, p. 105.

The Studio (1898) Vol. XV, 'Christmas Card Design', p. 126.

The Times (1880) 14 December, p. 4, col. f.

The Times (1883) 25 December, p. 5, col. c.

The Times (1895) 19 December, p. 14, col. f.

Thuesen, Peter J. (1999) *In Discordance with the Scriptures: American Protestant Battles Over Translating the Bible*, New York: Oxford University Press.

Tille, A. (1892) 'German Christmas and the Christmas-Tree', *Folklore* 3 (2): 166–82.

Twitchell, James B. (1996) *Adcult USA: The Triumph of Advertising in American Culture*, New York: Columbia University Press.

US-Iraq ProCon.org *2003–2007 Polls and Surveys of Americans and Iraqis on the U.S.–Iraq War and Related Issues*. www.usiraqprocon.org/pop/Resources-Polls. html#*. Accessed 20 May 2007.

Veblen, Thorstein (1899) *The Theory of the Leisure Class: An Economic Study in the Evolution of Institutions*, New York: Macmillan. (Republished New York: Random House, 2001.)

Voas, D. and A. Crockett (2005) 'Religion in Britain: Neither believing nor belonging', *Sociology* 39 (1): 11–28.

Waits, W. B. (1993) *The Modern Christmas in America: A Cultural History of Gift-Giving*, New York: New York University Press.

Walker, Alexander (1996) 'A thumping bad example from Arnie', *Evening Standard*, 5 December, cited in Rowana Agajanian, 'Peace on Earth, goodwill to all men', in Mark Connelly (ed.) (2000), *Christmas at the Movies: Images of Christmas in American, British and European Cinema*, London: I. B. Tauris, p. 154.

Watch Tower Bible and Tract Society of Pennsylvania (2006) 'Lesson 11: Beliefs and Customs That Displease God'. www.watchtower.org/e/rq/article_11.htm. Accessed 9 May 2007.

Weber, C. (2002) 'Flying planes can be dangerous', *Millennium: Journal of International Studies* 31 (1): 129–47.

Weintraub, S. (2001) *Silent Night. The Remarkable Christmas Truce of 1914*, London: Simon & Schuster.

Wernecke, Herbert H. (1959) *Christmas Customs around the World*, Philadelphia: Westminster.

White House (2001) Official White House Christmas Ornament. www.whitehousechristmasornament.com. Accessed 2 April 2007.

Whyte, Kenneth (2005) 'Q & A with Santa Claus', interview with Gerry Bowler, author of *Santa Claus: A Biography*, in *Macleans* magazine, 23 December. www.macleans.ca/culture/entertainment/article.jsp?content=20051226_118718_118718. Accessed 10 April 2007.

Wilson, W. A. (1895) 'A Christmas white elephant', *St. Nicholas*, Vol. XXIII, No. 2 (December), pp. 112–19.

Wrigley, Neil (2000) 'Four myths in search of foundation: the restructuring of US food retailing and its implications for commercial cultures', in Peter Jackson, Michelle Lowe, Daniel Miller and Frank Mort (eds), *Commercial Cultures: Economies, Practices, Spaces*, Oxford: Berg, pp. 221–44.

Zeitlin, Solomon (1938) 'Hanukkah: its origin and its significance', *Jewish Quarterly Review*, new ser., 29 (1): 1–36.

Ziska, Franz and Julius Max Schottky (eds) (1819) *Oesterreichische Volkslieder mit ihren Singeweisen*, Pest: Hartleben.

Contributors

CHRISTINE AGIUS is Lecturer in International Relations and Politics at the University of Salford. Her research interests include international relations theory and Scandinavian politics. She is the author of *The Social Construction of Swedish Neutrality* (Manchester University Press 2006).

GERRY BLOUSTIEN is an Associate Professor in the School of Communication, and Deputy Director of the Hawke Research Institute for Sustainable Societies, University of South Australia. Her cross-disciplinary research interests include the areas of cultural identities and gender, youth cultures, screen literacy and innovative ethnographic methodologies. Her monograph *Girl Making* (Berghahn 2003) is an international study of what it means to 'grow up female'. Her other publications include several studies of the television comedy drama, *Buffy*, and its fan base (*European Journal of Cultural Studies* 2002), an edited collection *Sonic Synergies: Music, Identity and Communities* (Ashgate 2008) and *Playing for Life: Youth and Music* (Palgrave, forthcoming).

TARA BRABAZON is Professor of Media Studies at the University of Brighton and Director of the Popular Culture Collective. She is a former national teaching award winner and a 2005 finalist for Australian of the Year. Her research interests in popular cultural studies include sport, popular music, creative industries initiatives, city imaging, multi-culturalism and education. Tara is the author of eight books: *Tracking the Jack: A Retracing of the Antipodes* (University of New South Wales Press 2000), *Ladies who Lunge: Celebrating Difficult Women* (University of New South Wales Press 2002), *Digital Hemlock: Internet Education and the Poisoning of Teaching* (University of New South Wales Press 2000), *Liverpool of the South Seas: Perth and its Popular Music* (University of Western Australia Press 2005), *Playing on the Periphery* (Routledge 2006),

From Revolution to Revelation (Ashgate 2005), *The University of Google* (Ashgate 2007) and *The Revolution will not be downloaded* (Chandos 2008).

BARRY COOPER is Professor of Music at the University of Manchester. As a musicologist he is best known for his work on Beethoven, about whom he has authored or edited six books, but he has published research on a wide variety of other musical topics from the medieval period to the nineteenth century. He is also a Fellow of the Royal College of Organists, with much experience of singing in and conducting choirs.

SARA M. DODD is an Arts Staff Tutor and Faculty Manager for the Open University in Manchester. She has published mainly in the area of nineteenth-century art and design: for example, chapters in *The Yorkshire Coast* (Normandy 1991), *Women in the Victorian Art World* (Manchester University Press 1995) and *Governing Cultures: Art Institutions in Victorian London* (Ashgate 2000). She has also made contributions to books on twentieth-century British and Russian art and theory: for example, an article on Vera Yermolaeva in the *Dictionary of Women Artists* (Fitzroy Dearborne 1997) and on Laurie Anderson in *The Routledge Companion to Postmodernism* (Routledge 2004); she has recently written on Victorian painting and the painter William Etty for *The Greenwood Encyclopedia of Sex, Love and Culture*, Vol. 5: The Nineteenth Century (Greenwood 2007).

FREYA JARMAN-IVENS is Lecturer in Music at Liverpool University. Her research interests include queer theory and performativity, psychoanalytic theory, and technology and musical production. Freya's favoured musical material for analysis ranges from opera to easy listening to alternative rock and hip-hop. She is the co-editor (with Santiago Fouz-Hernandez) of *Madonna's Drowned Worlds* (Ashgate 2004), a collection of new essays on Madonna's subcultural transformations, and editor of *Oh Boy! Masculinity and Popular Music* (Routledge 2007). Freya has also contributed regularly to the proceedings of the biennial International Association for the Study of Popular Music conferences. She is currently working on a single-authored book on vocality and subjectivity.

GEORGE MCKAY is Professor of Cultural Studies at the University of Salford, where he directs the Adelphi Research Institute for Creative Arts and Sciences. He writes mainly about cultural politics and popular music, his books including *Circular Breathing: The Cultural Politics of Jazz in Britain* (Duke University Press 2005), *Glastonbury: A Very English Fair* (Victor Gollancz 2000) and *Senseless Acts of Beauty: Cultures of Resistance*

Since the Sixties (Verso 1996). Among his edited books are *DIY Culture: Party and Protest in Nineties Britian* (Verso 1998) and, as co-editor (with Pete Moser), *Community Music: A Handbook* (Russell House 2004), and (with Neil Campbell and Jude Davies) *Issues in Americanisation and Culture* (Edinburgh University Press 2004). He is also an editor of *Social Movement Studies: Journal of Social, Cultural and Political Protest.*

JOHN MUNDY is Professor in Media and Head of the School of Media, Music and Performance at the University of Salford. His books include *Popular Music on Screen* (Manchester University Press 1999), *The British Musical Film* (Manchester University Press 2007) and the forthcoming *Laughter Matters: Understanding Radio, Film and Television Comedy.*

JENNIFER RYCENGA is Professor of Comparative Religious Studies at San José State University in California. She teaches in the areas of American religious history; religion and music; gender and religion; and lesbian intellectual history. She co-edited (with Marguerite Waller) *Frontline Feminisms: Women, War, and Resistance* (Garland 2001) and (with Sheila Whiteley) *Queering the Popular Pitch* (Routledge 2006). She has written for *Repercussions: Critical and Alternative Viewpoints on Music and Scholarship*; *The Encyclopedia of World Music*; *Progressive Rock Reconsidered* (Routledge 2001); *God in the Details: American Religion in Popular Culture* (Routledge 2001); *Keeping Score : Music, Disciplinarity, Culture* (University Press of Virginia 1997); *Queering the Pitch: The New Lesbian and Gay Musicology* (Routledge 1994); and *Adorno: A Critical Reader* (Blackwell 2002). She is currently working on a cultural biography of Prudence Crandall, a nineteenth-century Abolitionist educator and feminist.

JOHN STOREY is Professor of Cultural Studies and Director of the Centre for Research in Media and Cultural Studies, University of Sunderland. He has published widely in cultural studies, including seven books. His work has been translated into Chinese, German, Japanese, Korean, Persian, Polish, Serbian, Spanish, Swedish and Ukrainian. He is a Visiting Professor at the universities of Henan and Wuhan, China.

THOM SWISS writes on popular music and new media literature. His latest book – *New Media Poetics: Texts, Contexts, Technotexts* – was published by the MIT Press in 2006. He is Professor of Culture and Teaching at the University of Minnesota and author of two collections of poems, *Rough Cut* (University of Illinois 1997) and *Measure* (University of Alabama 1986). Swiss's collaborative new media poems appear online in such journals as *Postmodern Culture* and *Electronic Book Review*, as well as in museum exhibits and art shows. His new co-edited book is *Highway 61 Revisited: Bob Dylan's Road from Minnesota to the World* (Minnesota UP, 2008)

SHEILA WHITELEY is Visiting Professor at the University of Brighton. She is author of *The Space Between the Notes: Rock and the Counter Culture* (Routledge 1992); *Women and Popular Music: Popular Music and Gender* (Routledge 2000); and *Too Much Too Young: Popular Music, Age and Identity* (Routledge 2005). She edited *Sexing the Groove: Popular Music and Gender* (Routledge 1996) and co-edited (with Andy Bennett and Stan Hawkins) *Music Space and Place: Popular Music and Cultural Identity* (Ashgate 2002) and (with Jennifer Rycenga) *Queering the Popular Pitch* (Routledge 2006). She was Chair of Popular Music at the University of Salford (1992–2006), and is a member of the Advisory Board of the Music as Performance Working Group (MAP).

Index

Note: f stands for figure and n for note

Riddle, Nelson, 108
rituals, 1, 6, 7, 11, 108, 110, 140, 143
'River', 106–7
Rivers, Johnny, 183
robins, 5, 46–7
'Rock You Hard This Christmas',
    122–3, 125
Roman Catholicism, 100; see also
    Catholic League, Mary
romance, 109–11, 114, 118, 120–3
Ross, Marc Howard, 143
Roud, Steve, 30
Rowling, J. K., 109
Royal Guardsmen, 184
Royle Family, The, 155
Rudolph the Red-Nosed Reindeer, 2, 6,
    54
Rwanda, 150
Rycenga, Jennifer, 7–8, 71–87, 210

St Nicholas, 41, 44
Salvation Army, 105
Sandys, William, 21, 29, 92
'Santa Baby', 120
'Santa Bring My Baby Back to Me', 8,
    101
Santa Claus, 5, 21–2, 50–67, 108, 164,
    172
    and alcohol, 40, 59
    costume colours, 22, 40–1, 56–7, 59,
        61, 73, 168
    in films, 169
    hallucinogenic mushrooms, 77
    illustrations, 42f, 43f, 53f, 55f, 58f
    letters to, 1, 55f, 59, 191, 192
    masked, 162
    Secret, 157
    visiting, 20, 192–3
Santa Claus and his Works, 56
Santa Clause, The, 169
Santino, J., 146–7
Saturnalia, 6–7, 78, 111
Schudson, Michael, 65
Schulz, Charles M., 184
Schwartz, John, 153
Schwarzenegger, Arnold, 174–5

Scott, Derek, 100
Scottish Common Sense Realism
    (SCSR), 82–4
Scrooge see Christmas Carol, A
Scrooge; or Marley's Ghost, 167
SCROOGE (Society to Curtail
    Ridiculous, Outrageous and
    Ostentatious Gift Exchanges), 66
Searle-Chatterjee, Mary, 64
Secret Agent, 183
Secret Santa, 157
secularisation, 2, 12, 50, 83, 130–1
Seddon, Laura, 38, 40, 45, 46, 47–8
September 11, 11, 12, 129, 144–8, 150
Sesame Street, 109
sex, 111, 118–20, 121, 124–5
    and birthrate, 80
    casual, 110
Shaftesbury, Lord, 98
Shameless, 157
Sheridan, Jamey, 171–2
shopping, 22, 52, 53, 176; see also
    department stores
'Silent Night', 92, 93, 133, 167
Silent Night, Deadly Night, 165–6
Singing Nun, The, 180
'Sink the Bismarck', 184
'Sir Roger de Coverley' dance, 45, 46
situation comedies, 182–3
skating, 46
Sky News, 149
sledging, 46
Smith, Tom, 21
'Snoopy vs the Red Baron', 184
'Snoopy's Christmas', 184
snow, 113, 195
snowballing, 46
Snowy Day, A, 109
soap opera, 182
social networking, 153
solstice, winter, 6–7, 45, 79
Some Ancient Christmas Carols, 92
songs, 98–112
Songs of Christmas for Family Choirs, 100
space race, 63
'Sparky's Magic Piano', 109, 112n7